I0762941

# WHAT EVER HAPPENED TO EDDY CRANE?

# WHAT EVER HAPPENED TO EDDY CRANE?

*A Memoir and a Murder Investigation*

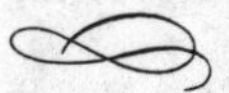

KATE CRANE

HANOVER
SQUARE
PRESS

ISBN-13: 978-1-335-44939-9

What Ever Happened to Eddy Crane?



Some names and identifying characteristics have been changed.

This publication contains opinions and ideas of the author. It is intended for informational and educational purposes only. The reader should seek the services of a competent professional for expert assistance or professional advice. Reference to any organization, publication or website does not constitute or imply an endorsement by the author or the publisher. The author and the publisher specifically disclaim any and all liability arising directly or indirectly from the use or application of any information contained in this publication.

TM and ® are trademarks of Harlequin Enterprises ULC.

Hanover Square Press
22 Adelaide St. West, 41st Floor
Toronto, Ontario M5H 4E3, Canada
HanoverSqPress.com

HarperCollins Publishers
Macken House, 39/40 Mayor Street Upper,
Dublin 1, D01 C9W8, Ireland
www.HarperCollins.com

Printed in U.S.A.

*For Marie Collins, Bob Crane, Yvonne Hughes, Gordon Porterfield, my grandparents, and my mother*

# TABLE OF CONTENTS

## BALTIMORE



## NEW YORK

## BALTIMORE

# BALTIMORE

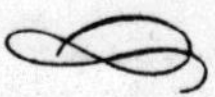

# PREFACE

I TRIED TO STAY SILENT. I never wanted to talk about this. I never wanted to think about it, much less write anything down. I didn't want to disclose or discuss our history, this story, to the people I held close or hoped to, who might look away in discomfort. Definitely not to an anonymous reader who could flatten me under a microscope and scrutinize. Scrutinize my family's destruction, scrutinize my failure to rectify or salvage. I didn't want anyone to know I might have made things worse.

For twenty years I tried to outrun 1987. First through amnesia, then through a deliberate forgetting. But everywhere I went, everything I did, every conversation I had, it was always in the room.

I say *it*; I say *1987*. That's shorthand for when childhood ended and something else began. I used to say that I grew up when I was twelve. "Overnight, I went from child to adult." That is baldly inaccurate, maybe even a lie. It wouldn't be the only lie between me and this story. I barely had a handle on how to survive menstruation, the cramps that woke me screaming in the dark. I drenched clean clothes and bedsheets in blood, stowed crusted red-brown pads and ruined underwear under my bed, where I, a child, trusted that no one would ever find them. I could not prepare any food for myself beyond PB&J; I'd never used the stove. I didn't know how to use the washing machine. I was so far from a latchkey kid that I did not in fact have a key to the house. I had started eighth grade days earlier. I was a little girl.

I constructed a narrative. It was safe—I rehearsed it often. I could look you in the eye right now and rattle off that story in fifty words or less without blinking or taking a breath. And your blood might run cold, yes, because there are no soft words for the facts of that night, or, at least, what facts I've been able to gather. Me? That narrative would not stir me an inch. Which was always the point.

I first became a writer by exsanguinating this story of its vitality and meaning. I needed the fundamental story of my life to be bloodless.

I buried it. It refused to stay underground. Twenty years after September 10, 1987, I came to a crossroads and a choice: die by silence, or survive by telling. I chose to live.

# HAND DRILL

I SLAMMED THE DOOR of my mother's Mercedes. For someone only four feet tall or so, a car-door slam was more about physics than carelessness—I was too little to close a car door with much precision. It was the early 1980s and, wearing my plaid Catholic-school poly-cotton jumper and white knee-highs, I was coming home from second or third grade. I'm not sure if it was spring or fall, but I don't remember struggling out of a winter coat.

Every school day Mommy drove me, and when she got old enough, also my sister, about ten minutes down Belair Road to St. Joseph, a Catholic school in a well-cared-for working-class area of Baltimore County. Until high school, I never rode a school bus except for field trips. Me, my mother, sister, father and Rottweiler were still living in the house I call the first house.

I thought I had the most normal childhood, that nothing could be more normal than our life and that little house on Silver Spring Road. Normal was, of course, good. But things were changing all around me. I was aware, as kids are, and unaware, as kids are.

White Marsh, a massive shopping mall, had opened in 1981, and Silver Spring Road, already a river of lead feet, was going to double from two lanes to four, which meant our driveway would shrink. As far back as I could remember, Mommy and Daddy had been planning a big house, a dream house, away from the car horns and the exhaust fumes. Expansion, escape. Blueprints covered the kitchen table as often as dinner plates. The idea of the new house filled me with joy—I'd have my own room, no more sharing. But I was also apprehensive.

"Daddy, will we have the same zip code?" I asked one day. Stout and serious and large, a graying bear of a man in a white undershirt, arms like delicatessen wursts bursting from their casings, he eyed me skeptically. There in his sagging blue crushed-velvet throne, the dank armchair parked next to the front door, he would almost certainly have been reading the classified ads. He loved to see what cars were selling for, call up their owners and ask them to give him a good reason why he should give up a Mercedes for a Chevrolet. "The day you show me a car that's better than a Mercedes, I'll stop driving a Mercedes."

I began to cry. I loved 21128. It was an artistic number—a palindrome with the infinity symbol at the end. 21236, an adjacent zip, was devoid of charm.

"How about you worry a little more about the C's you're pulling in religion class and a little less about our—" he growled, and here paused to regard me in disbelief "—zip code?" He looked at my mother. "Why are we paying for her to go to that school when she brings home those grades?"

I shrank at what seemed a willful misinterpretation of my report card, and at the scorn for my worry. I cared about Dad's opinion more than anyone's—his opprobrium stung. I didn't understand how I could be his favorite and also the occasional, unpredictable target of his judgment. 21128 was lovely—why couldn't he see? I got A's in reading and spelling. Who cared about popes and sacraments? I was already reading Shakespeare and writing a novel on a heavy blue typewriter in my grandparents' red-and-black-tiled basement.

A bookish nerdchild, I kept to myself in part because of preference and in part because I didn't have friends. My mother once set up a playdate—I wandered off to read a book and never came back. When I was immersed in *A Midsummer Night's Dream* on the faded floral sofa, my eccentricity was cute, and when I fretted about losing the zip code I dearly loved, I think my parents found me exasperating.

Today, though, I pushed through the front door, dropped my book bag on the staticky acrylic living room carpet, and began roaring toward snacks and *Scooby-Doo*. But something was weird. Dad was home.

This was not part of the school-week routine, which was: Dad was still asleep when I left for school, gone when I got back and usually walking back in the door when I was getting ready for bed. In the morning, I would kiss him goodbye on his sleep-sour, stubbly cheek before I ran out to the car with Mom.

My father's weight swelled and receded, but he was often close to three hundred pounds. So his presence could be audible: big man, big sounds. At other times it was like sharing a house with a mountain: Wordless, Dad would retreat into the blue armchair and vanish beneath his state-of-the-art plush black headphones, spiral cord lazing out to the tall stereo unit. He drifted to destinations unknown with Patsy Cline or Elvis Presley.

Entering the front door that day, I knew immediately he was there, but I could not hear him. I checked for his headphones—hanging on their hook. And the blue velvet armchair was empty but for the permanent impression of his corpulence.

The silence was loud. It was wrong.

"Daddy!" I knew he'd be happy to see me. Often I climbed

into the front seat of the tan Mercedes and we took car rides together, stereo playing rock 'n' roll as loud as it would go. I typed out stories on his secretary's typewriter when I went into Curtis Bay with him to his business, E & M Machinery—"Eve and Mary," Dad said it stood for, laughing. If it actually stood for anything, he never told me. I wrote my pen pal in Scotland that my father owned a junkyard, and Mommy and Daddy cried laughing. At E & M, glittering towers of truck parts were my first skyscrapers. They shimmered in the rain, ringed by toxic moats of rainbows and tadpoles. I loved it.

I rounded the corner into the tiny kitchen, all seventies oranges and olives, only a few steps from the front door of the house. My heart soared to see him, this constant in my limited world, solid in his body and the steady way he held a room. Cigarette smoke and Old Spice made my nose prickle. *The Sun* was spread out on the table where we ate, and a Viceroy smoldered in the glass ashtray. I stifled a gag. Even though that was the *nice ashtray*, as opposed to the black plastic ones that were in the garage or on the back brick steps. I was always trying to evade the reek of cigarettes that pervaded the house, our cars, our clothes.

"Hey, little girl. How was school?" He wanted to sound cheerful but it was forced, distracted. I could tell he was tense but not mad at me. He was concentrating, but on what?

For a few seconds I stood back, swaying with gladness. My daddy had deep brown eyes and crow's-feet and a slicked-back widow's peak. I always thought of his hair as jet-black, but if I looked hard, I knew it was streaked with gray. He looked a lot like the Elvis we both loved, but my dad's face had more worry lines than the guy on the LP covers. I loved him.

I started to go in to hug him and stopped short. Daddy was

holding something strange. And there was something peculiar about his hand.

"Daddy, what are you doing?"

I looked more closely, craned my head from where I stood. Dad was holding a metal tool. Medieval. It was a grim iron implement that looked like a pencil sharpener, or one of my Mee-Mom's baking tools. But I didn't see any cake batter. Just Dad's thumb. I lacked the vocabulary for what I was looking at: a thumb, yes, on my daddy's hand, yes. Discolored, it appeared to be pulsing.

That's when it clicked. The tool was some kind of key. And Daddy was going to use it to unlock the pressure inside his thumb. *Don't gag, don't cry*—and my stomach lurched. To impress him, I had to be tough.

No one had ever told me that sometimes we turned garage tools onto our bodies. If Daddy was doing this, I guess it had to be normal. All the same, an alarm inside me began to sound.

Daddy was gripping the drill. It looked like something an Edward Gorey villain would use to carry out a nefarious deed. My father's thumb was huge and blackened. The nail seemed to have expanded and warped and stiffened. Below the surface I could glimpse a hint of green and of red. Whatever was going on with that hand, I didn't want a good look, but I couldn't look away, either.

"What happened, Daddy?" I whispered, not wanting him to send me away.

The metal tip was nestling against the uppermost layer of his nail. His face was set in determination. The pain, which must have been extreme, seemed of no consequence to him. He sighed.

"Dropped a drivetrain on my thumb, prideandjoy." This man

with a drill bit poised to burrow into his thumbnail sounded about as perturbed as if he'd dropped a bag of groceries and realized an egg or two was broken.

I didn't know it then, but drivetrains put food on the table. My father was not, as I'd told my pen pal, a junkyard proprietor. Rather, E & M, which he co-owned with my Uncle Augie, bought, refurbished and resold heavy-duty truck parts. *Heavydutytruckparts* was one of my first words, along with *prideandjoy*, which meant me.

My father was losing interest in our exchange. "Hon, why don't you go in the other room."

Soon I heard a muffled snarl coming from the kitchen. But Daddy did not cry. If he needed follow-up care from a doctor, I never heard about it. Our bathroom cabinet held the holy trinity: hydrogen peroxide, Betadine and Neosporin. Provided he kept it clean, he might have pulled his home surgery off.

A menace had raged beneath his fingernail. He released it, rinsed it away. And eventually the ravaged thumbnail fell off.

The days filed by, one largely indistinguishable from the next. Life went on as before.

# MISSING PERSON

SEPTEMBER 10, 1987, changed everything for my anonymous, working-class Baltimore family. That's the night our family of four became a family of three, as if the kitchen table dropped a leg. Each of us was alone when it happened: My father was on an isolated truck yard in industrial Curtis Bay in South Baltimore. My mother was in their bed, an hour to the north in a rural corner of the county, waiting and waiting. She was the first one to realize. The unthinkable dawned with first light into her bedroom, a quiet, private space she shared with her husband. My sister and I were in our very own rooms, a very new thing, at the corner of our brand-new house, down two hallways from our mother. Fast asleep, we were unconscious to the new reality that was seeping through the freshly laid bricks, burrowing toward us.

We'd been living in the new house since last fall, but I slept in the same bed as always, a tiny twin from Sears. The house still smelled of timber, paint, concrete dust. Mom and Dad let me pick the color of my bedroom walls, and I had, surprisingly, chosen well: a pale yellow that amplified sunlight. So in the new house, I woke up each day to a lemon glow that evoked *The Wizard of Oz*.

But on an early September morning, a school day at the start of eighth grade, I opened my eyes and tensed. Something was wrong.

Mom usually called my name from the doorway until I made credible maneuvers toward getting up. This, in tandem with a beeping clock radio and a bowl of instant oatmeal, was the morning routine. Today, though, Mom was perched at the foot of my bed in her green belted bathrobe. I felt myself clutch for the warmth of the cotton Strawberry Shortcake sheets. They were safe. This deviation from routine was not.

I looked up and the fear pooled through me. What I could see, I did not like. My mother's face, fine boned, lovely, reserved but quick to smile, wore a haunted, strained expression. Her eyes were bleary and red. My mother had been crying. She had been smoking. I did not like this, the taut, wary look in her eyes that telegraphed something frightening. I did not like how very, very still she sat. I was afraid. My mother was afraid too.

When Mom spoke, her voice came out thick and mucky. "Katy . . . Dad didn't come home last night."

I knew instantly: Daddy was dead.

In my memory, I am stoic, but my mother is clear on this point: I let out a wail.

I weighed about ninety pounds. I was a child, and a sheltered one. I had a mommy and a daddy and a little sister and a dog. Now my daddy and my dog, a lovable hulking Rottweiler barely out of puppyhood, were gone. Sherlock went to work every day with my father. Where was my puppy? If Dad was dead, and I guessed that he was, then our puppy must be too.

In our family, and in my young life, practically nothing had ever been wrong. This was Perry Hall, Maryland, a blue-collar suburb in northeast Baltimore County. We had strip malls, a farm stand called Huber's, Persing's for cheeseburger subs, Santoni's for groceries. Sometimes we got Chinese at the Golden Bowl in the Perry Hall shopping center, where B&L Photo was, next to Woolworths and Michaels. There was a snowball stand on Joppa Road; a gas station and hardware store named Butt's; Klausmeier & Sons, an auto shop. There were no famous people, and crime was negligible.

We were as normal, I felt, as the loaf of store-brand sandwich bread that Mommy used to make my school lunches. My parents were both close to their parents. I spent Friday nights with my Mee-Mom and Pop, in the house where my mother grew up, sleeping alongside my four-foot-ten grandmother, who sang to me about Gina Lollobrigida to lull me off to sleep. On Sundays we often visited Grandmom Hilda, Dad's stout, white-haired German mother. Pappy, his taciturn father, had died a few years before, and Grandmom Hilda now lived alone with a bulldog named Sammy. I thrilled for her stollen, an arid flat cake riddled with dried fruit that looked like a tree root doused in powdered sugar, and her springerle, leaden Christmas cookies shaped like tiny Mount Sinai tablets, pressed with inscrutable etchings and flavored with anise. My mother called them an assault on teeth. I loved those cookies so much I hoped fervently that Grandmom Hilda would never die.

I knew Dad was dead because he always came home. He was not home all the time, but he always came home. He called at nine and then he showed up an hour or so later. He never slept at the office. He took exactly one business trip that I know of, to somewhere in Asia—he brought me back a yellow silk kimono. Every night, he called and then he came home. This was gospel.

He'd called Mom around nine to say he was on his way. Failing to complete the nightly ritual could mean only one thing.

If Daddy was gone, how would we live? Could we stay in this house?

My mother left my room to go tell my sister, who was about three years younger than me. Family outings had been a challenge as long as I could remember, as my sister became anxious and often got sick at movie theaters and restaurants. I resented her for this, never considering she might be reacting to something I couldn't sense.

I got dressed in a daze. On any other weekday I would be wearing a Catholic school uniform. But Mom was keeping us home. I chose something to wear from my little wooden dresser. I was an awkward kid. And even though my mother was stylish with excellent taste, she bought me clothing that was durable and reasonably priced, at places like Sears and JCPenney. The other kids harassed me relentlessly. So the uniforms were a blessing—they gave the bullies less to work with.

"What happened to Daddy? When is Daddy coming back?" my sister asked, her face hot and flushed, streaked with tears. Our closeness ebbed and flowed. Today we were allies of necessity. "Did Uncle Augie do something to Daddy?" she whispered. We were huddled shoulder to shoulder on the floor at my bedroom door, listening at the decent-size crack. We couldn't hear much. But, yes, I could make out something about Uncle Augie in the hushed voices. People were coming and going—my godmother, Mom's cousins. Someone had brought McDonald's, and this time I thought I'd be the one to vomit.

I had to be wrong; Dad couldn't be dead. Dad always came home. It was the Gospel of Eddy Crane: Phone home then come home. He had just gotten stuck somewhere. Any second, surely,

Dad's tan Mercedes would glide into view and start its rumbling, lumbering ascent up the gravel drive. It had to. Any minute.

It didn't.

The minutes and hours yawned, taut and terrible. Every time the phone rang, I prayed it would be Dad. I'd been enrolled at St. Joe's since nursery school in the incense-redolent church chapel, where every surface was gleaming and mausoleum-chilly. Over my short life I'd formed an obsequious but direct relationship with God. He was an almighty big shot who listened to prayers if you phrased them properly and enunciated. Every night my mother led me in a Hail Mary, Our Father and a shout-out to the dead: *Eternal rest grant unto them, O Lord, and let perpetual light shine upon them. May they rest in peace. Amen.* I wasn't sure how anyone could get eternal rest with perpetual light shining upon them, but I figured it would make sense when I grew up. Or died.

I prayed now: *Dear God, let Daddy call. Dear God, please send Daddy home.*

In early September in Baltimore, the days are long and humid, and they are contradictory. Summer is over, and also summer lives on. The night of September 11, 1987, full dark settled in slowly over our house, a velvet creep onto the fresh bricks and their mortar, a chic olive-putty color we'd chosen as a family. Shadows deepened from brown and green and slate orange to a full, final black. The new landscaping, in the middle of all those empty acres, vanished as night fell.

I wrote in my diary: *My father is a missing person. I keep hoping that I'm going to wake up and everything will be okay.*

Into my pillow, I moaned and wept. *My puppy, my puppy, I want my puppy . . . I want my daddy . . . I want my puppy . . .*

I never saw my daddy again.

# INTERCOM

MOM KEPT ME and my sister out of school for a week. She tried to hide it, but I knew she was terrified. She did not want to let me and my sister out of her sight, or at least not out of the house. Our new home, which had felt spacious and private before, now felt isolated.

We gorged on daytime television, gorged on the elixir of *The Price Is Right*. Studio audience applause bled all through the living room, and the white noise muffled our collective dread. Bob Barker would invite the next member of the studio audience to come . . . onnnn . . . *DOWN!* Cheers filled the space where my sister and I sat, in silos of fear. Someone would undulate and sob their way to Contestant's Row.

Would Contestant No. 4 win a new Buick Century station wagon? A top-of-the-line refrigerator? Would Bob kiss her on the cheek? Would she play Plinko?

From my fort of blankets on the periwinkle blue couch, I did my best to dissolve into the scratchy upholstery. I focused on those questions, which could and would be answered. If Contestant No. 4 made it to the Showcase, maybe she'd win *a new car*! She would at least go home with a lovely parting gift. She would at least go home.

Dad had not come home. No one knew where he was. No one knew if he was coming back. We couldn't visit friends, although I didn't have very many.

Before, Mom had encouraged us to take walks in this safe, bucolic homescape. The new house saved us from the speeding cars and exhaust fumes of an expanded Silver Spring Road. Here we could roam.

I know my father had dreams because we were in this house. This house and its surrounding acres were a dream come true. His parents were German immigrants who'd had two sons and a little house and a modest working-class life. Our new house embodied second-generation-immigrant dreams, and they had come true.

The front door opened up to birdsong and the perfume of sunshine broiling grass. Mom and Dad brought this place to life—from sheets of paper on a table to a multidimensional patch of heaven, a broad brushstroke of sky painted vivid over land, what felt like infinite land between us and anyone else.

IN THAT FIRST WEEK, we had two types of visitors: my mother's family and Baltimore City detectives. As far as I can recall, Dad's brother, my Uncle Bob, and his daughters, roughly the same ages as me and my sister, did not come over.

The Baltimore Police Department had classified Daddy as a missing person. But the two detectives, Ed Brown and Donald Kincaid, worked in homicide. Neither old nor young, one was white, the other Black. Despite the heat, each wore a suit and tie, dress shoes. They had walkie-talkies. Guns.

They greeted us somberly. Stiff, formal . . . I struggled to read them.

The sight of strangers was like a blast of sunlight after time in a tunnel. I was shy and overwhelmed. The distance between us was tough to bridge with words. I tried. "Are you going to find my father?"

Behind them, on the wall with the stone fireplace, shadows caught my eye. They weren't really shadows. In the time between the house being painted and our move-in, a bird had gotten trapped in the house. It flew around and around, smashing into the walls until it died. The blood got all over the fresh new cream-colored walls. The painters did another pass, but the shadows floated below the surface of the white.

These two detectives looked down at me, reserved or reluctant or just sad. They couldn't be blunt with a twelve-year-old, but still I hoped for something that would make me feel less hopeless. What I got made me feel even more hopeless. "We're doing everything we can, Katy," Brown said. "Everything we can."

AFTER A WEEK, we went back to school.

The year before, in seventh grade, I'd had Sister Frances Schiminsky for homeroom. She was tall with a commanding intelligence and a fierce smile in her eyes. I adored and feared her. She had a bachelor's in history and considerable expertise in grammar. In her English class I learned to diagram sentences, laying the foundation for my later career as a copy chief. Sister Frances disapproved of comma splices and sniffling, often intoning:

It's not the cough that carries you off /  
It's the coffin they carry you off in /  
So quit the coughin'.

Something violent—but what?—had surely happened to my father. He still had not called. I was waiting for him to call at the same time that I knew, just as I'd known in those first minutes, that he wouldn't. My father loved me more than anything, so if he wasn't calling, he had to be dead. This was what I had known in my waking moments, and denial could not shake a fact so true. This waiting-not-waiting-but-waiting eroded and remade me.

Why would the phone not ring?

The invisible violence was only just beginning to ripple out.

Every morning at St. Joseph Fullerton, the solemn voice of our spiritual and educational leader, Sister Georgine Marie Smith, principal, creaked from a metal box mounted in every classroom. At the time I thought she was impossibly old, but she was only in her late fifties. And formidable. She had a bachelor's and a master's in education, impressive for anyone, especially a woman born in 1928.

On my first day back to school, I was sitting at my desk, a few minutes into homeroom, when the PA system crackled to life. "Good morning, St. Joseph School. Today is Monday, September 21," Sister Georgine intoned. She announced an upcoming chicken dinner and reminded us to get in our orders for milk, plain or chocolate. Business as usual. And then . . .

*Students and teachers: Recently, Eddy Crane, the father of two St. Joseph students, was declared a missing person. He has not been seen or heard from since September 10. This is a difficult time for the Crane family. I speak for all of St. Joseph when I say that they are in our prayers. I ask each of you to pray for the Crane family.*

I kept my gaze trained on the blackboard and felt every set of eyes in that room pivot to me. I would gladly have melted into the black-and-white-checkered classroom floor. It occurred to me to simply get up and flee, but my legs were frozen.

I knew Sister Georgine meant well. But she'd just wrested from me and my sister our privacy, our power to control the most formative experience of our lives to that point. She had in fact extended the blast radius right over the PA system.

For years, I'd wanted their attention. All these kids who knew what *cool* was and kept it from me. When I needed my first pair of glasses in fourth grade, no one at the optometrist pointed out the Smurfs on the sides. My classmates noticed. Glasses were not cool back then, or at least they were fair game for bullying. So I now had four eyes and I'd managed to come to school wearing *Smurfs* too. Those children cooked me and my Smurfs over the open flames of their hard nine-year-old hearts until I one day "lost" my glasses in the clutter under my twin bed.

One year, I came to class-picture day in black leggings, a hot-pink tunic and ballet flats. It was pretty—I wear similar outfits today. But the mean girls in my grade could compliment and mock in the same breath. One day I got a love note in my desk from a kid named Tim, an actual caring person. Except the mean girls had faked it. I can't remember if I cried right there in class or held it in like a barf until I got home.

Mostly, though, these nice Catholic kids treated me like I was invisible.

Now I had their attention.

AT HOME, EVERYTHING was changing. I could not bear the new version of our lives. Mee-Mom, my mother's mother, came to live with us. It turned me hateful.

Mom stood in the kitchen, smoking, staring out the kitchen

window. My grandmother was crying on the phone to her friend Virginia. I couldn't escape her sobs. They still rise in my mind sometimes, naked and awful. "Eddy, Eddy! Lord in heaven help us! Poor Eddy!"

I scorned her anguish with an acid ferocity. I saw her as an invader and treated her as such. Of all of us, she is the only one whose effusive emotion I can recall. I read it as attention seeking. I didn't realize she might be reliving horrors. My grandmother was born in 1913. Her mother died in 1919, in the flu epidemic, and a little brother died, also of flu, soon after. Now she was seventy-four and witnessing the unthinkable yet again, a fundamental breaking of the family unit.

While Mee-Mom stayed with us, my grandfather was home alone. What about him? I insisted to my mother. He'd fought in World War II but he couldn't hard-boil an egg. He depended on my grandmother the way my sister and I depended on my mother. They lived fifteen minutes down Belair Road, and we visited them weekly. That was normal. This sleeping-in-the-guest-room business, leaving my grandfather alone, was an aberration. I would not stand for it. I acted as if her use of the phone was grounds for a one-way trip to the Hague. In my diary I wrote: *The phone bill is 4x as much as mom expected. Guess why? Dorothy, Virginia, Mil, Helen—Lord, she's more trouble than she is help!*

Mee-Mom's presence was the visible symbol of catastrophe. I couldn't fully dissolve into my fog because with her there I could not forget what was happening. A missing person is by definition not visible. My tiny granny and her immense heartache kept Dad's disappearance in the house at all times. Her tears made me hate her. And I felt, violently and adamantly, that this loss *belonged* to me, my mother and my sister. She had known my dad nearly a decade before I was born. He was her son-in-law. No one pointed this out to me, and I could not have held that fact, anyhow.

And so, in the fall of 1987, I experienced the loss of both my father and my grandmother.

# SHERLOCK

I SAT AT OUR kitchen table, still new. We'd lived here roughly a year. I was only twelve. Atop the table were neatly stacked papers that I understood to be adult and serious, along with the latest *Sun*. Each morning I scoured the paper for news about Dad. I stared down, my heart jackhammering. I'd found something.

The print was tiny and I was scared my sweaty hands would smudge it. I could almost hear it shouting up at me:

**FOUND: ROTTWEILER, FRIENDLY**

I read the little ad over and over, frozen still, as if taking a breath would spark the print to say something else. A Rottweiler had been found near BWI Airport. Dad's car had been located in the same area a few days after he disappeared. The ad said the dog was gentle and well cared for. Rottweilers were uncommon. How many of them could possibly go missing at one time? It had to be Sherlock.

"Mom," I called. She was talking to my grandmother. They were always huddled in private discussion now, which made me burn with resentment.

"Mom," I said again, this time louder. "Someone found Sherlock!"

"What?" My mother winced. "Katy, what are you talking about?" But she didn't want me to tell her; she wanted me to stop talking.

"Here," I said, holding up the newspaper. "Somebody found a Rottweiler."

"Katy, that's not Sherlock," Mom said, annoyed. "If the police find him, they'll call us."

Fury was a new emotion. I already understood that the Baltimore police were not omniscient, that they could not possibly read every classified ad. How could I know this so clearly while my mother refused to see? The person who had placed the ad had likely not phoned the police. Why would they? Not every lost dog was connected to a crime. People put ads in the paper or flyers in the grocery store if they found a lost pet. And chances are, whatever the police were doing, they were focused on finding Dad, not Sherlock. Why wasn't my mother listening?

"Why don't you just call?" I pressed. "Why do you have to wait for the police? We can call right now." I turned my head. The phone was next to me, mounted on the wall.

I felt ripped like a sheet of loose leaf between the imperative of obedience to my mother and a daunting new imperative: to do what had to be done, whether or not my mother gave permission. I didn't know if I could trust my mom. This was easily as scary as losing Dad. I was a kid and she was all I had left.

"No, Katy," my mother said in her strained, weary *you're giving me a migraine* voice. "That's not Sherlock."

It may have occurred to me to dial the phone number myself from the phone in my parents' bathroom. But that would be crossing a line that I was years from crossing. I was absolutely *not allowed*. Inside me, anger pooled like gasoline. This feeling toward my mother and grandmother was unfamiliar and overwhelming. I had no idea what to do with it.

I did not call the number in the newspaper. What brought Sherlock home to us was a miracle. A Doberman breeder—one of the only people almost guaranteed not to be intimidated by a Rottweiler on the loose—found him. There's a brief account in the September 30, 1987, *Evening Sun*: "His dog turns up, man still missing. Pet unharmed; hunt continues." Donald Kincaid, one of the detectives who'd come to see us, told the paper that Sherlock was "laying at the end of the driveway as if he were waiting for someone." He was waiting for Daddy or for me. "This is a very obedient dog," Kincaid went on to say. "He never would have left the owner. Someone had to take him away."

The person who found Sherlock asked around and then placed an ad in the newspaper. The ad I had read. *The Sun* says a tipster also saw that ad. The tipster was my angel. Because where I felt forbidden from using the phone, the tipster was in no way hindered. They called Metro Crime Stoppers.

Police gave Uncle Bob a ride to the station. Sherlock, not a large Rottweiler, knocked down Bob, not a small man, and licked him wildly, stubby tail going a mile a minute.

"You think that's the right dog?" one of the officers quipped.

Ken Glenn, who worked with Bob and Dad, picked them up from the station. When Bob let Sherlock into the car, he hurtled into the driver's seat and greeted Ken with the same elation.

"You think that's the right dog?" said Bob.

So, after three weeks, one of my two missing family members was home.

Sherlock had surely seen everything. And he couldn't say a word.

# THIRTEEN

I WAS SITTING AT the head of our kitchen table, both expectant and resentful. It was my birthday. Mom, in slacks, a turtleneck and Keds, had cleared away my dinner plate and gently placed a small package in front of me. "Haaaaaappy birrrrrttthhhdaaaaaay, Katy!" She smiled hopefully. It was early December. Dad had been gone for just under three months. I was now a teenager.

Mom's smile reminded me of the German pastries Dad had relished from Mueller's Delicatessen on Harford Road—fragile as first frost.

Tension hung thick in the house. It always did now. One of our neighbors had a bunch of dogs that lived outside in cages. They barked twenty-four hours a day. But the owners had cut their vocal cords. So the soundtrack to our worry was an incessant chorus of desperate rasps.

The pressure bearing down on me, my mother and my sister felt tectonic. I was Daddy's girl and my sister was Mommy's girl. Now she was Mommy's barnacle. Day by day, as they grew further entwined, I grew colder and angrier. I inhaled books about the supernatural and the unexplained. Werewolves, vampires, ghouls, spirits, spontaneous combustion. I could not get enough horror in library books. Reality, I found, was exhausting.

Tonight, at my birthday dinner, I was sullen and standoffish. I turned my gaze to the packet that my mother had lovingly presented to me and stared dubiously at the pink-tissue-paper lump on the place mat. I had gotten a Walkman the year before, and cassettes of Madonna and Cyndi Lauper.

I opened up the card first. *Happy birthday to you . . .* My mom always wrote the whole song out in the card, which I pretended was silly but secretly I loved. Usually it read,

*Love, Mommy and Daddy*

But this year's card was different. This year—just,

*Love, Mom*

Anger and disbelief. My mother had written my father out of the card. Somehow we had to proceed with things like birthdays.

"Thanks," I said.

I opened my mother's gift. A tidy wicker heart, like a wreath you might hang on the door, but much smaller. My mother had decorated it with ribbon and some dried flowers. She was crafty—every year before Christmas she made sophisticated arrangements with fresh winter greens, shiny baubles and candles for her small circle. She had applied her talents to this, my birthday present.

I can't remember my exact reaction. Maybe I was overtly hostile or coldly polite. If I feigned excitement, I doubt it was convincing. Blank and shut down are more likely, as these states were more and more my spectrum. What I definitely did not do, what I wish I had done: hug my mother and tell her what a wonderful gift she had made for me.

Mom knew I hated it. I saw the dejection deflate her and it just made me angrier.

"She made that for you," my sister hissed later in the bathroom we shared. "You could try to be nice."

I went back into my room and, intentionally or not, the little wicker heart wended its way under my bed. A month or so later, my mother found it, thick with dust. She went into her bedroom. I heard her crying.

I'd never felt so low.

# BLOOD

IN MY DREAM I was screaming. But then I was awake, still screaming, Strawberry Shortcake sheets tangled around my legs and all of it damp, all of it giving off heat. The screaming was no dream. The screaming was because of the pain, which was searing, stupefying. Real. Hard to spell—dysmenorrhea.

Two years prior, I sat on the toilet to pee one morning, panties with cartoon bears around my ankles, and when I wiped, the toilet paper turned red and smelled strongly of something wrong. My heart stopped for a second and then I called for my mother. I was eleven.

"Here, hon, use these for your time of the month," said my grandmother. I stared at her. She held out a clear plastic package with something beige and menacing inside. She and my mother chuckled. I didn't get the joke.

"What is it?" I asked, unbelieving, examining the package in my hands.

"Period underwear," they said, and dissolved into more titters.

The garment, which appeared to be a World War II relic, repulsed me. I was back in a diaper. What was even the point? When I bled through the thick Playtex pads I now took from my mother's stash in her bathroom closet—and bleed through them I always did, at times in what felt like minutes—the blood pooled in the sagging rubber of the ill-fitting brief. I felt them now, sticking to my scrawny butt.

One day we drove to White Marsh Mall. I sat in the back of Mom's Mercedes, chilled despite the heater and my jacket. Rain streaked the car window as I stared out. Tears streaked my cheeks. The pain, the mess, the smell—how could this be life now? Over and over, every month? "You'll get used to it, Katy," my mother said. I shuffled behind her, head down, as we went from store to store. From my waist down, I felt made of hot, wet cement.

When we got home, I sank into one of the wooden kitchen chairs and started to do homework. Then I heard my mother, cold and furious, from the back of the house where my bedroom was.

"What is it, Mom?"

"Get back here NOW."

I walked down the hall to my room. She was pointing at my bed, transfigured by anger. "Get in there. Look."

On the floor, in the middle of my messy room, was a used menstrual pad, brown and hardened with old blood. My face flushed with shame.

"What have I told you about cleaning your room? This is disgusting. We built this nice house and gave you a room and this is how you act? It's DIRTY, Katy."

I shrank back against my bed. It was true. I shoved things under the bed. I hated cleaning. And I also hated my mother for shaming me. *YOU'RE DIRTY* rang in my head.

"I'm sorry," I said, and it came out as a whine. "I didn't mean it."

And, then, the worst thing happened: Dad appeared behind her in my doorway.

"What's the commotion?" he asked. It had to have been a Saturday or Sunday, because of the mall trip and also him being there during the day.

"She shoved a used *menstrual product* under her bed," my mother spat, revolted. The shame and the cramps made me dizzy. I wasn't even sure my father knew till then that I'd gotten my period. And now he knew I had my period and I was *dirty*.

He shot my mother a look that was hard to read. "OK, so she shouldn't leave those things under the bed. Maybe drop it now?" And to me: "Keep your room neat and don't pile trash under the bed." And he disappeared back down the hallway.

Now, thirteen years old, I lay in my bed in a pool of my own blood. *Dad died thinking I was dirty*, I thought. Tears raced down the sides of my face, into my ears. Everything was wet. Every month now, when I bled, I had to stay home from school for a day or two. The pain kept me in bed, unable to get comfortable. I wanted to get away from my body. Sometimes I pictured the bald Mr. Clean muscleman raising an axe over his head and sinking it into my pelvis. It was like this—the agony split me in two. Attack by woodsman would make more sense than this did.

Already I knew by instinct that I had bled through the old towel and through the sheets, the mattress pad. How could I have so much blood to lose?

The house was dark and quiet. I tried to kick off the sheets, feeling a squish like wet galoshes underneath me. I swung my legs over the side of the bed and staggered up, dreading what came next. Hot, wet rivulets of dark ran down my legs. Blood on the new floors, blood on my Raggedy Ann latch hook rug. The hallway still had brown butcher paper in place of a rug. I felt less guilty about blood on brown paper than I did about carpet, but I'd have to see it now every day, the splattered evidence of this new hell. Dad was gone and I bled and screamed in the night every thirty days.

“Katy, what’s wrong,” my mother said, eyes bleary, a fuzzy shadow in the doorway. I wasn’t sure if she ever slept, but my screams had wrenched her out of whatever counted for her these days as rest. I didn’t want her help, when shaming might come with it, but her help was the only kind of help I could get now.

“The cramps,” I sobbed. “It hurts, it hurts, it hurts.”

How could something hurt this much?

# AMNESIA

Somewhere in this time, I forgot. My memory drifted out and away like so much sand. I forgot everything before September 1987, everything before my dad vanished. This was not Hollywood amnesia. I still knew the names of my relatives and our old address on Silver Spring Road. I still had the competencies appropriate for an eighth grader. What I lost was everything before. The forgetting settled in like snow while I slept, while I worried, while I wondered where my father was. A snowdrift of forgetting blanketed what was no longer relevant and too hot to touch: Birthday parties with ice cream cakes and Dad behind the camera. Walks with him through the labyrinth of trucks and hulking metal forms at E & M Machinery. Wandering through the backyard at his mother's, my Grandmom Hilda's, as night fell in summer, on the hunt for gnomes and fairies, fireflies blinking.

I missed my daddy with every cell of my body. The missing felt as biological as the wraith of menstruation. I think it had to be. At thirteen, loss was programming my mind. The bones that grew and the organs that developed and the height that came in and the feet that got larger all did so in mourning. Daddy underpinned my world. His expressions, his moods, his

Old Spice, his gait, his bravado on the phone, his Patsy Cline in his headphones . . . it was my ball of roots. Was he my world? Not the whole, no, but in losing him, it felt like the whole world had gone too. The sudden GONE felt unsurvivable and in a sense it was. To live, parts of me had to die or disappear.

Without my knowing it, my memories, each a precious treasure, evaporated. I could not stop missing my father, so instead my body deleted the context of his existence, of my happy life.

The past was irrelevant and now the past was gone. For the rest of eighth grade I slunk around the halls at St. Joe's, shimmying past other kids' pity and curiosity. I felt relief when the mean kids forgot me, and oddly I also felt forgotten.

I graduated from elementary school and got ready to start high school at John Carroll, a coed Catholic high school in Harford County, about ten miles to the northeast.

# SHERLOCK

Almost no one at my high school knew about my dad. I got picked on, sure, but not about my missing father. Rather, the bullies targeted me for being an awkward loner sad-girl goth—the usual. I didn't have a ton of friends in the conventional sense. But at any given time, I was corresponding with about two dozen pen pals. I poured out the depths of my teen soul to people I'd never met on loose leaf or whatever I could turn into stationery; almost anything could be stationery, I discovered with joy. Then I addressed envelopes to Karin (Brooklyn) or Osiris (Maine) or William (Washington State), asked my mother for stamps and plunked my missives into the mailbox at the end of the driveway, red flag up to signal for a pickup.

When I wasn't writing letters, I was writing in my journal, and when I wasn't writing in my journal, I was writing poetry. There was a rolltop desk in my room, glossy and handsome, alongside my dresser and the magazine cutouts of Sinéad O'Connor and Morrissey that I'd Scotch-taped to the walls. I felt too shy to write at the rolltop desk, as if I had to earn the privilege. Instead I wrote in bed, always covered with a thin brown quilt.

The quilt was a baby gift from my godmother, Yvonne, whom I called Auntie. She was a tiny bombshell, vivacious, with frosty hair, a comely gap in her teeth, gentle energy, a quick laugh. My brown quilt had pink yarn tufts and a pattern of girl and boy cowboys. It anchored me and bolstered my writing. I often adorned it by accident with pen ink. Those blots made me feel like a real writer.

One day I was on my bed laboring over an FB, the friendship books fundamental to the 1980s and 1990s pen pal scene. This was how we made friends: You'd fill out a page with art, your name and address, what bands and things you liked. Flipping through the stapled pages of the palm-size booklet, I took in the considerable art skills on display. I did my best with a rubber stamp or two, and attempted to gothify my penmanship with black Magic Marker.

From down the hall I heard the *click-clack click-clack* of Rottweiler toenails. Sometimes if I got too excited at Sherlock's approach, he would bound away, skittish like a stout little German deer.

Now he was panting in my bedroom doorway, looking like he had survived a war. And, well, hadn't he? My guess was, this purebred runt had cowered or taken off when the men with guns showed up that September night in Curtis Bay. My father ostensibly took Sherlock to work as protection. But this dog was a lover, not a fighter. I couldn't hold that against him. Sherlock found his way back home, and I loved him.

Sherlock rarely tried to get up on the bed; he was too big and it was too small and bouncy. But he would rest his face on the edge so I could caress his dense, velvety block of a head, stroke the satin of his ears, scritch the curt bristles at his chin and, if I was lucky, get a glimpse of his bottom front teeth, crooked like dollhouse tombstones. Worth the warm puff of Rottweiler halitosis. Sherlock accepted the affection, stubby tail wagging on medium high. His glossy, trusting eyes held me.

Since returning, Sherlock followed my mother everywhere. Dogs get PTSD too, and he had it bad. He'd seen his best friend leave this earth, I believe, and he wasn't going to let it happen again. When my mother showered, he stretched out, vigilant, on the bath mat.

Mom needed the support. She would lie on the couch with a cornflower-blue ice pack over her face. "I have a sick headache," she'd say, her voice far away.

*Sick headache* was my mother's term for migraine. I could see how the pain ate at her.

Superficial ties, which is to say most of them outside Mom's immediate family, had withered. The people who might have offered friendly parking-lot chitchat or invited her to casual group events stopped reaching out. Tall, close to six feet, my mom had endured teasing in school, and she carried a shyness with her into adulthood. That shyness became less tentative and more stony. As for God, we began to attend church only on Christmas and Easter—C&E Christians.

Every night she drew the curtains at the front windows. My mother's raison d'être was to protect her daughters. From prying eyes and potential danger.

Sherlock turned away from my head scratches and stepped across the room. He sat down beneath an enormous poster of the Cure.

He began to growl.

Growling was unusual for Sherlock. The sounds he was making were low, rumbling. Hateful.

What on earth was going on?

"Come on, pupper," I cooed from my perch on the bed. "Come on over here."

Sherlock didn't acknowledge me. He was staring down the creators of "The Lovecats" and "Friday I'm in Love," emitting a statement of grim intent from between clenched teeth. Otherwise he was statue still.

The hair on the back of my neck felt cold and tickly, and something was trying to flutter out of my rib cage.

Who did Sherlock think he recognized?

The fluttering knew before I had words. Sherlock thought he was looking at Dad's killers.

I pictured the headlines: *International pop stars the Cure taken in for questioning on the presumed murder of missing Baltimore businessman Eddy Crane.*

I felt myself choking up at the absolute cannot-be-happening of this. The little twin bed had been the boat I played mermaids on with my sister, had held me during chicken pox, cradled me when the bottom fell out of my life. Now I was clinging to this bed like a life raft as Sherlock tried to ID our dad's killers on a Cure poster.

For half a breath I thought: *Robert Smith would not kill my father. He wouldn't do that.* No. It wasn't that Robert Smith or any member of the Cure had been involved. The issue at hand was that Sherlock thought someone on that poster resembled someone from E & M Machinery.

But how could I figure out who? I considered the machine shop workers and night watchman and miscellaneous men I'd known at E & M. They were a blur of work clothes. I'd been twelve the last time I saw any of them, and in the couple of years that had passed, my memory had hemorrhaged. Still, I tried to force my missing father's employees into a mental lineup.

Nothing.

This was roughly 1990. No home internet. I dived into the materials available to me: a stack of Cure cassette tapes in clackety plastic cases, with their precious liner notes, a couple music magazines, *SPIN* and *NME*, and that poster. It was hard to match up the names in the liner notes with the faces on the poster.

The truth is, the look-alike could have been any of them, including Robert Smith, or none of them. Stripped of all the goth and the rock-star accoutrements, you could drop those men into Curtis Bay and they would look perfectly at home.

But the Rottweiler knew something. I was desperate to figure it out even as I knew I was wishing for the impossible.

All of us were struggling to cope. In sticking to my mother like a shadow and now trying to give me a witness statement, I realized how much this included Sherlock.

I told Mom what happened, and she told Uncle Bob. I know, because years later he remembered it. And what was true continued to be true: There was no news about my father. Limbo ruled.

# MERCEDES

On school holidays, I'd go to work with Dad. My sister stayed home—the line between Mommy's girl and Daddy's girl was demarcated hard in the sand. If pressed to ride along, my sister would balk. But I loved it. The hours in my father's tan 1975 Mercedes were all fragrant milk-chocolate-brown leather, music thrumming from the cassette deck and the car's custom speakers, vibrating right through to my marrow. Ash spilling out of the tray and drifting. When these drives show up in my dreams, the point of view is from halfway down the passenger seat, looking out the windshield.

This was long before the era of E-ZPass. Harbor Tunnel commuters had ticket books, whose pages looked like salmon-and-gold Monopoly money and had the heft of old Hallmark cards. Air, brisk with Chesapeake Bay salt and Baltimore grit, would rush in the window that Dad rolled down at the tollbooth. He'd tear out a ticket with a crispness, a flourish. He and the tollbooth attendant bantered. In his stretchy short-sleeve shirt, he was professional but practical—work clothes had to accommodate his girth. Hair going silver around the temples, driving a Mercedes, he was the picture of a friendly, authoritative businessman, someone well-off but who got his hands dirty. On the days I was with him, he was also a proud father.

"Thanks, Hoss," my father would say to the man in the booth. The attendant flashed me a grin and nodded my father's way as we drove off, as if to say, *Cute kid, enjoy it, they grow up fast, I've got a couple at home myself.*

My father, his meaty sun-reddened hands on the leather steering wheel, guided the shining sedan toward the tunnel, toward the entrance bounded by old-fashioned Formstone walls—the stuff John Waters has called the polyester of brick.

And then we were underground; and then we were underwater.

At E & M Machinery, a trailer, the original office, connected to a low-to-the-ground brick building. Truck repair happened across the gravel lot in a machine shop full of tools and vehicle lifts. There was an acid bath for cleaning parts and big rig trucks that lay like sleeping tigers. While Dad worked, I drew in my sketchbook and read my library books, vaguely supervised by the secretary, a thin woman constructed of Aqua Net and eye shadow. I hated her fog of cigarette smoke, how it fouled my hair and clung to my face.

But this was home away from home. I hung back from the men in greasy coveralls out of shyness, not apprehension. I was the boss's daughter, and E & M Machinery's rough-and-tumble crew treated me affectionately.

My dad was Eddy, not Edward. His mother, Hildegard, whom I called Grandmom Hilda, immigrated from Germany with my Pappy, August Crane, in the late 1930s. They named their firstborn son after Nelson Ackerman Eddy, a classically trained baritone who starred in musicals in the 1930s and 1940s, often with his great love, soprano Jeanette MacDonald. For a time, Nelson Eddy was the highest-paid singer in the world. Dad had that love of music, and at times he seemed like an undercover movie star.

At lunch, Uncle Augie drove me to his house in nearby Brooklyn to play. He had full-size arcade games in his garage, where I'd stand on a crate to play *Frogger*, maneuvering the pixelated frog across busy roads and hazardous waterways. Back at the office for the rest of the day, I tapped out my first stories on the secretary's clackety electric typewriter.

I saw Dad only now and then, to ask him for paper and pen. But after a rain, Dad and I would meander the metal hills made of car and truck skeletons. Giant truck bodies lined the lot, sci-fi sentries. All around, towers of truck parts caught the weak South Baltimore sunshine, the stacks of rusted metal like glittering scrap-heap diamonds. They dwarfed me. We crouched next to puddles; I saw my first tadpoles. They whipped and lashed in water that shimmered with benzene and naphtha.

What were our drives like for Dad? What went through his mind as he drove this small serious girl, thick glasses on her face and a stack of laminate-cover library books in her lap? Was he excited to leave sleepy Perry Hall and return to forlorn South Baltimore? I wonder if I, sitting next to him in the passenger seat, was a link, in Sears turtlenecks and corduroys, between the anchor of home and the gritty liberty of Curtis Bay.

# CRAZY

Patsy Cline told me when my mother was sad.

Mom put on a brave front. So much so that I thought she didn't care Dad was gone. I read her determined forward motion as indifference, and I judged her for it. Dad had vanished off the face of the earth, and Mom was making fish sticks on Friday, a Catholic thing, and staring out the kitchen window, smoking, cutting the grass on the riding lawn mower, doing laundry and watching TV. This was evidence of my mother's coping skills and ability to function as a single parent. Yet, with bitter disbelief, I read it as acceptance of Dad's absence.

Once in a while, though, I registered my mother's sorrow rising up from the basement through the ventilation system.

Dad collected vinyl records. He often brought me on his excursions to record stores, yard sales, the houses of other collectors. By 1987, he'd amassed some twenty thousand pieces of vinyl. As some of it was valuable, my mother applied herself to the laborious task of cataloging and selling it.

The basement was the size of the whole house. So when a Patsy Cline record played on Dad's stereo, a broken heart thrummed through every floorboard. The keening of "Crazy" tunneled into everything, acrid as smoke. In my room at the back of the house, door shut, I knew my mother's eyes would be red when she came back upstairs. Patsy Cline told me.

We never talked about it. The fact that we never talked about anything would soon come to a head.

# DRUGS

THE AIR IN the house changed texture over time. Tensions increased. My sister and my mother grew closer, and I grew away from them both.

One night I started to leave the kitchen to get ready for bed. My mother sat alone those nights at the table. She had always waited for Dad to get home to have dinner. She still ate late, alongside the empty place for him.

"Wait a minute, Katy."

My stomach gripped. I had a bad feeling. "What?"

"Don't WHAT me."

I stared at her. We didn't talk much, but there was an unspoken agreement that when I finished homework or got tired of the television, I would say a polite good-night, no hugs or kisses but an acknowledgment, and retreat down the hallway to my bedroom.

"I'm tired. I want to go to bed."

"You're not going to bed yet," she said. "You're going to tell me what drugs you're on."

I couldn't help it. I barked out a laugh.

"I'm not on drugs!" Then added, flatly: "That's insane."

I did not drink and I did not do drugs. I'd taken my friend

Nicole as my date to junior prom, much to the consternation and whispers of teachers and other kids. Nicole called me Sister Kate—as in, nun. Nicole did do drugs. One night we went to see Jane's Addiction and she collapsed near the mosh pit. It could've been heat or dehydration, and looking back, it could've been heroin. Nicole, broad and fair with lush red curls and a sharp wit, drifted through time and space. We'd nap together in her heated waterbed, never touching. She had a boyfriend, and I thought nothing of the intimacies, which seemed natural for teen girls. I loved her, but "lesbian" could have been a comet. If those feelings existed, I was oblivious to them. And also saw no reason why I couldn't take my favorite person to a school dance. What was the big deal? Recently, Nicole had ended our friendship, for fear that I would start taking drugs if we continued spending time together. She said she was honor bound to protect me. "You're too good, Katy. It's not safe for you to be around people like me."

Losing Nicole blindsided me. The irony of my mother's accusation . . . A friend who did use drugs had cast me off because I did not. I snorted.

"Wipe that smirk off your face. I see you. You sleep all day, you don't talk, you're spaced-out all the time."

I wasn't OK. But I wasn't doing drugs or anything else illicit. I did have a crush on an art boy from another high school. He wasn't Catholic. We'd sit on his bed, our backs touching, and listen to the Cure. When he confided to me that he'd had sex with someone, I was incredulous. I could not imagine it. Sex was another country.

"There are explanations for these things, other than drugs, which I am not taking," I said to my mother, stony.

Another friend, this one a far worse influence than Nicole, as she had the soul of a copperhead, knew where art boy's first love worked. She persuaded me to get her back—for what? Having a consensual sexual experience with someone I was not brave enough to pursue myself? Get her back for finding happiness during the hell of teen years? I agreed. One day after school, I drove there, and I sprayed her little hatchback with Silly String. I also scraped a Skinny Puppy sticker off her rear bumper.

"You are going to tell me what drugs you're on, and what is wrong with you, and you are going to stand there until you do it."

What an ugly thing I'd done. Touching someone else's car, ripping off a sticker that a girl had put there because she liked it. Defacing her car with Silly String, so she would stand out, at a time in life when standing out can be excruciating. I had tried to shame her for experiencing love.

Somehow, art boy figured out what I had done, and our friendship cooled. I was even more lonely, and this time I had only myself to blame.

"There is nothing to tell you," I hissed, venomous. "I want to go to bed!"

I had no dad, I had few friends, I did OK in school, I wanted to die but wasn't doing too much about that aside from the occasional sly cut on each wrist. My bedroom and its closed door were my sanctuary.

"Don't you dare move!" my mother snapped. "Tell me what drugs you're on!"

"I'M NOT TAKING ANY DRUGS AND I WANT TO GO TO BED," I spat.

She shot out of the kitchen chair and slapped me, hard, across the face.

# TERCEL

WE HAD CONSIDERABLY more space, fresh air and quiet than we did at the house on Silver Spring Road. I hadn't expected to worry about it. In an emergency, it would take three or four minutes to run to a neighbor. Since Dad had disappeared, I often worried if anyone would hear us if trouble showed up.

Then there was the snow.

Blizzards struck brutally. Among the last photos that Dad took: Sherlock, small but mighty Rottweiler, up to his shoulders in a pristine cloak of snowfall.

The main road got plowed, but we shared a long private road for which we were responsible. She paid someone to plow us out, and sometimes Mom relied on the kindness of neighbors.

I tensed every time I heard her on the phone. She'd say hello and laugh, and say, "Do you think you could plow me out?" It felt precarious. Whenever a punishing storm trapped us, we relied on other people. What if, one day, the neighbors just said no? And when my mother paid people, I had no idea if there was enough money. I was in the dark about our finances.

Snowfall turned up the dial on my sense of paralysis. White world, a white noise of being and going nowhere. Heavy snow illuminated limbo, living in a dream home where the basement would never be finished, and we would never have another family crab feast, where my mother would never again accidentally close the garage door on my dad while he was in the car. (Whoops.) We had gotten so close to the dream, and then God hit pause.

Sometime in early 1991, after I'd turned sixteen, a blizzard pummeled Perry Hall. I watched the snow dump down, blocking our only way in and out. I'd had a plan to do something at school. It might've been a play, maybe I was attending, maybe I had a small part in something. With those first snowflakes, I knew: I wasn't going anywhere.

I can't remember if I showed my mother I was distraught. She didn't know I was cutting my wrists. One morning I got to school, late, and the attendance nun, Sister Kostka, saw the Band-Aid I'd put across my wrist. She glowered and waggled a finger. Sister Kostka rises in my mind now and then, her index finger a bony metronome, her thin lips pulsing *tsk, tsk*.

My mother did know I was unwell. I'd withdrawn even further after the altercation in the kitchen. She sent me to a therapist, which I recognized as an act of care. But I could not relate to the man in the chair who expected me to talk.

As the blizzard turned our world a harsh white, my mother hatched a plan.

"You can go if I drive your car," she said. I agreed.

The event itself is long lost to memory. On the ride home, I sat in the passenger seat, rigid and sullen.

"Now, Katy," my mother said calmly, "hold on when we take the turn." She was referring to a bend in the driveway before the final ascent up a hill that was remarkable only when it was slick with ice.

"I don't need to hold on," I snapped.

I sensed my mother chuckle. "Just hold on."

Suddenly I was gasping, and gripping that built-in door handle for dear life. My mother had floored it.

"Mom!!!!" I cried. "What are you doing?!?"

The tomato-soup-colored Toyota Tercel was going so fast I feared we had taken flight. Somehow my mother had turned my first car into Chitty Chitty Bang Bang. As she maneuvered the small, tan steering wheel—no power steering—I had an overpowering image of her as Snoopy versus the Red Baron. Aviator goggles, leather flying cap, red scarf tossed rakishly over a shoulder.

"I told you to hold on." She smirked, and then began to chortle, pleased with herself. Who was this daredevil? This Evel Knievel in a hatchback? I choked out a sob and gripped the handle with both hands, a pill bug in a winter coat.

The uphill slalom was no match for my mother. And, as it turned out, neither was my own wall of ice. Despite my best efforts, I melted, just a little. I began to laugh too.

We were both in tears when the car thudded to a halt in a snowbank.

Now I wonder: Did my mother spend limited cash on a used car for me, knowing that it would allow me to escape—or that it might be a way for me to come home to her?

# DEATH PENALTY

In high school I found out about Amnesty International. I was astounded. You could write letters to presidents and prime ministers and dictators, and advocate for mercy? You could just say: "I oppose the death penalty," and explain your principled stance? I wrote letters to pen pals all the time. The possibility that my handwritten thoughts could save a life was electrifying.

With the support of my French teacher, Madame Donna Selway, I founded an Amnesty International chapter and led my little crew, mostly other AP students, in letter writing. In 1990 in Argentina, police disappeared at least one detainee, and the president pardoned a former army general awaiting trial on thirty-nine murder charges related to human rights violations. In Turkey, hundreds of political prisoners were sentenced to death after flimsy trials. In Jordan, dozens were detained without charge for opposing the government.

Again and again we wrote to ask for fair trials and the release of prisoners. Our letters gave me a sense of connection to the world at large.

Mom disapproved of my Amnesty work. "Why don't you do something closer to home?" she said one day in the living room.

"Because I like doing this," I said, defiant. Amnesty had given me my first sense of purpose, and my mother's distaste for this lighthouse repulsed me. I think she could smell the budding activist, and it made her nervous. If I got too invested in far-off lands, I might go explore them.

The little clock radio in my bedroom was another link to the broader world, and it told me big changes were possible. In 1989, the Berlin Wall came down, and in 1990, Nelson Mandela was freed. I listened to extended radio broadcasts of both events in my bedroom, awed. Could I too fight for justice? I felt I might like to find out.

Amnesty was an antidote to a subterranean "these things happen" message that choked me at home. Dad was gone, and authority figures, from my mother to the police, seemed to have accepted it. With Amnesty I got out my pen and said, "No, that's not right! You can't do this to people!"

Baltimore-area Amnesty high school chapters met a few times a year, a rare opportunity for me to meet people outside my limited ecosystem. I hit it off at one of those gatherings with an enigmatic kid with *Eraserhead* looks a year or two younger than me who went to a "progressive" private school between Towson and Pikesville. The Park School was a universe apart from John Carroll both in miles and approach to education—we did *Our Town* as a school play; they did *Antigone*. But my new friend's house was just a few blocks from Mee-Mom and Pop in Hamilton, northeast Baltimore. When he invited me to come have dinner with him and his parents, I lit up. We had already talked a blue streak about books and movies, and our shared interest in everything oddball and avant-garde filled me with a rush of possibility. Kids in Harford County generally did not gravitate toward *Riddley Walker* or *Bring Me the Head of*

*Alfredo Garcia*. And this kid clearly knew infinitely more than me about *culture*, a word I intoned with reverence.

The first time I pulled up at the house on Louise Avenue, I saw a fiftyish white guy in blue jeans, a Georgetown sweatshirt and white New Balance sneakers, sitting on the front porch of a sweet dusky-green house engulfed in trees. As I parked the car, he stood up and started waving. This man must be my friend's dad, I thought, a little confused. Because for some reason he was hollering my name.

"Katy Crane! Well, would you *look at that*—Katy Crane is here."

When I walked through the front door, it was like entering Doctor Who's TARDIS: bigger on the inside. Every room groaned with bookshelves that in turn groaned from the weight of the galaxies contained in the books upon them. Narnia. Oz. Encyclopedias of fairies. Birds of North America. Slavic tales. Children's fables like Beatrix Potter's Tom Kitten and Squirrel Nutkin, and her naughty Peter Rabbit. There was an extensive Holocaust studies collection and whole shelves devoted to Emily Dickinson. World War II, Sylvia Plath, Alan Watts. Elaine Pagels and *The Gnostic Gospels*.

I was mesmerized. I didn't know places like this existed. I had loved libraries forever, and I knew what a museum was. But the idea of home as a celebration of books, art and photography—it astonished me. Why didn't everyone crowd their home with story and color? The house on Louise Avenue was alive. Maxwell, the cat, bit me hard when I tried to pet him, but the house itself embraced me like a never-ending story.

"Katy, do you drink coffee?" asked Vicky, my friend's mom. She'd roasted a chicken and some vegetables, and served it with a rice pilaf. I thought she was a wizard. I started to decline the offer of coffee. And changed my mind.

"You know, I never have before, but tonight feels like a good time to start. Thank you, Vicky. And I think I'll take it black."

Gordon Porterfield—this was my friend's dad—roared. "That's the way to do it! Look at you, never had a cuppa coffee before in your *life*. But *Katy Crane* has no use for cream, sugar. That shit's for mortals!"

The steaming black liquid touched my lips and a hummingbird in my forehead began to flutter. I felt exhilarated and hopeful. Before walking through the front door at Louise Avenue, I thought home meant tension and isolation. As a teenager and a guest, I surely did not grasp that first impressions can be deceiving, that my experience as an outsider at a single dinner could not reflect the whole of a complex family dynamic. Nonetheless, I realized another kind of home might be possible: conversations, collaboration, sharing ideas, engaging with the world. Instantly, I idealized these new friends and hoped they could somehow take me in, as if I were a stray cat.

Almost certainly, Gordon and Vicky would have asked me about my parents that night. I can't remember if I talked about Dad. If I held back then, though, I soon shared my secret with them. I felt comfortable with these people. In Gordon, particularly, I sensed an ally, a potential guide with a lantern who might help me navigate all the darkness. When I went home after the coffee, I felt the glow of a lantern inside myself, a respite from sadness. I couldn't wait to go back.

At school, I never brought Dad up unprompted. Except once.

We had at least one religion class every year. Senior year, our teacher was a priest who coached some of the sports teams.

One day we were debating the death penalty. As founder of our high school Amnesty International chapter, I'd given the death penalty a fair amount of thought. I opposed it then, and I still do. Human beings are fallible; the justice system is racist and corrupt. People of color and the mentally ill are disproportionately imprisoned. Methods of execution often result in torture. And there's no undo. If the state puts someone to death and it turns out a witness lied, the dead victim of state violence stays dead. I also think years or decades without the freedom to go for a walk or take a drive on a country road in the middle of the night or bring home a kitten is all worse punishment than death.

My classmates did not share my point of view. The room was split into two halves, with about twenty desks on each side facing into a center aisle, which Father Ken Farabaugh paced throughout class, moving the dank air with his strides. Across from me was a football team's worth of Lukes and Chads and Bransons. They were sneering. John Carroll offered its students a quality education, should they apply themselves, but avid readers did not make up the majority. I suspect these particular young men picked up only as many books as passing grades required. Yet these Catholics were entirely confident that a person, any person, on death row deserved to die.

Back and forth we sparred, until the inevitable happened. I saw it coming and I knew what I would do.

Branson, a red-faced sports star with tousled brown hair, pointed a thick finger in my direction. "How would you like it if someone killed one of your family members?" Like a baseball aimed at my head.

My heart was pounding out of my face. I felt adrenaline sweat fouling the armpits of my regulation white Oxford shirt.

"My father was murdered four years ago," I said. I was a baseball bat, cracking his shot back at him hard enough to split wood. I was terrified in confessing my secret to these people—still mostly strangers—but my voice was loud, if unsteady. "My family will never recover. Killing the person who did it won't bring him back or fix anything."

You could have heard a pin drop.

Those boys looked taken aback and a little afraid.

Father Ken ended class early.

In homeroom, the talk each morning was increasingly dominated by college. I tended to tune out anything that seemed irrelevant to me. But then kids started asking me where I wanted to go to college and the reality of it struck me cold. I knew, with the kind of certainty I had known that Dad was dead, that there was no college plan for me. One day when I got home, I went into the living room and found my mother on the couch with her eyes closed.

"Mom, am I going to college?" I asked.

She was quiet for a second. Then she said, "I guess you'll go to Towson."

# REPORTER

THE SPRING OF my senior year, 1992, my mom said we were expecting a visitor. This was odd; almost no one visited us. More odd: The visitor was from *The Sun*. A newspaper reporter.

"Is something happening?" I asked, purposely vague. Our house was a battleground for information. My mother had it; I wanted it. I was learning, slowly and the hard way, that approaching my target from a side angle was reliably more effective than charging head-on. There was still no guarantee of success. But the wrong approach could lead to a fight and days of mutual silent treatment.

Mom didn't reply immediately. When she spoke, every word had a carefully considered quality, as if she were paying me in exact change: "The writer thinks a story in *The Sun* paper might get someone to come forward."

I received this statement in good faith. It was nearing five years since the night Dad didn't come home. Five years. No funeral, no grave site, no idea where he was. I often wondered if Dad got cold, wherever he was decaying. I knew it made no sense, and yet—the idea of my daddy falling away to bones somewhere without a cozy blanket and pillow was an unbearable sorrow that dogged me when I tried to fall asleep in my own little warm twin bed.

When the man from *The Sun* came to the house, he seemed as out of place as the detectives had years ago. But different. Where they'd seemed uncomfortable, this man—David Simon, he said his name was—exuded calm confidence. Sherlock lay at my mother's feet.

Simon's questions took us back to 1987. Our responses were the most any of us had spoken as a family about Dad's disappearance in all this time. Even now, it wasn't a conversation. Individual thoughts emerged from silence and silo for a moment, and we saw them, saw each other, flickering like things that fluoresce at the bottom of the sea.

"What do you think about what happened to your dad, Katy?" Simon asked me. I flushed, considering my own aspirations of becoming a writer. Simon wrote articles that appeared in the same newspaper where Pop had spent thirty years, largely in Linotype operation.

"People who do things like this never think how it affects anyone else," I replied.

Simon wasn't with us for more than two hours, but it felt like a before-and-after moment. I felt something hard to express and harder to hold: hope. Maybe, somehow, a writer could save us.

# LIBRARIAN

I WAS SHELVING HARLEQUIN romance novels. At the Harford County Public Library in Bel Air, we had an immense stock of these paperbacks. *Kiss of a Tyrant. Sun Lord's Woman. Perfect Passion.* People borrowed them in large numbers and at a brisk clip. The romance tales had a section of their own, three floor-to-ceiling shelves. It was not enough. When I entered the employees-only area of the library and saw carts packed tight with Harlequins ready to be shelved, I quavered.

This was a terrifying quandary. My job was to roll as many carts as possible out onto the floor and accurately, efficiently shelve the books that were ready for circulation. It was verboten to roll the cart back incomplete. And I got in enough trouble as it was.

In my performance review, my stern supervisor, Connie McEowen, wrote in a luxuriant cursive:

*After six months, Kate has to be reminded fairly often about socializing with patrons during work time.*

*Kate has difficulty arriving on time. She has been late at least six times in the past month.*

*She has at times forgotten she was to sub for another page and failed to show up.*

My first job was in fast food: running the cash register at a Roy Rogers that later turned into a Hardee's. I despised it—the smells, the fluorescent lighting, the grease that got into everything. I called out sick constantly until finally I quit. My manager, a skinny short kid with mud-brown hair, said on my last day with a withering glance: "You'll never amount to anything." I squirmed thinking of him and Mrs. McEowen comparing notes.

So I became adept at jamming these slim paperbacks so tight on a shelf that you almost needed a crowbar to remove one.

*Dark Betrayal* and *Rules of the Game* stared up at me reproachfully. I glared back and furtively stuffed them behind some Emily Dickinson hardbacks in the 800s.

I had a more pressing matter to navigate. I had decided to tell Ms. Schutzman about Dad.

Jan Schutzman was a trim librarian in her fifties with short salt-and-pepper hair and glasses. She was my favorite of the librarians. I was scared to approach any of them—the info desk seemed like high court. But whenever I had questions, I knew Ms. Schutzman would take me seriously. Also, she liked to talk about books and took an interest in my life that I craved from a safe adult.

"Hi, Ms. Schutzman," I said tentatively.

"Hello, Katy, how are you today?" She was bright and warm.

"Do you remember that story in *The Sun* I told you about?" I asked, scarcely above a whisper.

"Certainly I do," said Ms. Schutzman.

"Would . . . you want to see it?" I tried to act cool but it was a need I had no name for.

She told me she'd find me in the stacks when she had a few minutes, and back I went to my cart of Harlequins.

A little while later, I saw Ms. Schutzman nod in my direction, and, quick and quiet, I followed her. I felt like we were doing something dangerous. For me, it was.

We did not talk about Dad at home. David Simon's newspaper story, "Dead or alive? Businessman missing for years," was published May 31, 1992. Its two thousand words were a key. When my mother gave me a copy of the newspaper to read, it was like rushing into an oxygen tank after years of gasping for breath. Almost all of it was new information, flooding my mind the same week as I was graduating high school. Dad's absence permeated. With those sheets of newsprint, so did his presence. All of us read the story but we did not discuss it.

Now I was in a corner of the library, spreading out the family secrets in digitized newsprint to someone who was at once a relative stranger and someone I trusted.

A microfiche machine is like a cross between a movie projector and a TV. It takes pieces of film and projects them onto a screen. Ms. Schutzman disappeared for a moment, returning with the appropriate selection of *Sun* film.

The machine lit up and began to whir.

*Eddy Crane is at his desk inside E & M Machinery company in Curtis Bay, when he is confronted by at least two gunmen. They order him out of the building. Mr. Crane resists. They shoot once or twice to disable him, perhaps wounding him in his leg. He fights on and they fire again, killing him. They put the heavyset businessman's body in an office chair, then drag it out to a pickup truck and drive the body away.*

Simon wrote this part in the present tense, so every time I read those lines, I am with Dad in his windowless office at E & M, a room that holds mostly his desk and big faux leather chair on wheels. I'm there when the men with guns show up in that doorway, the only way out of the room. Today, so was Ms. Schutzman, in her neat slacks, sensible shoes and wire-rim spectacles. A chaperone.

I didn't want to stare at her, but I couldn't help it. I was starved to let someone in. I took in Ms. Schutzman's kind, intelligent face taking in the lines of type with care and gravitas. I caught flickers in her eyes—were they just words of type, reflected, or were they glimpses of shock, discomfort, sadness? I was, after all, still a child, and she was an authority figure, absorbing this horror under observation.

The pressure must have been intense. Jan Schutzman handled it gracefully.

*This is a story about what happens when someone simply and permanently disappears.*

*It's a story, too, about a family's frustration and suspicion in the months and years that follow.*

*Most of all, it's a story about the limitations of police and prosecutorial power and the chasm that exists between reasonable suspicion and reasonable doubt.*

William Walter "Augie" Augustin Jr. brought my dad into E & M Machinery, and the two were like brothers. Until 1986. That's when, the article said, Dad began suspecting his friend and partner of stealing money out of the business. At least one employee was fired, but money kept disappearing. Then one day, the story continued, Dad confronted Augie and there was a shouting match. At some point, the two began working opposite hours to avoid each other.

Reading this story had filled in so many blanks, and the light-bulb moment about Dad's schedule, a minor detail amid so many greater revelations, was huge for me. I hadn't understood why Dad went to work at night. I knew night shifts existed, but he hadn't worked in a hospital or factory, any type of place I associated with a graveyard shift. That he slept so late into the day and left for work in the afternoon had signaled to me that something was wrong. I'd been right.

*"Every time I hear about remains being found, I call the authorities before they call me," says [my mother].*

I scrutinized Ms. Schutzman especially hard when we scrolled to this section. Would she think, "Oh, of course. Of course Katy's distraught mother followed up with the detectives on a regular basis"? But this was not the mother I knew—the mother I fought with, whose silence devastated me. She called the detectives? This blew me away more than any other detail in Simon's story. I'd thought she had "moved on." It had not occurred to me that the front my mother presented to me and my sister might be curated. I took her wall of secrecy at face value. I had never considered that she constructed it to protect me.

I watched the librarian read these fundamental facts of my life, ones I had myself learned only weeks before. Lines of ink photographed for eternity or until the library threw away the film. My own statement, there in print:

*Katy Crane accepts that her father is dead, but the fact angers her: "People who do things like this never think how it affects anyone else."*

I thought of my Pop. I'm sure he never imagined that the newspaper he gave his working years to would one day chronicle so much grief in his own family.

On a tip, the Baltimore police had drained an acid vat at E & M—nothing. I learned in this story that an anonymous tip also told the police my father's body had been disposed of at a Curtis Bay soap plant.

Slow and steady, the librarian's eyes followed the lines of type.

The detectives wanted to charge the night watchman and

then pressure him to implicate others. They sought permission from Timothy Doory, who was chief of the violent crimes unit of the state's attorney's office.

*Mr. Doory demurred.*

That line had stuck with me. Mr. Doory demurred. Given my voracious reading, I knew what *demur* meant, but this context cemented it in my mind. *Demur*, to take exception. *Demur* is all civility and distance. My mother and sister and I could not *demur*. We could not hold ourselves at a cool remove from the ghost Mercedes rotting in the garage, the Rottweiler who could not testify, the father who never came home. Doory's *demur* was our shredded family, which might have interfered with his conviction rate.

*"A lot of money disappeared when he left," Mr. Augustin said about his missing partner, declining to be interviewed at length. "That whole thing was a mess and I'd just as soon forget it."*

The article said Augie knew he was a suspect but suggested Dad had run off with money he embezzled. Augie also demurred, right there in *The Sun*. So, my onetime "uncle" was telling everyone my dad was a thief. I had liked the man I knew as Uncle Augie. I was the boss's daughter and he was the boss's best friend. I felt comfortable at his house. When I visited the office, we would huddle over a sheet of paper and discuss designs for a writing desk he planned to build me. It occurred to me then that I was never getting that desk.

The week Dad disappeared, I understood quickly that Uncle Augie was involved. It still stung to hear the way he talked about Dad. The scorn was palpable. I'd never seen that side of him. It was a lot to hold.

I also learned about a buy-sell agreement that had existed between Dad and Augie. If either of them died, the other would buy out the widow's half of E & M with a $500,000 life insurance policy. When the insurance company released money on the policy, Augie sought some of it, saying Dad had stolen from the business. My mother settled.

I was a teenager and I understood: If Uncle Augie had in fact been involved, then he had gone on to demand a paycheck for killing my father. The brazenness of it . . . Every time my mind touched it, I wanted to take something sharp to my wrists, to drown out one pain with another. I glanced furtively at the most prominent white scar on my left wrist and then back at Ms. Schutzman. Her eyes behind her glasses, which glinted with my life story from the microfiche machine, were serious.

It was an active kind of quiet. For in watching Ms. Schutzman take in my catastrophe, I felt my own understanding of it deepen. Home felt sodden with denial; the librarian's face held something else: solemnity.

Reading along together, we got to the last quote from my mother. *"I've crawled into a shell and tried to keep my family at home. I don't want to go out anymore," she says.*

*"When someone dies, you have a funeral, you have a grieving period. We haven't had that. We are still in mourning."*

I thought I might cry. I had been so angry and hateful, and there it was: My mother told the world, or at least, Baltimore, Maryland, that she just wanted to keep us safe. To preserve what remained of the whole.

Ms. Schutzman turned to me. "Thank you for sharing this with me, Katy. I am so sorry for what you and your family have gone through. And I think you are very brave."

In the hush of the stacks, I let someone in to the family secrets, possibly for the first time. I didn't have to find the words to explain. David Simon had written them, had persuaded someone to set the type, like my grandfather had done at the very same newspaper, and print this story, the most important story I'd ever read. Newsprint got rumpled and thrown away, but now our story glowed, preserved for a time, on the screen of the microfiche machine.

Ms. Schutzman and I returned to our separate posts in the small suburban library, dwarfed and muffled by the rustling of thousands of other stories.

For a moment, I felt less alone.

# SLEEP

I PARKED THE CAR as close as I could to the door and eyed my surroundings before getting out. I was at 1433 W Hamburg Street in the Pigtown area of Baltimore. Just like Curtis Bay, where Dad had worked, there were lots of trucks and warehouse-looking windowless buildings low to the ground. The sky was a cathedral, and tonight, a biker bar was church. This area was perfect for rock or punk shows—deserted after dark, no neighbors to complain. But I always felt like a moving target walking to and from the car. With bands making eardrums ring inside, no one would hear you scream.

My edginess was common Baltimore sense, unlinked to my father's disappearance. My friend Autumn and I had been mugged a few years earlier after leaving Louie's Bookstore Cafe in Mount Vernon. Neither of us got hurt physically—the guy who took our wallets had a knife that glittered under the moon below the Washington Monument—and the experience rattled me. I learned to be more aware of my surroundings. A lot of random, it's-nothing-personal sorts of crime took place in Baltimore. Whatever had happened to Dad was different—that was personal.

In spending time in Baltimore City, I could also get closer to Dad. I went to punk shows, artist-run cafés and museums that were significantly closer to E & M than my mother's house. There was no graveyard to visit, but I could wave at the Key Bridge when I went to see Candy Machine and Trenchmouth at the Rev or, like tonight, Lungfish at Memory Lane.

I'd graduated high school in May of 1992 and started at Towson State that fall. The transition felt colorless. My friend Brady had died in a car crash that January. I wrote a eulogy for him in the high school newspaper, and his parents created a writing award that I received at commencement. There was a photo of me hugging Brady's brother, my thick, russet curls cascading down the back of my white robes, in *The Aegis*, a Harford County newspaper. I'd taken Brady's death hard, and my sense that life was grief only, rinse and repeat, deepened. I still lived with my mother and sister, as Towson was a twenty-minute drive away. A night owl even then, I struggled to make my morning classes and would relentlessly tailgate the other cars also driving to school. One of my victims once whipped their parking permit off the rearview mirror and waved it at me in protest—i.e., I'm going exactly where you're going.

I was the first person in my family to go to college, and I took this seriously. I was also receiving another kind of education. Punk was a solace and a source of meaning. Amnesty International had led me to it. I got my first exposure to leftist politics through Riot Grrrl and DC bands in the sphere of the Dischord Records label, co-owned by Fugazi's Ian MacKaye, a living icon in the scene. I was reading Angela Davis, Assata Shakur, Frantz Fanon, bell hooks, Gloria Anzaldúa, before I ever took a women's studies class.

Lungfish was political in the way of a street-corner prophet on LSD. I took them more as religion, and I treated Lungfish shows like mass. That night on Hamburg, I double-checked that the car was locked and took purposeful strides toward the entrance, where a cheerless neon sign proclaimed in black letters on a white background: MEMORY LANE, and below it, in smaller letters, 50s AND 60s. I pushed open the door and handed a stout biker with a crabby face my ID and five dollars. It might have been Fudgie, the man who took Memory Lane from a biker bar with a stripper pole to a nationally renowned punk club in the early nineties.

Memory Lane was a grimy hole-in-the-wall so thick with cigarette smoke you could cut it with one damp pinky finger. Except for the headlight glare of the stage lights, it was dark. A few dozen people milled about with beers and smokes.

There he was, setting up: Daniel Higgs, head gleaming, haloed in a dense hedge of salt-and-pepper hair, beard dense like boxwood. In a black jacket and trousers, I read him more as priest than rock star, though none of the fathers or deacons at St. Joe's had as many tattoos.

After an eternity, the music started. A droning, the crack of percussion. The crowd began to move as if we were one creature. A low howl emerged, from nowhere and everywhere. Daniel Higgs nurtured that howl like a flame; it gained speed, filled the room. Vibrations washed over us all. I was there and not, drifting out of deep freeze and into trance. I was floating and I was above everything, running across my grandparents' fragrant green lawn with the garden hose in the heat of August, opening gifts under the tree while Mom and Dad smiled, seeing Sherlock for the first time, Dad grinning ear to ear like a little kid. Daniel Higgs helped me travel back in time. It was easier to hold the rage at what I'd lost. And the sweetness of it.

But I could never see a future.

"BYE, JOHNNY!" I waved at the jolly, clean-shaven bear of a man who was one of the servers at Donna's Coffee Bar, where I was a barista. He was older than college age, making him a minority here, had thinning hair, was kind. I was always glad when he was on the schedule. He treated me like a light in his day, and his gentle acceptance surprised me. I couldn't shake the nagging sense that I was bad, essentially damaged. Sometimes that job felt like the worst of high school. Like the time a rumor started that I had a crush on Randy, a frat boy with curly hair. "I don't like dykes," he told me, in a bland grunt, as I passed him at the prep station, as if he were telling me table 5's roasted vegetable sandwich on toasted olive bread was up. Ashamed, I went home that night and cut a line in one wrist for the first time in several years. The straights at work took the opportunity to judge me as weird, and the gays as suspect. Except for Johnny.

When there weren't thunderstorms, July afternoons in the Baltimore metropolitan area tended to be hot and sunny, and today was blazing. Leaving the café, I was loaded up with lentil soup, roasted vegetables and a stack of books I'd brought because I carried books like Linus carried his blanket. A little unstable with my full arms, I took special care to look both ways as I crossed the street. My car was in a narrow lot reserved for a bank, and we weren't supposed to park there. But parking in Towson was tricky, and Donna's got busy. I was more likely to get a ticket because I didn't make it to the meter with fresh quarters in time than I was to get towed.

I leaned into the back seat and secured the books and the food as if I were fastening a toddler. The tub of Donna's lentil soup was so hot the plastic was soft. The heat radiated through the crisp white paper take-out bag.

I felt a tap at my hip.

*Tap tap . . .* I must have forgotten a book. Raymond Carver's *What We Talk About When We Talk About Love* looked up at me from the seat where I was still contorted inward. *Tap tap . . .* Maybe I had forgotten my tips. I'd made about fifty dollars that day. *Tap tap . . .* It must be Johnny.

I called over my shoulder without looking, "Hey, did I leave something in there?"

I paused my back-seat fiddling, waited. Silence. And then: *Tap.* More insistent. I realized what I felt at my hip was not the index finger of a friend.

Then came the voice, low and serious.

"Give me your keys."

I froze. I imagined my hip bone and the head of my femur exploding into the back seat, splattering Raymond Carver and my lentil soup with blood, muscle, cartilage.

*No, this is the only car that has ever worked properly! No, this car runs! You can't have the car that runs.* I felt the begging on my face and knew he didn't care. I had something the man with the gun wanted and he was going to take it from me.

Devastation. Which switched to panic.

Then and now, I often put something down and two minutes later require half an hour to find it. I had no idea where my keys were.

"I . . . I don't know where they are," I said.

He pointed the gun a little higher. "Find them."

This wretched negotiation was taking place in between cars, off a side street in a suburb that was not particularly busy. No one was coming to help. I flinched, wondering what would happen if someone did accidentally come up on the scene. What if someone startled him? I had to find my keys—immediately—and I had no idea where my keys were. I tried not to dwell on the possibility that this man might take my car and shoot me anyway. And then Dad and I would both have bled out alone from gunshot wounds. I swayed.

An eternity later, I sat on the curb, stunned and deflated, as the car I adored sped off, driven by an unsmiling gunman who had taken it from me by threat of death. I knew I was lucky to be alive and the grief tore a gash into my heart. The 1987 Nissan Sentra was stalwart. I felt safe in the car. That car was how I got out of the house, and maybe how I might one day move on.

Some greater force was not allowing me to leave. I sat on the curb and wept.

I SAW AS many punk shows as possible, often driving to DC, now in a used Plymouth Sundance that my mother had bought with the insurance money after the carjacking. A few nights before was Sleater-Kinney on a side stage at a new club, the Black Cat. Enthralled, my friend Abby and I had pressed against the back of a stage barely big enough for the trio. I loathed myself for accepting the car from my mother. But it made experiences like this possible, so take it I did.

One night in the fall of 1994, a show at the Beehive Autonomous Collective in DC went late. I was tired from driving and tired from listening to young men from good homes in the suburbs scream into microphones. Brad Sigal, a friend in the punk scene with grumpy-old-man vibes, offered me a place to stay. "People sleep on the couch all the time," he assured me. Brad was like a big brother. I said yes and followed him back to Arlington, Virginia, where he led me into a dark two-story house that I'd later realize was held together, almost literally, with duct tape. It was humble but pin neat even though some eight people lived there.

Brad and I tiptoed up the stairs so he could show me the bathroom. "If you need to pee," he said, in an urgent whisper, "it's this door. But, listen"—and he turned to make sure I was listening. I nodded, rapt. "You have to jump from the doorway to the toilet area. Can you do that?" I gauged the space. Nodded.

"Why?" I asked.

"The whole floor will come down if you step on it. Don't forget. JUMP!"

That night me and my full bladder successfully vaulted from doorframe to toilet area. It seemed like a sign. Soon I was Positive Force DC's 112th or so housemate.

AROUND THIS TIME, I visited friends for dinner in Mount Pleasant. Positive Force was in Virginia, and underneath all the punk flyers and punk crust, the building itself was charmless. In Mount Pleasant, the DC neighborhood about half an hour away over the Potomac where most of my friends lived, the houses were rambling turn-of-the-century Victorian row houses. They had enchanting details, and some were built into hills and accessed by steep brick stairs, perilous when icy. I was over here often, as two women friends shared the house with members of a prominent hardcore band.

While we were savoring our tofu curry and brown rice, and chatting about bell hooks, the front door slammed. I tensed. Back in Baltimore County, my family were experts at communication via doors and cabinets. When the male roommate, a vocalist for the band, entered the room, he radiated anger.

I took a "speak when spoken to" tack with guys like this. He was famous; I was not. I respected him without questioning it. I knew most of the words to most of his songs, which challenged authority and spoke truth to power. The singer had never been warm to me, but people in the DC punk scene were largely aloof. I was used to being ignored. I was, however, entirely unprepared when this man began to berate me.

"YOU'RE ALWAYS HERE. DO YOU PAY RENT HERE? NO YOU DON'T PAY RENT HERE. DO YOU PAY FOR MY FOOD? NO BUT YOU SURE DO EAT MY FOOD. DID NO ONE EVER TEACH YOU NOT TO FUCKING TAKE WHAT'S NOT FUCKING YOURS? WHAT THE FUCK IS YOUR PROBLEM?"

He had crossed the room much too fast, and now he was close. I froze, ice on a collision course with lava. I took an uncertain step back, stumbled. Somewhere behind me, I knew, was a wall. Where could I go?

I thought about his accusations: Those bowls of tofu stir-fry I'd devoured but never offered to pay for. The nights I had crashed in a sleeping bag on the floor of their basement, often with bands that were in town for a night or two.

I was mortified.

I had found fury in DC punk. I found mine, and I found others'. Sometimes it was solace, and other times it was just more danger.

Someone had finally called out my fraudulence. Who was I to be in this subculture of creativity? I was a hanger-on. I'd also come to believe that if Dad could be murdered with zero repercussions from the justice system, I must somehow be bad. Otherwise, how could someone be allowed to get away with murder? I'd always known that someone would figure out I was a phony.

Over the days and weeks that followed the incident in Mount Pleasant, my despair spread like a pool of ink, blotting out the sun.

The final straw was a bottle of body lotion.

I'd found it underneath the bathroom sink at Positive Force and commandeered it for my room. My housemate Wendy either left a note or mentioned at a house meeting that things of hers were going missing. Even after I returned the lotion, the shame was the crack that undid me. I stopped getting out of bed. In certain ways I had grown up at twelve—in others I had not. Here I was, twenty, and I had stolen a seven-dollar health-food-store product from the communal bathroom. The confusion of it sent me over a precipice into my futon bed in my unheated room. I understood that people you called uncle sometimes killed a parent and got away with it. I knew nothing, however, about the etiquette of sharing space in a group living situation.

I felt like I was missing an essential sense, without which survival was impossible. And why survive? My dad had been successful. Being successful had not worked out for him. People in my family did not go to college. I had no idea how to be an adult.

Sleep let me live and die at the same time. I stopped eating. I stopped talking to people. I started threatening suicide, in a matter-of-fact way, to my friends. In a letter to Andrew, a punk kingpin in England, that stayed tucked in my journal, I wrote:

*I've become indifferent to most of my friends . . . It seems all too clear that when I have needed my friends most, they just aren't there. I feel very alone. If I survive this, I'm not sure that I will ever want to trust other people again. It's fucking not worth it.*

Then, comically:

*I really hope you are well.*

*Get in touch when it's convenient for you.*

I never sent that letter, but I'm fairly sure I mailed some other doom-and-gloom doozy to London, and a once-close friendship died off.

The sense of my worthlessness got heavier and heavier. These feelings dominated—lead balloons, clamped tight to my wrists and elbows and shoulders. There were lead balloons in my lungs too, and in the pit of my stomach.

I'd transferred from Towson to a Quaker college, but, miserable in Greensboro, North Carolina, I was doing an internship for the National Lesbian and Gay Health Association in DC. There I made databases and did administrative tasks. Slowly I stopped showing up. I was too ashamed to quit. I was too ashamed to go. They were so much better off without me. Shame kept me in bed more and more. At the worst of the depression, I was sleeping twenty-plus hours a day.

I was sick, and I was also immature and petulant, and I was in the middle of an arduous, soul-level lesson about what friendships should and should not contain.

I slept in my Positive Force futon bed for three months, getting up only to use the bathroom. I dropped at least fifteen pounds and I was already small.

*Live or die, but don't poison everything.* That Saul Bellow line appears at the beginning of an Anne Sexton poem. I was at a crossroads, and that was the signpost. I had to choose. Kill myself or live. No more of this mewling, useless in-between. I had to pick.

I visited the Whitman-Walker clinic for LGBTQ people, and they gave me a list of queer-friendly mental health professionals. I found it overwhelming—shame that I was weak, not sick. Terror that I would be mocked. How would I pay for help? I didn't deserve help. All of this layered over with the desire to sleep. Every day I made one phone call to a therapist on the Whitman-Walker list. At last I found one. She had a lilting European accent, and she taught me two terms: major depression and post-traumatic stress disorder. The psychiatrist said I had both. My mother agreed to pay for the sessions, which insurance would partly cover.

I decided suicide should wait. I pictured it like a Goldenberg's Peanut Chew, the power snack of the punk rock vegan. I'd put suicide in my back pocket like a Peanut Chew. I could always take it out again later. For now, I started talking to the psychiatrist twice a week.

# VWs

I WAS IN A deep squat in my black T-shirt, worn black jeans, grimy black canvas shoes. Me and my perpetually stuffy nose were buried in the minifridge that was my responsibility and my realm at Donna's, the café where I was once again working. I felt like I was at the bottom of a pool that smelled of old vegetables and Mocha Java. Above me was a tinnitus of laughter, clinking forks, Sarah McLachlan and urgent shouts in the kitchen.

That happy hum, the sounds of meals and life and workday, was torture. I was suffering from a kind of claustrophobia: Every time I turned my back on anything, I felt the phantom muzzle of a gun against my hip.

Where in the hell was the unopened box of soy milk?

I was also certain I had prepped a tub of iced coffee. Somehow that too was gone. I was foggy, so, so foggy. My mind was shrouded in mist. I could no longer think crisply. I had no idea what was fresh trauma, what was old trauma, what was some physical illness that the doctors were dismissing as stress and fatigue. It was easier to believe I was defective.

I stared into that refrigerator as if it might reveal what was wrong with me or where my father was if only I stared hard enough. The minifridge said nothing, not even where the soy milk and iced coffee were.

Then, the inevitable.

I felt a light shove from behind. I launched upward and spun, uncoiling like a spring. My hand flew out in a limp, shaky slap and just missed a sorority girl named Jenny.

"What the fuck is wrong with you?" she snapped, glaring.

Good question. My heart was going hard. I hated drawing attention to myself, hated being called out, rebuked. It was hard enough feeling worthless without seeing it on other people's faces. I took measures to make that impossible—for years I had worn glasses, fairly necessary for me to see, only when driving a car. If I kept my corrective lenses off, and I could not see the world, then maybe the world, in turn, could not see me. I'd read somewhere that James Dean did this, which seemed romantic.

"Oh no, I am so, so sorry," I said, but I was talking to the sorority girl's back.

The psychiatrist's diagnoses, major depression and PTSD, felt ominous, and I wasn't entirely sure what they meant. I was finding out, though. Every shift I worked at the coffee shop, I parked in the same lot where I'd been carjacked. I arrived on edge, heart racing, fighting off tears. Flashbacks. When I went back to my car, the same thing. I was making about ten dollars an hour. There was no other feasible parking option.

Even so, I was beginning to stabilize. After an ill-fated attempt at Paxil, the psychiatrist had prescribed an old-school tricyclic, imipramine. It gave me cotton mouth, and I got dizzy when I took stairs or stood up quickly, but the depression symptoms were slowly lifting. I still drove to DC once a week to see the psychiatrist, and for the moment, I was living with Mom again. I'd gotten a failing grade for the internship and would not go back to Greensboro. Instead, having realized that proximity to Baltimore and DC contributed to my academic success, I planned to reenroll at Towson State in the fall.

I was determined to get my degree and to live on my own. I assumed my sister would be close on my heels.

"There's nothing wrong with living here," she said when I asked about her plans one day in the bathroom we shared. "I like this house." Our eyes locked in the mirror. "Going to school doesn't make you better than everyone else."

My sister would come to her senses, I thought. She also had a point. Some part of me did believe that going to school made me better. Or at least that it made me right.

I was attuned to my mother and sister like a tree is attuned to the soil. I read the silences, the tensions, the resentments, the energy building up at fault lines. Almost ten years had passed since my father's disappearance, and I still slept in the room where I first learned he had not come home. Same twin bed, same lemon-yellow walls.

I began to connect the leadenness of it all with my desire to sleep. This was the point of the antidepressant: Relieve the symptoms so I could uncover what was causing them, before it was too late. Still, I was terrified I'd start sleeping again all the time—and what if I couldn't pull myself out of it?

I loved the house my parents had built. I loved the tranquility of the land around it. And I could not live there.

"HON, DID I hear you say you need a room? You should give my friend Harold a call."

It was Jane, one of the bakers at Donna's. Jane turned out the featherlight scones and the deep trays of ganache that I furtively excavated with a tablespoon. Her brownies, half butter, could charm the knickers off a queen.

I trusted Jane, a tiny woman with a shiny chestnut-brown bowl cut and maternal curves. Unfamiliar with craigslist, I wasn't sure how to find housing. She wrote a phone number in neat blue ballpoint on a Donna's napkin.

WHEN I ARRIVED at the door, Harold's house seemed askew. I squinted upward, convinced the tilt must be an optical trick.

Off in the distance I heard the noises of York Road, four tight lanes with constant traffic. This place straddled the city-county line. The weeds grew tall. The pointy attic with its little window smiled out at the sky—hey, hon. Everywhere I looked, there were old Volkswagens. Blue ones, tan ones, a pink one, a cherry-red one. A Bus, two Bugs, a Karmann Ghia.

Before me was a beat-up brass knocker. I grasped it and rapped a couple times. No one came, and inside was quiet. It was hazy, early summer, still light out, the humidity almost visible. Fireflies were beginning to blink, fluttering harbingers of night.

I waited.

Maybe I got the time wrong, I thought. I was turning away when the door flew open.

The man who appeared in the doorway was wiry, leathery, brown from the sun, and had brown eyes that flashed through a mane of black curls and a beard that stretched in all directions like a tomato plant in August. And although he would have been in his forties, a few years younger than my mother, he seemed unspeakably old.

"You Kate? I'm Harold!" He pronounced it with a *T* at the end, as if his name were spelled Haroldt or Harult.

I liked the room, and the rent was four hundred dollars. This was double my rent at Positive Force, but I didn't have to pole-vault from the doorway to the toilet at Harold's house, which also seemed less likely—slightly—than PF to be razed in the near term. My mother still gave me some money every month.

I moved in.

Harold grew ivy in his bedroom. I ringed my own windows with Christmas lights and was delighted with the effect. To save money, we kept the thermostat on fifty degrees, and we stapled plastic over all the windows, trading oxygen for a lower Baltimore Gas and Electric bill. In my room I had a bay window. I had coveted this since I was small, when I'd read book after book with girl protagonists who curled up with novels in bay windows behind curtains.

Not long after moving in, I sat on the dining room rug and examined one of Harold's bookshelves. The bottom row stood out to me: *The Fellowship of the Ring*, *The Two Towers*, and *The Return of the King*, by J.R.R. Tolkien. I'd heard they were good.

"Oh hey! I love those books!" Harold was streaking past in a cloud of motor oil and Chandrika, an Ayurvedic soap with patchouli oil and sandalwood, on his way to a forest-green Beetle in need of repair. I was still wary of Harold—it was so hard to know what to make of him. Pure creative energy, lightning atop a string bean. But I was living at an auto shop, albeit an unusual one, and Harold's house felt like home—an echo of the Mercedes in my parents' garage, the trucks all over the grounds at E & M.

I looked at the paperbacks in my hands. They felt warm, a little tingly.

"You should read them! Aw, man!" His face burst into excitement under all that black hair. "They're beautiful. Like nothing you've ever read. You'll read them over and over!"

The next day, I woke up in my futon nest, wandered to the

kitchen, poured Erewhon cornflakes and soy milk into a bowl and went out to the back porch with a *Lord of the Rings* paperback socked under my arm.

Between the house and Harold's garage was a long, lush garden, growing and growing with the passing of the summer days. Moving through the rows of tomatoes and snap peas in a deliberate sway was his dog, Gypsy, wresting her breakfast off the vine, her sinewy old frame rocking with the effort.

THE TOWSON STATE course catalog was a dense book with onion-thin paper and print. I pored over it, a tub of vegan ice cream at my elbow. Choosing classes was a thrill.

A special English course was on offer in fall 1995. Virginia Woolf. I had heard of her. Woolf sounded cool. Woolf sounded *literary.* She sounded like the kind of writer who, if I studied her hard, would help me be smarter. And I liked the idea of an entire semester devoted to the work of one author.

There was a catch. *Instructor permission required*, said the catalog, menacingly. My stomach sank further: The teacher had the sparkling, sophisticated name of Jacqueline Wilkotz. I shrank in my chair, defeated. Why would *Jacqueline Wilkotz* want me in her class? There was no way I was qualified. I could never live up to the expectations of this mysterious Wilkotz.

But then I figured, what did I have to lose? I picked up the dining room phone, the only one in the house.

When she said hello, I heard intellect and refinement flowing across the line, and I knew in an instant that I would not pass muster.

I stammered. I should hang up. But that would be rude. Oh, God, this had been a terrible idea.

"I would like to take your Virginia Woolf class," I said, "but I saw that I need permission. I'm sure I'm not qualified."

"Why would you like to take the course?" she asked, summer-lake serene.

I stammered some more. My face burned. Virginia Woolf was not for people like me. But I got a few sentences out.

"Wonderful," Dr. Wilkotz said, and to my amazement, she sounded delighted. "I look forward to having you as a student."

ONE DAY WHEN Harold was out working on an artist friend's Karmann Ghia, I called Mom.

"Would it be OK if I have Dad's cameras at some point?" I asked. Dad had a number of 35mm single-lens reflex Nikons. He had been the family photographer. "I would really like to start learning photography, and it would be great to teach myself or take a class using his cameras."

Silence on the line.

I had agonized over my tone and choice of words. I aimed for deferential—I could not say in words or tone that my father's cameras should be mine, dammit, and it was ridiculous that they were sitting in a closet when I could use them. Except that's exactly how I felt, and I was roughly twenty-one and so-so at tact.

My mother spoke, voice tight and suspicious: "What do you want them for?"

"Like I said," my voice getting edgy, "I would like to learn photography, and it would be great to have Dad's Nikons."

"You have a camera already," she said.

"That's a point and shoot," I replied, my voice sharpening. "Dad's cameras are manual. I would like to learn real photography. I would like to learn on my father's cameras."

"No," she said. "I'm not comfortable with that."

"Why?" The frustration and tears were fluttering their way in. Deferential was out the window. "They're just sitting in your closet. I could be using them."

"You've never been interested in photography before. I don't understand why you want them now. That's expensive equipment and I don't want it to get broken. No. They're staying here."

A couple weeks later, I wound up at a pawnshop somewhere off West Fayette near the Poe House. I came back to Harold's with a Pentax K1000, the classic student camera.

I bought a book, tried to wrap my head around shutter speed and f-stops, and I started to take pictures. I'd drop my film off at B&L Photo in Perry Hall, where Dad had gone. Barbara handed me envelopes of black-and-white prints. Harold in beard and flannel. Billie the cat—short for *Hillbilly*—staring plump and contrary from the dining room table. "These are good, Katy," said Barbara. I kept shooting.

This is how I spent the summer after the major depression. *Live or die, but don't poison everything*, I repeated to myself over and over. I sat on the back porch and read while Harold fixed VWs and Gypsy and Billie snoozed among the squash and tomatoes. With each page I turned, as Frodo and Sam found the courage to face peril, I moved back toward the light.

My life was manageable: I went to my job at the coffee shop. I drove to DC to see my psychiatrist, although I struggled with some fundamentals of responsibility, such as putting gas in the empty tank. I looked forward, with genuine excitement, to Virginia Woolf with Jacqueline Wilkotz. I was also going to do an independent study on Black feminism with a professor I knew already, Judy Beris. Slowly, I began to build visions of myself and of the world, of who I might become and where I might go.

THROUGH IT ALL was Harold. Once he took down the ceilings without notice. I came home to an indoor snowfall. Plaster dust was everywhere. A housemate, Jeff, was apoplectic—his DJ equipment was engulfed. Some of my books still hold the now-ancient silt. Another time, Harold shoveled out the entire street the day after a blizzard so I could take a road trip. Once he plummeted straight off the roof while I was napping. Then there was the time metal shavings got into his eyes; our housemate Amy and I had to hold him down to administer eye drops. Harold didn't shrink from climbing on the roof or using a blowtorch beneath a VW near his eyes and beard. The eye drops were kryptonite.

One night I came home to find a prehistoric moth impaled with a butcher knife to the kitchen table. And a scrawled confession: THIS IS WHAT HAPPENS WHEN YOU LEAVE THE SCREEN DOOR OPEN. The impaler was Jeff. Harold, a vegetarian and the world's biggest animal lover, sobbed over that slain moth. Shouting a blue streak of Bawlmerese, he evicted Jeff loudly enough for the whole block to hear.

I began to suspect that Harold was not only a *Lord of the Rings* fan—he might also be Gandalf, or at least an eccentric second cousin.

I was lonely—punk had given me a sense of identity and a facsimile of family. The illusion had shattered when I'd gotten sick. I listened to Excuse 17 and Heavens to Betsy on cassette in the car, but the people I hung out with in the punk scene were scattering. For now, my job was to recover my health and to achieve my bachelor's degree. So I took comfort in Billie, Gypsy and Harold. I worked. I ate good things from the garden. I got stronger.

MY UPWARD TRAJECTORY had its bumps. On June 15, 1995, I heard Harold muttering in the living room. He was in the recliner next to the TV. On the screen, the O. J. Simpson trial. Testimony about leather Isotoners. And then the big moment: O. J. tugs on the gloves, which do not fit him.

I exploded. "He killed her and he's going to get away with it because of . . . *gloves*?"

Whatever station we were watching cut to footage from June of 1994, of O. J. in the white Ford Bronco, speeding away. "Does anyone ever go to prison for killing another person in this country?" I went upstairs and curled up on my futon.

I felt so tired sometimes. A fatigue bigger than me, bigger than the city of Baltimore or the entire Eastern Seaboard. This was the world, I was realizing. Men with guns hurt people and got away with it. Men with guns murdered fathers and wives, and, it seemed to me, faced no consequences.

I had fought so hard to survive that winter of sleep at the Positive Force house. On days like this, I wondered, why? I was going to have to fight my whole life to stay safe from men with guns and knives. Complicating my uneasy relationship with sleep—I was sick more often than not. I began having nonstop sinus infections, joint aches, urinary tract infections. My sense of shame at the winter of sleep made me want to keep sleeping, but the terror that I wouldn't get another chance propelled me forward.

I never felt judged by Harold. He was glad I was there. Harold wasn't a dad substitute, but he was safe.

DONNA'S COFFEE BAR employed half the artists in the Baltimore metropolitan area. One of them was an enigmatic thirtyish sculptor named Martha, a chef. My height and all muscle, she kept her fine ash-blond hair under a hat. Her glasses were a set of severe Bauhaus rectangles that intensified her scowl. Instant overpowering crush.

"So, uhhh, you're an artist?" I asked one day. I was sitting at the coffee bar eating a roasted vegetable sandwich on focaccia that Martha had made for my employee meal. We all got sick of roasted vegetables—in Donna's lingua franca, RV—but, mother of God, those sandwiches, also served on olive bread or sourdough, with a lashing of balsamic vinaigrette, were otherworldly delicious.

Martha leaned over the marble bar and regarded me gravely. "Never get an MFA," she said. "Poison. They kill your ability to make art." If she were a cowboy, she might have spat in the dust for emphasis. "Promise me," she hissed.

I stared at her, eyes saucer-wide and reverent. Clearly, she had *life experience*. "OK, I'll stay away from MFAs," I assured her, as if I were denouncing cocaine.

Once she brought in a book of collage art by Hannah Höch, a German Dadaist, to show me. Another week it was photographs by Nan Goldin. The art of Louise Bourgeois, Kiki Smith, Cindy Sherman. I was minoring in art history at Towson, and these books captivated me. I would eye the schedule to see when Martha and I were working, and daydream ways to seem cooler. Cautiously, I confided to her that I hoped to one day be a writer. She seemed to approve.

Dating in Baltimore was difficult. I was not interested in men, and sometimes it seemed like there were no lesbians. Either that, or they all chain-smoked. My childhood aversion to cigarettes had intensified. That Martha didn't smoke seemed miraculous in the mid-nineties.

"WHATCHA READING, KATE?" Harold had flown in, a cyclone of beard and motor oil.

"It's not quite as good as *The Lord of the Rings*," I told him, "but it's still pretty good." I handed him my stack of $7.95 Harcourt Brace & Company paperbacks, all by Virginia Woolf, and he perused them with keen interest.

Upstairs in my treasured icebox of a room, I'd set up an antique rocking chair I'd bought for thirty dollars in Richmond, Virginia, on some punk thrifting expedition next to my three big windows, with my quilt from Auntie Yvonne. The Christmas lights I got at the Caldor department store up York Road winked around the window frames. I was alive. I was back in school. I was reading my first Virginia Woolf.

MARTHA LIVED IN a big house not far from Gordon Porterfield and my grandparents. One night she and her housemates, a painter who smoked heavily and a distinguished gay man with a sinister Russian Blue cat, had a party. I was nervous. Martha was a decade my senior. I knew what the invitation to the grown-up artist party might mean. But what could she see in me, a skinny twenty-one-year-old basket case with home haircuts who always had black hair-dye stains around her ears?

I felt her take my hand under the tiki lights. "Do you want to stay over, Katy?" she whispered.

Ten million jittery crickets came to life in my rib cage, but I played it cool. I caught the roommates exchanging a smirk. They thought I was a child. They were not wrong.

I have never liked sleeping away from home. But Martha's bed had clean Company Store sheets, whisper soft from years of use. The sound of Baltimore summer nights—insects, backfiring cars, the occasional faraway shouts—held its own beneath the music Martha chose: Spain and Morphine, moody and chic.

Martha slipped off her worn Gap khaki shorts. I held my breath. What would be underneath? I wondered. I had never seen a girl naked. Soon I saw boy underpants, dark under a white belly that glowed in the dark of her room. Off came her holey black T-shirt, revealing a racerback sports bra. This seemed very in line with what a lesbian would wear beneath street clothes.

Then she slid into the flannel sheets with me. She smelled nice, like laundry. I froze.

I was eager to cast off my virginity and make my lesbianism official, as if a laminated card would arrive in the mail after my first gay orgasm. But who touched who, and how? I thought back to early-childhood experiences with astral projection. Sex must be like that, I thought, like leaving my body, and doing gymnastics in slow motion in space.

The first time I had sex with Martha was also the first time I had sex. Despite all the body and sex positivity in punk and Riot Grrrl, I had practically zero experience.

I was tense but open-minded—and fascinated to see a naked woman. My boy crushes were always pencils in hipless corduroys. Martha looked like an ancient Greek statue, all chiseled muscle.

"That was so great," I said. "I think I came. Wow!"

Martha snorted. "You didn't come. We barely had sex."

. . . Oh. Overwhelmed with embarrassment, I pretended to go to sleep.

Soon after, we began to discuss living together.

# NEW YORK

# MISSING PERSONS

An autumn night was closing in swift outside the floor-to-ceiling windows of my office near Central Park. I dialed a now-familiar 718 number—mine—from my desk and waited for the voicemail to click in.

"Hey, Mar, it's Kate. I need to run an errand after work. Don't wait on me for dinner. I'll figure out food when I get back. Love you." I placed the receiver gently back in the cradle. Did I love her? The question nagged at me.

Our first year together, I had driven up on weekends from Baltimore and stayed with her and our friend Clarence, a cat lady and copywriter, in a fifth-floor walk-up on the Lower East Side. My routine was to pick up a tofu-rice dish from Café Zen in Belvedere Square and devour it with chopsticks as I tore up I-95 North and the New Jersey Turnpike. I lived on three hours of sleep and continued to suffer from ceaseless sinus infections and brain fog. Somehow, though, I dined by chopsticks at highway speeds with trivial spillage, a point of pride.

The primary-colored bowls I'd bought at a vintage store in the East Village lived in that apartment on a metal shelf. They were a promise in Pyrex that I was going to have my own apartment someday soon with Martha. Now, after a year and change of dating, my pretty Pyrex had a home.

Martha and I lived together in a narrow floor-through on a sooty stretch of Metropolitan Avenue in Williamsburg, Brooklyn, an area barren and bereft of trees in comparison to lush, forested Baltimore. Eighteen-wheeler trucks barreled past our street-facing bedroom windows at all hours, leaving grime on the sills and traces of Curtis Bay in my mind. I'd viewed this place alone, in the midst of a gut renovation, and saw its potential. The construction had uncovered charming columns near the living room, hardwood floors, and a deep violet-blue flooring from the early twentieth century in the kitchen. I was proud of my first New York apartment. But the dreaded lesbian bed death had already set in. Though Martha and I had been together under two years, she criticized me relentlessly, and I was uncomfortable with her drinking.

What do lesbians bring on a second date? A U-Haul. At twenty-two, I learned that old saw by living it. I hadn't really known Martha before we moved in together. I had little relationship experience, and I wasn't sure if it was normal to be so unhappy with your girlfriend.

"A lightly trained monkey can do it" was what our friend John told me about temping. I'd applied to internships at magazines like *Lingua Franca* and got no reply, not even a rejection. I assumed, without a hint of self-deprecation, that I was not good enough. I did not have a single friend in the world of media or publishing to explain to me how many people apply to internships, how biased the selection process can be, how an editor might choose a family member or an alum from their college. I really did not want to go back to restaurant work. So I'd clung to John's words when I moved to New York, and he in turn introduced me to his contact at the temp agency.

Bright enough, friendly enough, and a people pleaser who mostly showed up on time, I found I had steady opportunities for receptionist and administrative assistant gigs. Which is how I came to explore dozens of office buildings throughout Midtown Manhattan. I returned home with free socks from Donna Karan one week and an indestructible golf umbrella from a real estate company the next. Subbing for a linguist-cartographer with calligraphy for handwriting led to a full-time job at the private equity firm where I now sat in khakis and a cobalt-blue blouse from the Gap. I made about $45K, which seemed unthinkably rich, and I had a retirement plan and health insurance.

The assistants all sat at an interior bank of cubicles. To see the dumbfounding splendor of Manhattan, I would slip into an empty office when everyone else had gone home. The firm was at least thirty floors up, maybe fifty, and from up here, the city entranced me at any time of day or night.

I answered phones, booked travel with an agency run by an upbeat and exceedingly patient duo, reserved Town Cars, filed expenses. I smiled politely when an elderly lech, one of the managers, draped himself over my desk and murmured how much I resembled his wife when they were lithe young lovers.

Martha would be irritated with me for getting home late. But I pushed thoughts of her out of my mind. I had personal business to take care of.

I packed up and hurried down a long corridor of glass and polished wood toward the elevators.

"Good night, Katharine!"

I waved at Irene, an ebullient blonde from Staten Island who ran the office with a salt-of-the-earth sparkle. The elevator doors opened, and I stepped into the hush. My stomach dropped as I sailed back down to earth.

My mask dropped too. I crumpled as I hit the street and strode toward the subway, tears starting. It was November 1997, and I'd been in New York full-time for under six months.

On the seventh, a week or two previous, a TV news segment had stopped my heart. Camden Sylvia and Michael Sullivan had disappeared. The couple lived at 76 Pearl Street, in Lower Manhattan, in a rent-stabilized, 1,400-square-foot loft just off the East River, like my dad's trucking business was just off the waters of Curtis Bay. Camden and Michael, thirty-six and fifty-four, respectively, paid $304 a month on the fifth-floor space; my rent on the Metropolitan Avenue apartment, half the size of theirs, was $700. Winter was setting in and with the Pearl Street loft bitterly cold, Camden and Michael threatened to withhold rent over insufficient heat. Then they vanished. Wallets, passports and a set of keys were all still around. So was a video they'd rented at 4:20 p.m. on the seventh. It was as if the couple had stepped out for an errand. Yet they were gone, and so was their landlord, Robert Rodriguez.

Strings inside me came untied.

I couldn't tell my girlfriend. She had no patience—*What do they have to do with you?* she would say. There was no room for this kind of strangeness in our domestic partnership.

I was beside myself, raw and agitated. On the subway, I looked around. *Did you hear about that couple who disappeared?* I wanted to say. *That happened to my dad too. Did you know that people can just vanish?*

There was a vigil tonight, and I was going to support them—two brand-new missing persons, and all their loved ones, whom

I would welcome, wordless and from a respectful distance, into this awful club.

I slid into a window seat on the N train at 57th and kept my face averted. It was a local with frequent stops. At Whitehall Street, I got out and walked, studying the directions I'd written down on luxe private equity firm stationery. I didn't know the Financial District well.

People went missing all the time, I told myself. And I could not ignore these echoes.

A few minutes later, I found my way to a triangle of pavement with a bunch of grieving strangers. I felt like a firefly with my birthday-cake candle. I was pretty sure Camden and Michael were dead.

Standing there in the brisk late-fall night, my fingers going numb, I had transformed from executive assistant to wraith of death. *You're never going to talk to them again*, I thought. *You're never going to see them alive again. Maybe you'll get their bodies back. But they're gone, and there won't be any justice.*

I said nothing to anyone, wishing only to bear witness. I held my candle and wept freely. I was crying for Camden and Michael, and for their family and friends, for whom my heart was breaking. And I was very much crying for me.

# HOMICIDE

At the other end of the apartment, Martha was half-way to the bottom of a bottle of Gato Negro from Tro-janowski, the liquor store on Bedford Avenue, prepping a tortilla casserole for dinner—a tasty standby of beans, tomato sauce, cheese and anything else we had, zucchini or spinach or rice or eggplant, that was filling and cheap. We knew how to eat well on little money, and Martha was a superlative cook.

We also thought we were drinking well. We called Gato Negro, at about $8.99, the good wine.

Life on Metropolitan Avenue was sedate, almost suburban in its rhythms: We both had nine-to-five jobs and did laundry on the weekends, hauling it over to Driggs Avenue in a wire cart we named the Jazzy. Aspects of the neighborhood, like Radiac, a short-term storage facility for low-level radioactive waste, gave me the creeps. Yet Williamsburg was so full of artists, book-stores and quirky coffee spots that I had warmed to its Curtis Bay elements.

On this particular night, as my girlfriend made dinner, I was watching the TV in our bedroom, sitting on the floor on the pumpkin-colored wool rug from IKEA.

*Homicide: Life on the Street*, the prime-time police drama

about Baltimore, was based on the book by David Simon, the reporter who'd come to our house and written the *Sun* feature about Dad in 1992. I watched every episode. This one started off with banter between Richard Belzer, Kyle Secor and Jon Seda. Yaphet Kotto enters and summons detectives to his office in his muted, authoritative way. Then shots of "the board," where the names of the murdered appear, in red if the case is open, in black if it's been solved.

To underscore the hard-boiled vibe, Belzer makes a *Maltese Falcon* quip that sails over Seda's head.

The wife of a writer had come to the police. No one had seen her husband for five days. In a small office, a colonel, called in for the high-profile nature of the case, says that L. P. Everett is missing.

"Not missing—dead," she corrects him. "My husband was murdered."

Detective Ballard: "OK, he's been murdered and the body is where, exactly?"

Mrs. Everett: "Well, that's what I need you for."

Cut to the first commercial break. I didn't think much of it. A murder without a body. Just like my dad. But it's a generic detail, and besides, my father wasn't a writer.

Incredibly, it was the seventh season of *Homicide*. I felt connected to this TV show, because of the location, and because, with that feature story, Simon had unlocked a door to life-altering knowledge.

*Homicide* didn't interest Martha, but she didn't mind if I watched it. She knew very little about this part of my background, which, in my early twenties, was the dominant force in my life. I didn't know how to talk about it and I didn't want to try. Martha, however, was more open about her past. One night, in the dark at Clarence's apartment on a futon, she whispered to me: "I ran away one summer when I was little, Katy. I lived in a cave with a Sasquatch." I knew my Bigfoot lore—her account tracked. I believed her.

I also thought what had happened to my father was stranger.

The episode resumed. The wife, Patti D'Arbanville in a smart hat and veil, tells the roomful of police officers that when she last spoke with her husband, he was at his office in Canton.

They watch a video in which the missing husband says that he believes his literary agent is going to kill him, and if anything happens to him, that's where investigators should start.

Privately, the detectives express skepticism. "We have real murders to work. I think we should dump this on missing persons," says Ballard. "Ten to one, this hack is at a Vegas craps table with a bimbo on each arm."

Huh. My father was murdered in his office. And Canton is right on the other side of the Harbor Tunnel from Curtis Bay. And the cops didn't believe he was murdered. And they told my uncle that he had probably run off with some woman.

A feeling drifted in like fog. Something was wrong. I started to sense my jaw setting into a clench.

Ballard and another detective, Gharty, go talk to the literary agent, who's incredulous that his missing writer has pointed the finger at him from a VHS tape. The detectives say that Everett hasn't been seen or heard from in days, and his Jaguar isn't in the garage. Huh. My father was a Mercedes fanatic, and his car, the tan 1975 Mercedes 300D, was missing for the first week or so.

It couldn't be. But the more I thought about it, the more it made perfect sense. David Simon had already written about my dad. Now he had a television show. About Baltimore. Of course he would be likely to dip into the stories that had interested him, affected him.

Sitting on that scratchy IKEA rug, I realized I was watching a dramatization of my father's murder. Maybe to Simon this was some kind of tribute. Yet as I watched the circumstances and investigation of Dad's disappearance unfolding in front of me on the TV screen, I didn't feel honored. The fog gave way to shock and rage.

I could not look away. I had to take in every second of it, compare truth with TV. I'd been asleep when Dad met his end. Tonight I was a witness, reluctant but riveted.

*This cannot be happening*, I thought.

Every bit of dialogue confirmed the oily churn in my stomach. I knew Martha would be calling me to dinner any minute. It didn't occur to me to call her in for support. I knew my girlfriend would not understand the uneasy exchange I was having with the television.

At the next commercial, I got on the phone long-distance to my mother. Our family dynamics had further shifted with my move to New York. I left. She and my sister stayed. I thought my move might expand our collective worlds. I pictured trips to the MoMA, pizza at Grimaldi's. But my mother didn't like to drive on the highway or ride trains.

"Hello?" I heard it in her voice. She was watching it too.

"Are you seeing this?" I asked.

A pause. "Yes."

"I'll call you when it's over."

When Everett's car shows up in long-term parking at BWI Airport, near where Dad's turned up, cops take it as further evidence that he skipped town. But eventually it dawns on them that they might actually have a murder, or at least a truly missing person. So detectives Ballard and Gharty head down to Everett's office.

From the second they flung open the doors and turned on the light, I saw what they didn't. I knew what was coming.

Ballard lounges on the couch and laments, "There is nothing out of the ordinary in this office. There is no blood. No bullet holes. No signs of a struggle."

The desk chair is missing, bozos.

"THE CHAIR IS MISSING!" I snarled at the screen.

I heard a startled clatter in the kitchen.

"Katy, what's going on?"

"Sorry, Martha. I'll tell you later," I said, trying to keep my voice even.

"No chair," says Gharty. "The desk chair is missing." Wow, they muse. We've been looking for what didn't belong but couldn't see what should have been here! But why would a leather desk chair be missing? Blood cleans up easy off of leather.

Police never recovered my father's chair, and its disappearance probably had to do with his size. Two grown men would have struggled to carry him out the door. He would never have walked out with them.

Gharty gets a clue. "A bullet hole," he says. "If you put a couple slugs in that chair, there's no repairing it." He clears off the desk with a theatrical sweep of his arm, revealing multiple bullet holes in the wooden desktop.

"Bingo."

Then Gharty backs into the office doorway.

"Semiauto. He stood right here and he walked the shots up." He makes his hand into a gun. Cocks it.

"BOOM." A gunshot sounds.

"BOOM." Another shot.

"BOOM." And another.

I'd been watching this show for years, and it had never occurred to me that one night I might see my own life unfold on the screen. I felt dazed.

Martha wandered in, wiping her hands on a dish towel. When she saw my face, she winced.

"What's wrong?"

"This episode of *Homicide*," I said, choking on tears. "It's about my dad."

She raised her eyebrows in doubt. "About your dad? Why would the TV show be about your dad?" She shook her head. "I'm sure you're misunderstanding something. Come and eat. And it's your turn to do the dishes. And to vacuum. And we've got to get up early tomorrow." Her friends, also artists, were coming up from the Jersey Shore.

I felt like I was having my own Bigfoot experience. Our little sixteen-inch television was beaming my dad's murder back at me in no uncertain terms, while my girlfriend assured me such a thing was impossible, here, have some cheese and beans, and a dishrag for later.

I wanted my father to stay out of my apartment, and I also desperately wanted to be alone. I was in Brooklyn; I thought I was safe. How far away did I have to move to actually escape Baltimore?

# CHARAS

My relationship with Martha ended within a year of that *Homicide* episode. I'd normalized the baseline unhappiness and constant criticism, but then she left for an art retreat for part of a summer. The relief was staggering, and what's more, my friend from high school with the amazing dad had moved to Brooklyn. The fun we had was so far from the quality of my time with Martha that I dreaded her return. The nail in the coffin was a woodworking dyke down the street whose yellow pit bull had a heart of gold. That went nowhere but Heartbreaksville for me; twice, in fact. But it was the push I needed to break up with Martha.

Sometime in 2001, I met Jaime. A bike messenger in her early twenties, she hung out at the same vegan café on Bedford Avenue that I frequented. She thought she was straight. She was wrong. And now I was riding a custom fixed-gear bike she gave me and learning how to fix bikes in my spare time.

I moved on from my illustrious temping career when a public relations firm hired me as a researcher. My boss there noticed both my editing skills and my boredom with the role, and kindly introduced me to a friend on the creative services side of *The Wall Street Journal.* Suddenly I was copywriting and proofreading marketing materials, work I found interesting and challenging. The feedback I got from my coworkers gave me confidence: I was good at this work.

On September 10, 2001, there was a torrential rainstorm. I got soaked coming home from the *Journal*'s office on 6th Avenue in the forties, and again when I met friends for dinner at Oznot's Dish to mark the anniversary of Dad's disappearance. Where I got very drunk. The next morning, when I woke up and turned on WNYC, I froze. *That can't be right,* I thought, and all the same, self-conscious at my overreaction, I left my boss a voicemail saying I thought I should stay in Brooklyn. I got dressed and walked down to the water. The skyline was charcoal with smoke, and, impossibly, one of the Twin Towers was gone. I was still getting my bearings when, with a nauseating sizzle, the other tower dissolved to the ground. All around me, screaming. The woman next to me, we had wrapped our arms around each other. I recognized her from Mousey Brown, the hair salon on Bedford Avenue where both of us got our chic Jean Seberg cuts. We wept and held each other. I never got her name.

I knew instantly that the US would drop bombs somewhere, and I craved the company of activists again. I'd done nothing particularly political since the Beehive had folded under the pressures of transient membership, gentrification that our presence exacerbated and my first taste of leftist infighting horrors. In the days and months to come after 9/11, I found my people again.

I fell in with a crew of anarchists on the Lower East Side. Artists, tuba players, authors and theorists like David Graeber and Eric Laursen, squatters like Michael Schenker and artists Fly and Seth Tobocman, who'd fought to keep their buildings and won. I met independent journalists, community gardeners and all-around rabble-rousers. We came together to try to stop our government from starting another war. We also fought to preserve gardens and public space.

One fall day, I was on my way to a protest. As always, I was running late.

I flew west across Houston Street on the fixie that Jaime had given me and taught me to ride. That bike, royal blue with an air horn, was fast. Fixed-gear means no brakes. I had strong legs. As I never wore a helmet, I may or may not have had a death wish. *I am part of the flow of traffic*, I mused. *I am traffic.* A yellow cab disagreed, swerving into my lane and nearly taking me out. I thwacked it with a fist and kept riding, adrenaline surging.

I was rushing to a street party in honor of Charas, a beloved community center on the Lower East Side that was under threat of closure by its sale to widely reviled real estate developer Gregg Singer.

Finally, dripping with sweat, I locked my bike and waded into the crowd. And then I made a beeline. Fell into the arms of one Bradley Roland Will. Tall, bespectacled, charismatic, lanky. "Have you been running from cops again?" I asked as we hugged. He laughed; I beamed.

"Every day, Kate!" He reached into his bag and produced a juice container. It was half full of something murky orange. "I got you a present!" I raised an eyebrow. "Carrot juice! From behind Dean & DeLuca." The dumpster. "Sorry it's half gone—I got thirsty," he said.

"All good," I said. "Thanks for thinking of me." I meant it.

We turned to listen to whoever was speaking. The future of the Lower East Side was at stake. Charas/El Bohio, the former P.S. 64 on East 9th Street between Avenues B and C, was the beating heart of the neighborhood and beyond. A gigantic building, it was home to a kaleidoscope of activity: artist studios and theater groups, community organizations, holiday parties, after-school hangouts. Whatever the need, Charas offered the space. Locking its doors would deal a devastating blow to the Lower East Side.

In New York City, nothing is more dear than affordable space. And in the months following 9/11, determined to combat xenophobia and war mongering, we congregated regularly at Charas. I was bouncing between *The Wall Street Journal*, protests and interminable anarchist meetings. I slept two or three hours a night. When no one was looking, I churned out flyers for protests on the *Journal*'s Xerox machine. My return to activism was, in part, trauma. My city had been attacked; it changed me. I was also having a ball, living out the same love of social justice that had begun with Amnesty International and grown in the DC punk scene. As for Brad Will, I was not in love with him, and I loved him, in a way that expanded my heart. Sometimes I'd catch him out of the corner of my eye at some six-hour meeting full of speechifying and I could swear he was glowing.

# MERCEDES

One late summer night, I was out for a walk with a friend I'd met in the DC punk and Riot Grrrl scenes. I'd been living alone in my apartment on Metropolitan, and this friend lived a few minutes' walk down Roebling in a loft near South 2nd. I was surrounded by friends new and old, with whom I shared meals almost every night of the week. I lived on Planet Thai and Bean, the Mexican spot on 8th. The owner's mutt, Champ, was a flaneur like Harold's Gypsy and looked like her too. I often cooked at home, serving my rustic vegetarian experiments to friends at the 1950s dinette table I'd bought off the back of a truck on Lorimer. New York still felt like an artist's utopia, where you could temp at a reception desk by day and write or paint at night, with just enough cash for mole burritos, shows at Brownies and nine-dollar bottles of red.

At some point, I'd started finding needles on my bathroom floor. The tile was dusky shades of blue that reminded me of the ocean. Sharp lengths of metal did not belong; my copy editor's eye seized on them. Jaime. I learned what my girlfriend looked like when she'd been using, and suddenly I could spot it on anyone. I felt like I had walked through a sliding glass door and now saw the world with sharper lenses. Ones that hurt. Jaime swore that ibogaine, a controversial psychedelic treatment for heroin addiction that she'd undergo in London, would cure her. I was skeptical but went along with it. She returned, elated, and soon began using again.

Finally I realized that heroin would be part of my life as long as I was with Jaime. It was my future or hers. I ended the relationship and locked my home against heroin.

I was a million miles away from Baltimore. Hopeful and optimistic, I thought this time would never end. Upon leaving Jaime, I dated a blur of women, but no one serious. I also experienced my first layoff, when my entire department was cut from *The Wall Street Journal*. At the going-away party, I drank too much gin, a novel substance. When I began crying uncontrollably, Celia Currin, the venerable head of our department who exuded the grit of a Marine, issued a withering rebuke. "Pull yourself together, Katharine!" I blanched and swore off gin.

One of my bosses sent me an ad for a proofreader at *New York Press*. I'd never heard of it, but I applied. Soon after, I was copy chief at the scrappy low-budget competitor to *The Village Voice* where my new boss offered me a column on local activism called "Louder Than Words." I made peanuts but I'd never been so happy. I profiled a harm-reduction program in the Bronx, Jews for Racial and Economic Justice, Sylvia Rivera Law Project, Rebicycling, a program where artists taught kids to strip bikes, rebuild and customize them at the Bronx Museum of Art. I got fan mail. Life could get no better, I felt: using my talents to spread the word about New Yorkers who were helping their communities. I also wrote about food, music and movies, and contributed essays to special issues. My entire life was writing and editing—me, from Baltimore, the first person in my family to go to college. My heart was full.

Tonight, me and my old Riot Grrrl friend walked companionably. Summer was receding. A few weeks before, we'd driven to Virginia for the funeral of our friend Nathan Maddox, who at age twenty-five had died dancing in the rain on a Broome Street rooftop. "Storm Trouper: Mystic Saw Lightning's 'Beauty' Before It Killed Him," barked *The New York Post* in all caps.

We strolled alongside warehouses with black windows like lidless eyes, the watchful silence of mixed zoning. We took our time, stopping now and again to sit on a stoop or a loading dock, then walked some more.

"Oh look, weird!" My friend was pointing to something up ahead.

I froze. Parked at an angle, one rear door swinging open like a slack jaw, was Dad's car, the tan 1975 Mercedes. Here on South 1st Street. I felt a sudden crack, the snap of a quick earthquake, my body buckling.

*Is it sleeping or is it dead?* I thought.

An energy was shuddering through me. I was shaking enough that I thought I might fall and maybe, blessedly, close my eyes to this scene. But I couldn't look away.

*The day you show me a car that's better than a Mercedes, I'll stop driving a Mercedes.* I heard Dad's voice in my head, an echo from decades away, when he'd call people from the classifieds about their Buick or Pontiac. Dad had stopped driving a Mercedes, that was fairly certain.

Yet his sedan lay lifeless in front of me in South Williamsburg. How?

I heard my friend's voice as if through water. "Isn't that the car that belongs to your friend who owns Atlas—Walter, right?" Oh, right. Yes, my friend Walter did own Atlas Cafe, a place where I loved to work and read. And Walter did drive a Mercedes quite similar to my daddy's. A logical explanation, I told myself. On closer examination, it wasn't a 1975. It might have been a 1977 or a 1973—similar, but a couple years off. And then I realized that the car in front of me, which had definitely been tan when we rounded the corner, was now navy. This was a dark blue Mercedes, not a tan one.

Dad's car had been found not far from BWI Airport at a fast-food restaurant. Sitting with its lights on, staring into eternity. The other silent witness to whatever violence stole my father from me and my sister and my mother. Dad loved his Mercedes and his Rottweilers almost as much as he loved the rest of us. Maybe the same. And when his life came to a sudden end, at least those friends were with him. The 1975 Mercedes and the shy, runty Rottweiler had been helpless to alter Dad's fate, but I'd like to think that at least he wasn't totally alone. I only wish those witnesses could have given statements.

My sense of dread deepened, like feet in a puddle, black wet seeping in, moving up the ankles, Ella Fitzgerald crooning about cyclones and beating rain. It hit me and I gasped: Something terrible was going to happen if we got too close to that car.

"What do you think we should do?" my friend asked. "Shut the door, right?"

I did not want her to know the state I was in. Was I even really there? I murmured a noncommittal hmmmm, as if I were giving serious consideration to her question. But I knew: Touch that car and we were finished. We would disappear or incinerate or electrocute. We could not touch that car.

Sometimes when I feel horror that is too big for me to hold, I hear screaming in my head. I don't know when or if I have ever screamed like that, but it's me. I heard it then. Screaming, screaming, screaming. Ragged screaming.

"Kate? Kate, honey, what's going on?" My friend was staring me in the face, hands gripping both my elbows, looking up at me.

"It . . ." My mouth was working but I struggled to make sound. "It looks just like my dad's car. I feel afraid. I don't think we should touch it. Could we just go?"

She took my hand and walked me home.

# NIKONS

MEE-MOM DIED IN 2004, after a slow, heart-crushing decline. I drove to Baltimore to see her in the hospital, crying the whole way; the lady whose heartbreak had so offended me when Dad first disappeared was impossibly fragile now. From her wreath of tubes and wires and things that beeped, she was overjoyed to see me. I held her fairy-light hand. My grandmother pointed to me and crowed to the nurses: "*Wall Street Journal*! *Wall Street Journal*! My granddaughter works for *The Wall Street Journal*!" and beamed pride. I in turn felt ashamed. *It was just the creative services department*, I thought. *I was just a copywriter. I got laid off. She thinks I'm a journalist and now these hospital workers do too.* I know I had explained my job to her in the past, and either she didn't get it, or it didn't matter. Her granddaughter worked for *The Wall Street Journal*.

Early in 2006, I drove down to Baltimore for a couple days to see Mom and Gordon. At some point she beckoned me back to her bedroom. "What's going on?" I asked.

"You'll see," she said.

I shrugged and followed her, down the hall, toward her bedroom, then into a large closet. Curious. I followed her in. We sat on the floor, our knees almost touching. She handed me a box, and then another and then another.

Dad's cameras! I couldn't believe it. There were two, and several lenses, honorable Nikon glass. I held each piece in my hands with reverence, admiring the heft, the craftsmanship and the infinite potential.

Photography ran in our family. Dad's father, August, shot medium format, making beautiful images of his family. In the May 16, 1943, Sunday edition of *The Sun*, a writer named A. D. Emmart reviewed an exhibit at the Municipal Museum of photographs of Baltimore, and mentioned Pappy: "August Crane has produced a really interesting new view of Mount Vernon Place," in a show that Emmart said "caught a good deal of what is essential . . . as well as the 'spirit' or 'mood' of Baltimore." Some years, Pappy made photography holiday cards, shooting a young Eddy and Bob next to a board that read: *Merry Xmas, the Cranes.*

With this gift, my mother was handing me tools to interpret the world around me. The K1000 I'd bought in that pawnshop was a stalwart friend. I liked experimenting with expired film and lots of grain. With Dad's cameras, I had new ways to communicate in images—and tangible connections to both him and Pappy. I was overwhelmed, for once in an entirely wonderful way.

"Thank you, Mom," I said. "Thank you so much. I will take good care of them and I will use them and I will love them. Thank you, thank you." I hugged her.

I drove back up the turnpike with my precious cargo wrapped in blankets in the back seat of my hatchback. Now I was in a relationship with someone new and old—a drummer from the punk world. I was on an indefinite hiatus from women, having hit my limit on emotional abuse. I thought men might be less trouble.

When I got back to the Jersey City apartment I shared with him, I opened up the newer Nikon to examine it. I was holding a state-of-the-art camera, by the standards of twenty years ago. Dad loved technology. We had a VCR before most other families, and a video game system called Bally.

Tucked in the packaging, I found a receipt, made out in handwriting I knew well—Barbara at B&L Photo in the Perry Hall shopping center. Then I saw the date and stopped breathing. September 3, 1987. Dad had paid for this camera a week before he died. In my hands was his final high-tech toy.

As I tried to figure out this new treasure, something sandy trickled out. I recoiled. What? I had no idea what I was looking at. Until I realized it was emanating from the battery compartment. Acid. It was battery acid. Dad had set it up and a week later he was dead and then his new purchase hibernated for nineteen years.

I used a Q-tip and alcohol and cleaned everything out as best I could. The acid had eaten a hole in the metal camera body, something no Q-tip could mend. I showed it to a photographer friend, who signed off on my cleanup efforts. "But there are tiny particles of acid in there," he said. "They'll continue eating away at the camera for eternity."

I could never get all the acid out. It would keep destroying. *I'd better use this while I can*, I thought. And so I got started.

# WILL

JUST BEFORE HALLOWEEN in 2006, I got a call from Eric Laursen, a good friend from my activist life. We often collaborated on grassroots media work. He was a writer too, and a gentle, generous soul.

"Kate, are you sitting down?"

"Eric, what is it? I don't need to sit down."

"Just do it, OK?" Leery, I sank into my boyfriend's favorite armchair and waited.

Brad Will was dead. He'd gone to Oaxaca, Mexico, to cover a teachers strike for Indymedia, and plainclothes police shot him in the torso. He was filming.

"It's on YouTube, Kate. Don't watch it."

I got off the phone with Eric and I watched it.

After all these years of wondering what happened to my father, I could see what happened to Brad. I could see what happened to this person I loved so much. I had watched him eat the food out of my fridge, run from cops at protests, sing folk anthems in community gardens, flirt with cute anarchists and cruise the streets in the monthly Critical Mass group bike ride. Now I saw the gun go off in a flash, heard him cry out and watched him die.

Roughly eight years previous, I had seen David Simon's dramatization of what happened to my dad on prime-time television. That was pure shock. Tonight, in my Jersey City apartment, as an explosive grief mushroomed, in the shock there was a kernel of horrible solace. I didn't have to wonder. Brad documented it. Brad put it on film. I did not have to wonder.

Nonetheless, I unraveled.

In the weeks that followed, friends from that world pressured me to help out with protests. "Justice for Brad." It made me feel sick.

"I have to work," I told one of them, truthfully, when she wanted me to attend a press conference to call for accountability around Brad's killing.

"Brad needs you!" said this woman, who was independently wealthy.

"Brad's dead," I said, empty, and hung up the phone.

Justice. For a foreigner who had been shot by plainclothes agents of the state. I had been down a similar enough road with my father. Justice? Unlikely! That my activist friends were oblivious to this fact embittered me. In the past I'd felt consolation and connection as we fought for community spaces and spoke out against racism and xenophobia. Their zeal now alienated me. Murder was a black hole, not a group project. Brad's death had ripped the Band-Aid off my mourning for Dad. Unfairly, I resented the others' good-hearted wishes to do right by our friend and work through their own pain in productive and communal ways.

*New York Press* had ultimately imploded. My boss had quit when the publisher disciplined him over a cover story celebrating the imminent death of Pope John Paul II. And just like that, I was at the helm. The editor in chief role fell to Alexander

Zaitchik, who made me his editorial partner. For the coming nine or so months, that newspaper was ours. That is, until new ownership fired us to make way for a replacement. At first, the publisher sat me down and begged me to stay on, lauding me as the *institutional memory* of the paper. I'd been there four years. I smelled BS but I needed my job. They fired me and my institutional memory a few weeks later. Soon the new guy quit too, also in some act of defiance.

At the time of Brad Will's killing, I'd been working with *SmartMoney*, the personal finance magazine of *The Wall Street Journal*, for a year and a half, since winter 2005. *New York Press* paid so little that I needed a significant amount of freelance work. A week a month of copyediting for a kindly rock 'n' roll fan named Hugo Moreno was a godsend. I'd help Hugo at *SmartMoney* from ten to six and then go to *New York Press* afterward and stay past midnight. Hugo saved the day when I lost the *Press* by hiring me full time. I was over the moon to accept $50K for a low-pressure copy editor role. I was in treatment for adrenal failure; *New York Press* had half killed me.

One day I'd stumbled on someone else's notes and notebooks in one of my drawers. Curious, I asked Hugo who Stephanie Williams was. His kind face turned serious.

"She had that office before you," said Hugo. "But a couple years ago, she died." At thirty-one, in 2002, Stephanie had found out she had under two years to live. Cancer. Her dream had been to write a novel. So she got to work, doing much of it from a hospital bed. *Enter Sandman* was published and in her hands three weeks before her death. Stephanie didn't live to see *The Boston Globe* call her novel remarkable and compelling. But she'd lived long enough to see it come to life.

I often found fragments of her work life in that room, stashed in file folders or the backs of drawers. As if we were roommates of a sort.

In fall 2006 and winter 2007, as the months passed and my grief for Brad stretched out like arsenic taffy, hard questions began to nag at me. What was I doing with my life? How much time did I have? Brad and I had both assumed he'd be outrunning the cops for another few decades. His absence was unthinkable. Stephanie Williams had been traveling Italy with the boyfriend she'd planned to marry when she got her death sentence at basically the same age I was now.

We never know how much time we have. Stephanie had gotten her novel out despite terminal cancer. Brad had done tree sits in old-growth redwoods, worked with people's movements in Bolivia, hopped trains, built squats. Brad had made his life mean something. I managed too much mysterious illness and pain to aspire to tree sits or train hopping. What did my life mean? My answers left me cold.

Just under nine months later, something unexpected bloomed.

# BALTIMORE

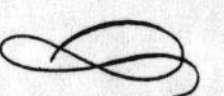

# ALARM CLOCK

One day in July 2007, I checked the calendar. September always crept up on me. Bad dreams, dread and the haze of New York City summer sparked an internal alarm clock. I used to get drunk each September 10, but the gesture felt childish and hollow. I'd feel sick and ashamed of myself the next day. After 2001, September 10 and September 11 became back-to-back challenges. I could not handle two days of alcohol; my health had continued to decline. So the drinking ritual was out, but I had not figured out another means of surviving September 10.

Something was different about this September. There was an actual ringing. I heard it in my head and felt it under my skin, the way an old-fashioned fire alarm at school gets into your teeth and leaves a metallic tang. I was buzzing with the ringing. At first I chalked it up to being sickly. Maybe this was some depressing neuropathy that no one would be able to treat. Then I took a second look at the calendar. July 17, 2007. September was coming, all right, but this was a September unlike the one before: It was September 2007. In eight weeks, it would be twenty years since Dad disappeared.

Twenty years . . . A coldness swept through me. Those detectives in Baltimore had said they were doing everything they could. They would let us know about any developments. It was always possible for new information to come in, they said. I had held on to these assurances, determined not to poke at them too closely lest they crumble. But now? Twenty years! Were the detectives who worked on Dad's disappearance still on the force? Were they even still alive?

Agitation surged. I knew the term for this. My dad's disappearance was a *cold case* now. Two decades, and he was no closer to walking through the front door or being properly buried than he was when I was twelve.

Waiting on Dad as the years crept onward had instilled in me an oceanic patience. Looking at the calendar, realizing the magnitude of the date—that patience was gone. In its place I felt a live-wire sense of urgency. I'd held on to the periodic and tepid reassurances from the detectives, reassurances I now realized were old. Very old. In that moment, I released them. It was time to face reality: Those detectives in Baltimore had long ago given up and moved on to other crimes.

The adults had failed the child me. But at thirty-two, I was an adult now too. One minute, I didn't know. The next minute, I knew: I had to do something for my father.

Help? Find? Avenge? Solve? The certainty that it was on me fractured into questions. Yes, I had to do something.

I despised the voyeurism of the nascent true crime genre. The plague of true crime podcasts was a decade off, but you could throw a rock and hit an *SVU* rerun. I loved Alfred Hitchcock and Sherlock Holmes, and I'd just finished reading all seventy-some Nero Wolfe books. Mystery and detective stories were close to my heart. But the kind of work that glorified murder, along with the phrase "girl detective," set my teeth on edge. I did not want to be Nancy Drew or Trixie Belden or Olivia Benson.

I was a writer, though. Right? At what point could I call myself legitimate? My work had appeared in *New York Press*, a newspaper that was available in boxes on the street all over the city. I'd written for *The Brooklyn Rail* and *Time Out New York* about music. I had an essay about swimming in a real literary magazine, *Post Road*. Did any of it credential me? My confidence was shaky. I was afraid that professionally, I didn't compare with people who'd gone to fancy schools, who surrounded me at work.

Despite all the self-doubt, I felt sure that any path I took to help Dad should involve writing rather than pretending to be a detective.

What did I even know about Dad's disappearance? I got out a notebook and made a list. This exercise did not take long.

Most of it came from Simon's 1992 *Sun* article. Dad and Uncle Augie had fought about money. There was a screaming match in front of E & M employees, and then Dad started working at night to avoid his partner. Then he was gone forever.

There had to be more to the story.

Over the coming days, I formulated an initial plan. I would call my mother, Uncle Bob and the Baltimore Police. No doubt after those phone calls, I'd have a better sense of next steps. Recently, Mom had sent me a five-hundred-dollar savings bond from Augie, from when I was a baby. It gave me the creeps—I did not want his money. I resolved to use it on a private investigator. If I was going to stir up the past, I owed it to my family to try to find out how much danger that might entail.

After all that, I thought, vaguely, I could probably write some kind of magazine article. Writing something could be like a grave marker. Not made of stone. Better: made of story.

SWITCHING TEAMS HADN'T improved anything in my personal life; I was making poor choices that had nothing to do with sexuality. I loved to talk a blue streak, while the boyfriend I lived with preferred never to talk. I didn't discuss my dad or much of anything substantial with him. I felt alone.

I called both my mother and my uncle on July 26.

My uncle was a constant in my childhood, but a distant constant. There was some mutual dislike between him and my mother that both of them managed to simultaneously hint at and deny. Bob, a couple years younger than Dad, had a booming voice and a boisterous personality. Where Dad was heavy with a round face, Bob was angular. Not skinny, but as if he'd been sculpted to have sharp edges, including a prominent nose that he'd inherited from Grandmom Hilda. Uncle Bob called me *honey* and always sent cards at the holidays and my birthday, signed in confident, blocky print. But I can't recall ever taking a ride with him or eating a meal with him and his two daughters, my cousins.

I had to get his number from my mother.

"Uncle Bob?"

"Hi, honey, how are you? How's work?" He sounded glad to hear from me, and I felt bad for calling with an agenda, especially this one.

"Uncle Bob, it's coming up on twenty years since Dad went missing. I feel like I could write something. The cops didn't come through. I feel like I have to try to do something now."

"Baby, I could talk your ear off for hours. I'll tell you whatever you want to know. But dinner's ready. Let's talk in a few days, OK, honey?"

I was ebullient. I was as certain that my mother would tell me nothing as I was that Uncle Bob would tell me everything.

When he called me back later that week, his whole demeanor had changed.

He said it was too dangerous. But then he kept talking. And talking, and talking. The words poured out of him. I listened, floored. A week earlier, I'd stopped in at a big art supply store in the West Village and chosen a hefty spiral-bound 11x9 notebook with blue plastic covers as home base for my Dad project. As Bob talked, my pen raced across its pages.

*Eddy and Augie had this bond over thievery.*

*Your dad got arrested for stealing hubcaps. He wanted to be a state trooper, but they wouldn't let him because of that arrest. He went to work for a Chevy dealer, but he got arrested for stealing.*

*Then he went to work for the White Motor Company. He was a salesman, and he got involved with some scam where they'd take brand-new trucks and paint them over and sell them as used. I don't know where the profit was in that. He got fired, and he went to jail, but I'm not sure if he did time or not or if he was just in jail overnight.*

*The customer base at E & M was lousy. When a customer didn't pay his bills, your father and Augie would steal a truck and cut it up to get their rear back. It was easy to dispose of a truck and get their parts back. They knew where the serial number was located on every truck. Mack trucks were the worst—they have serial numbers everywhere, even on the bumpers. They never wanted to steal Mack trucks. But they stole so many trucks and cut them up.*

*They called it their self-payment plan.*

*Augie is a kleptomaniac. I've never worked with anyone like him in all my life. He couldn't help himself. We'd go somewhere, and I'd say, "Augie, don't embarrass me." It didn't have to be big—he'd steal pens, saltshakers. But he always had to be stealing.*

*That was the bond that started their relationship.*

*The political regime Augie was involved with, all the way up to the mayor, was corrupt. And I think there had to be some corruption in the Homicide department. Augie was tight with a city councilman named Willie Myers, and he had connections to William Donald Schaefer, the former mayor of Baltimore, turned governor of Maryland.*

*The guy who I believe pulled the trigger, Archie McAleese, worked in the shop at E & M. From what I heard your father and Augie say, he had been indicted on three or four murder charges and gotten off on a technicality. He had been on the run from a recent incident—he'd stabbed a guy in a bar—and the FBI was looking for him and apprehended him some months before your dad disappeared.*

*He started showing up at E & M. He was driving a reefer from a company in Nebraska two weeks before your father went missing.*

*After I showed your father how Augie had been stealing, your father was so blinded with hate for him. He was coming in to work later and later, and Augie was coming in earlier and earlier. When your dad would show up, Augie would leave and not come back.*

*Your father had a really bad temper, and he was very unforgiving. He got into this screaming, nasty, ugly verbal fight with Augie.*

*Archie McAleese came into the office about two weeks before your dad disappeared. He picked a fight with your father. Your father carried a handgun. When McAleese saw the gun, he backed down and left.*

*One day, prior to your dad's disappearance, I remember Augie screaming at Myers on the phone. "You'd better take care of it!" He kept screaming at him that he'd better take care of something. I don't know what it was.*

*Supposedly Augie had two prior partners who both died mysteriously. One with a gun in his hand and a bullet in his head, ruled suicide, and the other that fell off a roof, ruled accidental.*

*I don't think you can understand how ruthless these people are, Kate.*

*You don't have the slightest idea what these people are like. They would think nothing of picking you up, raping you, cutting your throat.*

*If your father was capable of murder, I think he would have killed Augie before he murdered him.*

I got off the phone with Uncle Bob and raced to the bathroom. Diarrhea. It felt like everything I had consumed for two months rushed out of me in a gruesome river. I lay down when the sickness passed and wondered: *What the hell am I getting myself into?*

I dreaded calling my mother infinitely more than I had dreaded the call to my uncle.

When I told my mother my plans, she was horrified. "Please don't, Kate." She adamantly opposed whatever I was setting out to do. "Do not use my name," she said. "I have risen above the shame and anger I felt. I have established something better for myself. I've moved on," she said. My mother was clear on another point: "I don't want to feel threatened again."

# WORDEN AND NOLAN

After the nerve-racking calls with my mother and uncle, I moved on to my next step: reaching out to the Cold Case Unit of the Baltimore Police. I had absolutely no idea what to expect. Would I get a phone tree? A secretary who would take my name and contact information? Would someone tell me to fill out a form and mail it? I barely knew what to say, in the event that I did speak to an actual person.

In my big blue notebook, I had carefully printed a few questions to ask. Had my father's case stuck with them? Did they perceive my dad as a good person? Was his disappearance connected to organized crime?

I was sitting in my office at *SmartMoney* magazine. I'd gotten a promotion, from copy chief to associate editor. My windowless space was far away from my coworkers, which was dreamy—I loved the silent refuge, padded by carpet and the murmurs of the HVAC system. But there was a real downside to that room: I couldn't see anyone coming. My boss or one of the half dozen interns or reporters I managed could easily appear in the doorway at any moment. A microwave was inexplicably parked just outside my door, at the end of a hallway. So I was often a captive audience to those who felt like chatting while their tuna melt nuked.

I got up from my desk, poked my head into the hallway and, reassured that no one was coming, screwed up my courage and dialed the number I had written down.

"Cold Case. This is Worden."

It sounded like an older white guy. He delivered those six syllables—compressing his name almost to one, emphasis on the "*wor*"—in an accent that said Highlandtown or one of Baltimore's other predominantly white, blue-collar neighborhoods.

"Hi . . ." I faltered. "I'm calling because I'm starting to write something about my father's murder, which happened in the eighties. I was hoping there might be someone there who could talk to me about his case."

"Who was your father?"

"Eddy Crane."

"That's not a murder," he flashed back at me. "That's a missing persons case."

I stared past my desk. Whatever I'd been expecting, it wasn't this. I could hear my voice quaking. "You know my father's case?"

"O' course I do. I just had the file out the other day."

"Oh!" I said. "I didn't think anyone would remember."

From there it was a short conversation.

Worden told me that he had been in the department at the time of my father's disappearance and now freelanced for Cold Case in his retirement.

I had been braced for rejection, rudeness, runaround or "sorry, we can't help you." I had not dared hope for this—a larger-than-life presence on the other line who not only knew my father but also seemed willing to help. The questions I'd jotted were there in my big blue notebook, but the words swam on the page. The questions would have to wait.

"Could I come down there and see you?" I asked, suddenly afraid he would say, *No, don't call here again*. Donald Worden said yes. I hung up the phone, amazed. This was something. It wasn't much, but I'd done *something.* All this time, and only a telephone call had separated me from at least one source of intel on my father. He even seemed likable.

Worden said he'd been looking at the file. When that alarm clock in my gut had started to ring, I'd feared that any detective who'd worked on my father's disappearance had retired or even died. Worden had retired, yes, but still worked cases. And he was still puzzling over my dad. Until that moment, I had no idea if anyone other than me cared or even remembered. I was rank with adrenaline. My body was hard at work trying to process what this phone call might mean.

I knew one thing: That exchange with Donald Worden had tilted my world on its axis. A stranger, 180 miles away, knew my father instantly—I was different now. I did not know how yet, but I knew I was different.

Worden wasn't the only surprise that week in my little office. One of my next steps in this project, as I awkwardly referred to it, was to google my dad. In 2007, these searches had not suffused every molecule of life. Besides which, there had been no media coverage of Dad since the 1992 *Sun* paper story. I had no reason to believe anything at all about him would be on the internet. For the most part, I was right. But not completely.

In the search bar I typed: "Eddy Crane." And stared in wonder at the results that flashed onto my monitor.

*The Wire* was probably the most popular TV show in America at the time, but I had never seen it. I didn't have cable, and I was leery of David Simon television after that *Homicide* episode.

The link appeared to go to some kind of script database: "s04e04 - Refugees - The Wire Transcripts." Transfixed, I clicked in.

*Where's he putting the bodies, Bunk? In the sewers? Rogue funeral home, maybe? Yeah, they teach that fancy-ass Latin at them Catholic schools.*

*You remember the Eddy Crane case? Word was they put him in an acid vat down near Curtis Bay.*

I knew who'd created *The Wire*—anyone from Baltimore did. And just like that, my lingering anger for David Simon evaporated. All these years later, he remembered my dad, and by name. Yet again, Simon had included him in a TV show. I couldn't believe it. In one week, I'd found not one but two whole people who remembered my dad and seemed to care about him. The world was different. I made a note to contact Simon through HBO.

"HEY, LITTLE GIRL," the smoky voice boomed through the telephone line. "Wait a sec." The handset clattered to what I knew was his kitchen table. "Jake! Hey, Jake!" I heard him shriek. "Leave that cardinal alone!" I grinned. That yawp might be enough to scare the cardinal into accidental salvation.

This was Gordon Porterfield, a garrulous, chain-smoking playwright, actor, poet and novelist who'd taught drama in city public schools for forty years. I'd met him back in high school, through his son, my friend in Amnesty International. Over the years, he had become my closest friend, and very much a substitute father. Occasional phone calls became regular phone calls, and those in turn became ritual. Though he was more than thirty-five years my senior and had three children, six grandchildren and many solid friends, Gordon generously folded me into his life. We'd talk for hours, sprawling dives into music, books, film and creativity. He got me, and he encouraged me to take risks and pursue my dreams. I'd also become close to his former mother-in-law, Marie Collins, with whom I exchanged handwritten letters. Her family, the Tołodzieckis and the Kołodziejkis, were from Fairfield, adjacent to Curtis Bay, when it had been a verdant, tree-lush place to build a family. Across from their house on Remley Street, her grandparents planted a modest orchard. Marie graduated from the Union Memorial Hospital School of Nursing in 1961, then completed a nursing degree program at University of Maryland in 1970, all while raising young daughters. Her education and long career, including a role as nursing supervisor in obstetrics at City Hospital, marked a level of academic and professional achievement rare for women of her generation. Marie loved E. B. White, Georges Simenon and outings to Barnes & Noble and the Ivy Bookshop in Mount Washington. Petite with rimless glasses and snowy hair, she cheered on my every endeavor with ferocious sparkle and warmth.

Gordon was a cat man. His boy Jake, more lynx than house cat, patrolled the outdoors during the day, to the peril of the birds, squirrels, other cats, and dogs of Louise Avenue.

"OK, I'm back. Jake won't leave the birds alone. What's happening, Katy Crane?"

"I called Cold Case, Gor. At the Baltimore Police." I felt shaky, the paranoia tickling my insides, like my mom or my sister or Augie might have my phone tapped, might start yelling at me. "The guy who answered the phone knew who my dad was!"

I heard Gor exhale hard. "Can you believe that?" he said. "After all this time . . . Isn't that something. Well, what are you going to do now?"

Good question. There was the easy, adrenaline, gut answer—I am getting in the car and coming to Baltimore and talking to anyone and everyone who will possibly talk to me. My family would be against this. My mother had expressed staunch opposition to my plans. Uncle Bob would be upset too. My sister? I was afraid her anger would be explosive.

"They said I could come see them. Could I stay with you next weekend?"

Of course I could, he said. I was always welcome there. Gor smoked like a chimney, inside now, since he and Vicky had divorced, and those putrid Carltons he relished drove me nuts. Even so, that house, groaning with books and pictures of his children and grandchildren, continued to enchant me.

I did not tell my mother I was coming. If I did, she might insist on going to see the detectives with me. I knew in my bones that this would conclusively shut down any conversation. So I kept this plan to myself.

I was wading into murky waters. Baltimore's Inner Harbor was vivid in my imagination. It licked at my ankles, my calves. I didn't know how deep the water was and I wasn't about to worry about it. If I thought too hard about any of this, I might stop. I was determined to submerge.

I was paying for it. The guilt was astounding. So was the diarrhea. I'd had it for over a month now, and every time I shuddered in misery in the bathroom, I thought my insides would never find solid ground again. I felt guilty for upsetting my mother. I felt guilty for potentially putting her, my sister and my uncle in danger. I felt guilty I was going to Baltimore and not seeing my mother. Yet if I did, I would go numb and crave sleep.

I also felt guilty that, whatever I could do for my father, it would be inadequate.

After another couple of phone calls back and forth with Worden, I got ready for a road trip.

IT WAS A HUMID, sunny day in Baltimore. I walked into the visitors entrance of the Baltimore Police Department at 601 East Fayette Street. I didn't feel nauseous, exactly, but my breakfast wasn't secure in my belly, either. I felt out of my body, like I couldn't precisely locate myself in space, and my hands were cold. I was seeking the truth, and it felt unsafe. The nightmares, which howled that Augie knew my plans, that he would come for me and kill us all—they felt as real as the ground beneath my feet.

What was the right outfit for dropping in on a couple of old homicide detectives to chitchat about a parent's murder? I'd learned to always wear something I'd feel comfortable in. So I wore black skirt pants, a simple black jacket and chunky black ankle boots. It was a step up from the punk days of thrifted corduroys, although I always felt overdressed or under, out of step with what other people wore. For years I'd had short hair like Mia Farrow in *Rosemary's Baby*. If I didn't signal some femininity through fashion, I often got mistaken for a boy.

I'd gotten lucky with street parking and even remembered to cram a bottle of water into my leather tote bag.

Ready. Well—I don't know if I was ready or not, but I was there.

A person inside at a podium regarded me, wordless, took my name and made a phone call. For several excruciating minutes I watched Baltimore through smudged glass and held my breath. The waiting area felt like a cell phone store. Small, unspecial entry space, designed to make you feel bored and anonymous, if it had been designed at all. *Municipal*, I thought. And waited.

Then a trim African American man, who at sixty-eight could have passed for fifty-five, was standing in front of me.

"Hello, Miss Crane," he said, shaking my hand. "I'm Sergeant Nolan."

"Thanks so much for agreeing to see me," I said, trying to strike the right combo of likable, smart and deferential. I followed him to the elevators and up to the floor where the homicide detectives worked.

The Cold Case Unit held aging, generic furniture in beige and ivory and steel gray. Sergeant Nolan led me to an area that was more or less like a conference room, surrounded by file cabinets. At the time, in 2007, there were between three thousand and four thousand cold cases in Baltimore, I later learned. Those unanswered questions and grieving loved ones strained at me through the metal drawers, where their stories had been filed away.

"Be right back, Miss Crane," said Sergeant Nolan, offering me a seat at a table. "Let me go get your father's file."

My digital recorder was in my bag. But I was paralyzed with fear. I was afraid of being inappropriate, of breaking the rules. I was already breaking a rule, the Mount Everest of family rules: Don't talk about Dad. And definitely don't make friends with Cold Case detectives. I was dreading what would happen when I inevitably disclosed this visit to my mother and sister.

I snapped a few covert photos . . . of filing cabinets.

Sergeant Nolan returned with a thick manila folder and placed it on the table between us. The Eddy Crane case. My father had been reduced to a couple hundred pages detailing the worst and last day of his life. A macabre paper doll. And my heart still leaped to see it.

I reached out to take my father's file into my hands.

"I can't let you have that," he said, and my hand froze. "I can go over it with you, but this is still an open investigation."

*What?* I thought, taken aback. Was it such a trespass, to pick up my own father's missing persons file? The thick collection of documents in front of me was a holy grail. This whole exchange felt off somehow. I nodded and apologized. "No worries," I said. "What can you tell me?"

I tried to shake off the sense of rebuke by studying the man on the other side of the table. Across from me was a force: watchful, reserved. Roger Nolan, son of a longshoreman, had served in Vietnam in the Marines and joined the Baltimore Police in 1968 at age twenty-nine. In a career that spanned forty-two years, he was a constant in that office, using his vacation days if he got sick. Nolan had founded Cold Case and supervised it since 1995. Known for his care toward victims' families, he also had a reputation as stern, which I'd just glimpsed.

I sensed integrity. This was someone worth knowing, I thought, and found myself hoping I might know him a little.

Sergeant Nolan reviewed the well-worn facts with me, turning pages in the file folder, close enough for me to see but not read. My father had called my mother the night he went missing to say he was coming home. They suspected the night watchman, Roscoe Woolard, had something to do with what ever happened after that call. The detectives had followed Roscoe off and on for years but had never gotten anywhere with him.

"No one would talk," Sergeant Nolan said. He was not defensive. "We did work this case."

As I closed my notebook and he carefully reassembled the documents, he said, "There are a few things I'd like to go over with you when Donald Worden is around. I need to look for something that might prove useful."

"It's an easy drive," I replied. "I'll come back next week."

I RETURNED TO Baltimore on a morning blessed with sunshine. Coming over the Susquehanna River, on the bridge between Cecil and Harford counties, the sun was a searing gold, and mist suffused everything. *How will I ever tell this story?* I thought. I was at a loss even to sketch its shape. Anxiety fanned out all around me—that I was incapable of finding words for any of this, that I was in over my head. Then there was the cloud of danger. I'd always looked over my shoulder; the sense of my own vulnerability since I started this quest had only intensified. At least once a month, I told the man who owned the UPS store where I rented a mailbox never to disclose my actual address to anyone. A Jersey City native and a tough guy, he agreed and asked no questions.

Now, as me and my silver Honda Civic approached a five-dollar toll plaza, I thought of the tasks that lay ahead and frantically tried to conjure Dad's voice in my mind. "Eddy Crane," he'd say when he answered the phone. I heard it as if from far away. He always sounded self-assured—a swagger, a "don't mess with me" quality. I thought of him in the driver's seat approaching the Harbor Tunnel toll, saying, "Could I get a receipt, please?" The same thing I was about to say. Except now I was the one driving, and I was getting a receipt because I was going to Baltimore to do something that was ill-advised, or pointless, or selfish, or unreasonable, or potentially calamitous. All of it. I just didn't know.

I was no less nervous when I arrived at police headquarters. This time, when the person inside the front door phoned upstairs, the elevator doors opened up to the man I'd first spoken with on the phone: Donald Worden.

An image of a video camera came to mind. I sensed that this person was recording every detail of his surroundings at all times, which meant he was reading me as much as I was reading him. The tall, imposing figure, mostly bald with a halo of snowy white hair and a white mustache, was no more effusive than ex-Marine Roger Nolan, but he let a little more warmth slip. I felt comfortable instantly.

"Hello, Miss Crane," he said quietly.

"Hi, Detective Worden!"

I beamed and stumbled toward him, ever the klutz. The hand I extended disappeared into his much larger one.

I was hoping to project an upbeat demeanor: Here we have a bright young journalist with professional experience but hometown credentials. I wanted to convey that I was happy and normal. I felt I should hide the mania behind my project. But I was not above playing daddy's girl if that might help me create a rapport or get answers. Which, a long time ago, I was.

Up we ascended to the Cold Case Unit. When he retired in 1995, Donald Worden had been with the department for thirty-three years, starting in 1962. David Simon wrote about his then-imminent retirement in the September 9, 1995, *Sun*, calling him "the Big Man, the last natural-born police detective in America, a huge, gap-toothed, Hampden-born polar bear, blessed with instinctive street moves and an elephantine memory." Twelve years later, he continued to work cold cases with his old friend Roger Nolan.

"Good drive down?" he asked as he led the way to a conference room.

"Yes, I love to drive," I said, smiling for real. This topic was easy. "And I live in Jersey City now, so it takes less than ten minutes to hit the turnpike."

I was hoping this trip might yield more information than the first. Maybe in spending more time with me, these veteran detectives would treat me, if not like a peer, then at least as someone worth candor and conversation. And Sergeant Nolan had alluded to another reason for my return—I was curious.

Sergeant Nolan was seated at a table, in front of Dad's file, calm and businesslike. We settled in, me across from the two detectives. The men exuded the closeness of a long work partnership. Nolan could have been a college history professor—watchful, discerning, every word weighed out. And if I'd seen Worden, also in his sixties, at a gathering of the cousins and elders, I'd have taken the broad bear of a man with the ruddy complexion and bright blue eyes for a long-lost relative on my mom's side.

"I can't believe your father and Augie were best friends," said Nolan. "It's not that your dad was classy, exactly, but he wasn't like Augie. How did he get involved with that guy?"

I pictured Dad in his work pants, stretchy black trousers. He paired them with stretchy shirts, often in ivory, with his brass ballpoint pen clipped in the pocket. His chosen fabrics could take the beating of a formidable man who worked with heavy machinery and came home marked with truck grease. Dad gave Orson Welles in his *Third Man* era a run for his money—cocky self-assurance, stocky good looks.

Sergeant Nolan was looking at me expectantly. I shook myself out of the reverie.

"From what I've gathered from my mom and my uncle," I told them, "Dad wanted to go into the military or become a cop, but then he got caught stealing hubcaps, or something similar, and wasn't allowed. He got a job at the White Motor Company, and also at a Chevy dealer, where my uncle said he got arrested. Somewhere in there, he and Augie first met."

Neither Nolan nor Worden looked surprised, and I wondered if they were gauging how much I'd already figured out.

In the August 26, 1970, Court Docket section of *The Evening Sun*, above a half-page ad by the Hardware Fair for an 88-cent stock-up sale, is an entry titled, "Probation Report Due in Stolen Truck Case." It says that Eddy R. Crane, 29, pleaded guilty to a charge of receiving a stolen truck tractor. The truck had been stolen in New Jersey. Dad purchased it for two hundred dollars and then switched the serial number plate. He got caught when he tried to get a title for the truck in Pennsylvania. This lined up with my uncle's account of Dad getting arrested and going to jail for theft.

"That's unfortunate," Sergeant Nolan said evenly. "I don't think your father and his partner were the same kind of person. When it came to the embezzlement, Augie probably couldn't help himself. He probably felt like, if we steal from others, why shouldn't we steal from each other?"

"I don't know if you know this," I said, "but Uncle Bob says he showed Dad invoices that proved Augie had been stealing."

Sergeant Nolan nodded. "Sometimes we confuse audacity with intelligence." It's not that no one cared or tried to get somewhere on the case, Nolan went on. "Ed Brown was looking at it in terms of what he knew. But a murderer like this was just not in his world. It's good to work cases the same way over and over, but you have to be able to change course. There are A–R murders. And then there are XYZ murders. You have to turn on all the jets and think of everything you can do." He sighed and opened his hands in that universal "leveling with you" gesture.

"In cities like this, if we get an intelligent murderer, we're in trouble. We should have known we were outdistanced. We should have brought in the feds."

I was scratching notes as quickly as I could without a complete devolution into scrawl. In the moment it was too much to absorb. I did not expect an admission that a crew of lowlifes had gotten the better of experienced murder detectives. Outdistanced—a writerly word. The finality of it made me, suddenly, very sad.

"I'm an old-time cop," Worden said. "I trust nothing. I have to be able to prove everything beyond a reasonable doubt. But the application of reason would not work on Augie. He's the kind of guy you have to have something on. You have to have him by the toe or the little finger."

Sergeant Nolan nodded. "He's like a Damon Runyon character. A gangster, locked into a persona."

"I met him twice," said Worden. "He was just so unbelievable. He didn't register the slightest discomfort. He came off as this gangster, shyster, bullshit artist."

I'd grown up around Augie. Kids don't differentiate between the family members who are blood related and the ones who aren't. The man that everyone was now telling me was a gangster had just been one of my uncles. I'd never been afraid of him, never hesitated to go anywhere with him. If anything, I'd found Uncle Augie a little more interesting than other grown-ups: When he talked to me, he took me seriously. And then, wham, one day Dad was gone and I realized I'd never see this uncle of mine again, either, because somehow he was responsible for why Dad was gone.

"Your mother . . ." Nolan trailed off. Looked at me hard. I knew what he was about to say.

"Your mother had the 'I want to move on, I don't want to be involved' vibe almost immediately after his disappearance," Nolan said gravely. "It was as if she knew it was going to happen—it was as if she expected it."

I felt laughter, pitch-black, bubbling up. When I first told my mother that I wanted to find out what happened, she said, "I've moved on." And she was saying it twenty years before, in 1987. It had struck me as cold through my teens and twenties. Now the light bulbs were starting to go off. My mother would have wanted nothing to do with anything criminal. Now she had two children to raise alone and a husband to grieve. But if there was any upside, it was this: an opportunity to distance herself from her husband's seedy friends and business associates.

"Eddy Crane has become campfire lore around here," said Nolan. "The four or five guys who are still around talk about 'what the hell happened to Eddy Crane?' The perfect means of disposing of a body was right there. Shredders, acid. It seemed like if the object was to kill, why move the body?"

Because, they went on to explain, it's very difficult to dispose of a body.

Burn a body? There will be remnants of charred bone. Put a body in a bay or ocean? It might float. Years ago I interviewed oceanographer Curtis Ebbesmeyer about the severed feet that regularly turn up on Vancouver's shores. When a body is in water, he told me, it eventually disarticulates at the joints, typically into ten pieces. A foot in a sneaker essentially has a built-in flotation device; the rest of the body washes away.

"If there's one place on this earth where a body can vanish forever," Nolan continued, "it's Curtis Bay."

A headline in the October 3, 1951, *Evening Sun* declared, "Flowers Wilt, Nylons Run in Curtis Bay Smog." The neighborhood where my friend Marie Collins had been a little girl changed radically in the mid-twentieth century, becoming the most polluted part of Baltimore. Heavy industry—solvents and coal and medical waste—killed off the orchards Marie adored, leaving only street names like Birch, Hazel, Filbert and Elmtree as a clue to the past. The Curtis Bay of 1987 was split between row homes and medical waste incineration, chemicals, an open-air coal terminal and the city's only rendering plant. In an area like this, there wasn't one particular site where a body could vanish—the neighborhood was defined by them.

"The object right now," said Worden, "is to prove your father is dead."

Hold up. I felt foggy. The object right now? I didn't realize there was a right now. I had come down here expecting to talk about the past. These courteous gentlemen detectives were also starting to talk to me about the future.

"What do you mean?" I asked. "Are you saying there's still something that could be done?"

"We want to show you something," Sergeant Nolan said in reply. "A skull was found in spring 1988. We went down there, to Virginia, to take a look at it, and we had a reconstruction done. We all thought it kind of looked like your dad, but your mother and uncle said no. Same height and weight, same relative age, but the dental record was slightly wrong. The skull had a full upper and a full bottom denture, and your dad had an upper and two partials, according to his dental records."

I'd never heard any of this. That part wasn't a surprise. After all, I was here because I was so fully in the dark. It was still a startling revelation. While I was struggling through eighth-grade math problems at St. Joseph, these detectives had gotten a lead that was worth traveling out of state to investigate, one that was promising enough to merit the cost of a reconstruction. This whole universe had been spinning while I studied with the nuns.

I paused for just a moment longer. How was I going to feel if the reconstruction looked like Dad? How would I feel if it didn't? Only one way to find out.

"OK," I said, and my voice sounded small. "I'm ready. Let's see the pictures."

Sergeant Nolan opened the folder and slid a couple of color drawings toward me. And there in front of me . . . was a man with dark hair. Who could have been my father. And could just as easily have not been my father. But there was an undeniable likeness.

"Yes, it looks like him," I said. They exchanged a glance and nodded, because they thought so too. "I'm not certain, but it's close enough to warrant looking into, don't you think?"

"I do think so," said Sergeant Nolan.

I looked at Sergeant Nolan hopefully, and he nodded.

"Let's do this."

*OK!* I thought, giddy. *Let's do this! What are we doing?* I was confused. I'd been operating under a mantra: *I'm a journalist, not a detective. I'm a writer, not Nancy Drew.* The writer was now spending a great deal of time in close quarters with detectives. The lines were blurring.

I knew that I had to say yes and figure it all out later. An opportunity to actually do something about Dad? Maybe find him? What if it were possible?

"Well, I'm a writer—do you want me to write to someone? The commissioner?" I asked.

Nolan shook his head in an emphatic no.

"If you write to the commissioner," Sergeant Nolan said, "they'll dive under desks and tell me to give you someone's head on a plate."

Love the commitment to justice, to closure for families, I thought, struck by what this indicated about Baltimore Police Department priorities.

I kept those observations to myself.

"Write to the office of the medical examiner in Virginia," he said. "Copy me. Let's see if we can find that skull."

This was a long shot for more than one reason. After twenty years, the medical examiner's office may have lost the records. Surely that body had been buried somewhere—what if they didn't know where? But for me as an inveterate letter writer, this was an effortless action to take.

The detectives and I talked a little while longer and sketched out a game plan:

- I'd look through Dad's 1975 Mercedes, still in Mom's garage.
- Sergeant Nolan would track down the evidence box.
- I'd write the letter to the Office of the Chief Medical Examiner of Virginia.
- Nolan or Worden would question Augie.

Detective Worden photocopied a few pages from Dad's file and handed them to me in an orange envelope. We said goodbye, and Sergeant Nolan escorted me to a side exit of 601 East Fayette. We stood together in the doorway, the artificial cool of police headquarters behind him, the baking heat of summer and the sounds of early rush hour behind me. I wasn't sure how many more times I would see this man, if he was about to become a regular part of my life or if one day he would abruptly disappear too.

Sergeant Nolan looked at me in the somber, reserved way I was coming to know. "You lost your father," he said, "and not much was done about it. And that's the case 60 percent of the time. Whatever comes of this, you know you're not going to get those twenty years without your father back."

I had been so poised in the Homicide Unit, through the conversation about disposing of bodies and an artist rendition of someone who might be my dad, and the jarring new fact of a skull that I had signed on to try to help find. Now I was fighting the tears, and not all that successfully. "Yeah. I know." I thanked Sergeant Nolan and left.

What weren't they telling me? I wondered, already sweating in the late-day sun as I brushed away the tears and dug in my bag for my keys. What did they agree in advance to say and not to say? I was hungry for whatever went unsaid, and I also knew some doors would stay closed forever.

Gordon and I went to dinner at the Hamilton Tavern or the Chameleon, two much-loved standbys along Harford Road near his house. That meal and our conversation are lost to me now. I'm sure it was a comfort—I avoided discussing this with almost everyone but him. Gordon's interest never felt leering; I could safely confide to him even the most sensitive details.

I grappled with the subject of my father's body for a host of reasons. When we talked about a body, we were talking about my daddy. Two simple two-syllable words, one signaling comfort, the other horror. The *body* that people had *disposed of* had been a person who loved Rottweilers, pastries, Nikon cameras, Mercedes, listening to rock 'n' roll loud through good speakers and his family. I had to do feats of emotional gymnastics to discuss Dad in this way calmly. I couldn't seek information around Dad's disappearance without confronting this facet of it, and I also knew that whatever kind of story I ultimately told, voyeurs would seize on the lurid elements as the cheap thrill du jour. It all made my head ache.

That night I surged with a sense of agency—brisk, intoxicating. I was going to be the one who propelled the Cold Case Unit to act. Perhaps they'd find Dad; perhaps there would be justice. I was going to *do something.*

I crawled into the guest bed, flattened. I wrote in my journal:

-i have a plan

-new york seems a world away

-i feel like i could sleep for a week

-i have never understood so deeply how human our criminal justice system is

# SOME NEWS

A WEEK OR SO later my phone rang at *SmartMoney.* It was Sergeant Nolan.

"Miss Crane, I have some news," he said. "We looked into getting the box of evidence from your father's case. Unfortunately, it's been destroyed."

*Unfortunately, it's been destroyed.* Four words. I felt like a truck hit me.

"Destroyed?" I asked, naked dismay in my voice. "What does that mean? How?" The "how" was somewhere between a cry of pain and a shrug. I was reeling. I already knew that however many questions I asked Sergeant Nolan, the answer wouldn't restore the box of evidence.

Rage and helplessness and disappointment were rushing in. I felt the rug pulling out from under me in real time.

"Destroyed how?" I repeated.

Sergeant Nolan used the phrase "procedurally destroyed" and said that Cold Case was not consulted. He framed it as something that the evidence room had done to save space after the case had been dormant for a certain period of time. I couldn't understand it. How could some administrative wing of the police department just destroy evidence, procedurally or otherwise, without getting approval from investigators? It defied comprehension.

This was another before-and-after moment. It clicked into existence like a closing door.

For a little while, a speck in time, I'd thought there might actually be a chance to reopen Dad's case, and an even smaller chance to solve it. A chance all the same. It had never occurred to me that actively investigating Dad's murder was possible. Until it was. And now, suddenly, it wasn't again? Whiplash.

At the first house, Dad would get comfortable in his blue velvet armchair and I'd sit at his feet. We'd watch old Looney Tunes cartoons and crack up. In his ill-fated pursuit of the Road Runner, no dialogue except for the Road Runner's beep-beep, hungry old Wile E. Coyote would plot and scheme, and use ridiculous ploys. Inevitably, that sad coyote got smashed by his own Acme anvil. It was one of Chuck Jones's rules: "No outside force can harm the coyote—only his own ineptitude or the failure of the Acme products." His obsession left him flattened, over and over. Dad would convulse laughing at Wile E. Coyote, every time like it was the first time, sometimes until he cried.

From under the anvil, I wasn't laughing.

"Let's see about that skull," Sergeant Nolan said gently. "Bit by bit, little things come to me that I can do."

# CURTIS BAY

THE DIARRHEA AND the nightmares were beginning to recede. In their place I felt stained and depleted, as if I'd been submerged in poisonous floodwaters. Even so, I was relieved. I seemed to be making peace with my decision to track down what I could about Dad.

On the other hand, the mania was not easing up. I was following this path, wherever it was going to take me, and the sense of . . . *being* . . . electricity was a new default. The phrase "vessel of lightning" came to mind. It sounds firefly pretty but felt like hell. Holding dual realities—a disruptive private quest and a demanding ten-to-six job—was physically and emotionally draining. I'd only barely recovered from adrenal failure the year previous. Each day I raced from Jersey City to Columbus Circle, a mile of walking and two trains, then more walking. Outside was the big city, but every time I closed my eyes, I saw the stony skies over South Baltimore. I knew at some point I would leave *SmartMoney* magazine, and probably the boyfriend too. Something had to give.

Curtis Bay tugged at me with black-hole insistence. I had to go. I had to set eyes on E & M Machinery again. The reasons were not entirely clear to me. I certainly did not expect to find a memorial plaque or a signed confession, laminated and posted at the entrance to E & M. I did, though, think seeing the place with adult eyes might knock it down from horror-flick proportions to something less ominous. And I had no cemetery to visit. I longed to see the place where Dad had died.

A secret part of me also harbored an irrational wish: What if I could feel Dad's presence? I didn't want to play ghost hunter any more than I wanted to play detective. Still that wish scorched me from within. I mentioned it to no one.

That August, I got into my five-speed Civic and once again hit the Jersey Turnpike. I would stay in my room on Louise Avenue in Hamilton. Gordon was fully supportive of my project—in fact, he was adamant I take it on. So was Marie Collins. The two of them, Gor close to seventy and Marie almost eighty, were my silver-haired cheerleaders—not to mention two of the only people still allowed to call me Katy. Gordon was fired up to go with me to Curtis Bay. Marie would have liked to come with us, both for the adventure and to see the place where she'd been a little girl in the 1930s. Marie was delicate, though. We decided the trip would endanger her safety. I did not invite my mother along.

One humid morning after waking up to birdsong and cigarette fumes, I zipped down Northern Parkway to Belvedere Square for a brown paper sack of Greg's bagels, Baltimore's finest, and some coffees. Fortified, Gor and I stood over his atlas at the same kitchen table where I'd had my first cup of coffee fifteen years before. We felt like a couple of wartime generals, strategizing over maps.

The longer I lived in New York, the more I kept my Baltimore geography fresh by driving around with Gordon. He taught me a neat mnemonic: *Wolf down, wash up*. Wolfe Street was a southbound route, and Washington Street was its northbound counterpart. And while my mother taught me how to drive, it was Gordon who'd taught me manual transmission. We would cruise around the Loch Raven Reservoir, low pressure and low speed, over and over in his four-door Honda Civic sedan, as I got the hang of a clutch and choosing gears. Reverse was my nemesis: I stalled out dozens of times before it clicked.

Hamilton and Curtis Bay are both in Baltimore, but the city is complex, and Dad had always driven me to E & M. Gordon had been a taxi driver before he became a drama teacher—and before he himself was much of a stick driver, to the dismay of his passengers and the lamppost he once assailed. Unlike me, he knew Baltimore like the back of his hand. Almost—even Gordon Porterfield didn't know Curtis Bay. So there we were in the kitchen, combing his beat-up city atlas, yellow legal pad and pencil at hand.

I drove. Down Harford Road, through Hamilton. A languid four-lane artery, this stretch still felt like a small-town main street, albeit not the most pedestrian-friendly one. The side streets all led to the houses or former houses of 99 percent of my relatives; this neighborhood was ground zero for my German and Czech predecessors who immigrated here, put down roots, became plumbers and house cleaners and tailors and home aides, and raised families. Gor and I passed St. Dominic's, the Catholic church where my parents got married in the 1960s and where I used to go to Latin mass with petite, eternally chic Mee-Mom. There was the Blockbuster where I used to rent videos with Gordon and his son. Pete's Cycle, where my mother bought me a ten-speed the year after Dad disappeared. That bike embodied my mother's caring effort to preserve normalcy, and I couldn't push past the anguish to simply pedal. I'd learned to drive a stick-shift automobile but never to shift the ten-speed's gears. It gathered dust in the garage until Mom gave it away.

Gordon and I didn't talk much on the drive to Curtis Bay. He sensed my growing agitation and let me be. I'd pointed the hatchback toward a parallel dimension. Until today, I'd driven to Curtis Bay only with Dad. Now I was with a different father figure. Now I was behind the wheel.

After a few wrong turns, we found ourselves heading down Pennington Avenue under the same slate-gray skies of my dreams. Then, there it was: the corner of Birch Street and Curtis Avenue. E & M Machinery loomed from a low hill. Ludicrously, nonsensically, I remembered the first line of *Rebecca*: *Last night I dreamt I went to Manderley again*. A chill swept through me.

A high, white metal fence and a chain-link gate concealed the business itself, and a retaining wall partly encircled the property. Tall weeds and coarse grasses covered the hill. A weather-beaten sign hailed all comers, however few: *E & M Machinery*, in a combination of old-fashioned block letters and cursive. Below that, *MD. STATE & D.O.T. INSPECTION. TRUCK REPAIRS. REBUILT REARS and TRANS*. Then the phone number, the one I dialed for the first years of my telephone-using life when I wanted to talk to my daddy while he was at work.

"Let's get out and look around," Gordon said. He was intrigued. Since retiring, he wrote novels and plays, doted on his six grandchildren and taught part-time at Johns Hopkins. This was fun for him, a lark. Meanwhile I was flooding with dread. But we'd come this far. I had to at least get out of the car, I told myself. My legs, though, refused to cooperate.

All I could do was stand in the shelter of my Civic, hands gripping the doorframe, wondering at the physicality of panic:

I felt it in my trembling knees, in full-body cold that had descended from nowhere. Then, eerie voices in my head began to clamor. *Let's go, let's go,* they chattered in a chorus of dismay. It sounded like me and my mother and my sister all chanting together. *Let's go let's go let's go! LET'S GET THE HELL OUT OF HERE!* The voices and the sound of my heart thumping muted the world.

It hit me then. It hit me so hard. What I was doing was incredibly dangerous. What if the simple fact of pulling up to this place could get me killed, and Gordon too, and my mother, my uncle, my sister? I'd assumed coming down here would mitigate my paranoia. Twenty years later, how scary could an old truck company be? Instead of crumbling in the light of day, the paranoia roared up like a great white from the depths, all jaws and razors. There was no reasoning with this level of terror. Death was imminent.

"Gordon, stay near the car," I pleaded in a whisper. I couldn't see anyone up on that hill, but that didn't mean no one was watching. If I'd needed to scream, I don't think my voice would have risen to the occasion. And no one would have heard anyway. I watched as Gordon wandered farther and farther away, a lit Carlton in one hand as if we'd just left dinner at the Owl Bar, back in cheerful Mount Vernon.

*This was the place.* Right here. This was the place where he left work for the last time, dead or dying, likely in the back of the company pickup, which bore traces of blood when the police later tested it. "If they try to kill me, I'll make them do it in the office," Dad told my mother and uncle; he wouldn't let them take him off the property. And so he was most likely hauled out of here like a truck part.

I clutched my car like a rosary bead, scanning in every direction for approaching vehicles, for signs of movement up on the property, for any indication that someone had registered our presence.

"Gordon, come on, let's go!" I begged, crab-skittering from the car to tug at his sleeve.

He lumbered back, and, as if through water, I heard him muse: "God, what a strange place this is."

I got us buckled back in with shaking hands, locked the doors and shifted into first. We'd been in front of E & M Machinery for roughly five minutes. I had gotten a cold drink of reality, all right, but not the kind I expected. Yes, I was having a panic attack. And yes, I was drenched in paranoia. But there was not a doubt in my mind: My pursuit was dangerous.

I hadn't felt my dad, not one bit. Only terror.

"You turned into another person back there," Gordon said.

I was shaking too hard to reply.

# ECKHART TOLLE

IT FELT WRONG to keep my mom in the dark. I had to tell her what I was doing. She deserved to know. The sense of danger I'd felt in Curtis Bay left a knot in my stomach. I had so many murky emotions for my mother, including an ocean of love. I did not want to hurt her.

At thirty-two I could organize a protest, moderate a panel discussion in front of hundreds of people, write newspaper columns. I was finding my voice and my power. I could be loud when the moment demanded it. My mother, in contrast, was a reservoir of quiet and privacy.

Could I be OK with what I was doing if my mother was not? I had spent so much of my life rebelling from her, and leading my life differently from how she led hers. I put hundreds of literal and metaphorical miles between us. But all the rebelling and moving away from her made her a kind of lighthouse.

I tried to think logically. If something happened to any of us, given my father's well-documented disappearance, suspicion would fall upon my father's former business partner. Particularly since I was already in contact with Cold Case.

Whatever the actual level of risk, I had to update my mother. So a few weeks after my visit to E & M, I drove back to Baltimore to see her.

I mostly would stay with Gordon on these trips. The instability of my dynamic with my sister and a steady grief at going back home kept me away from my mother's house. Staying there again was a tentative shift. "Try to see your mother more," Gordon urged. Long estranged from his only sister, he pushed me to embrace my family. The first time I tried to stay with my mom again after a long absence, though, I got into bed and erupted into a thousand sneezes. I realized the sheets hadn't been washed, probably in years. So this time, I was surprised, and moved, to find that my sister had generously put clean sheets on my old twin bed. "No problem, it was easy to do!" she said, hugging me, when I thanked her.

I followed my mother back into her bedroom and hovered nervously while she folded and put away some laundry. Finally, I got up the nerve.

"So, I've been spending some time with the Cold Case detectives," I told Mom, who was sitting on the bed.

"Oh?"

My mother could pack more meaning into a single syllable than a doorstopper by Dostoevsky. It never ceased to astonish me.

"They showed me a little bit of Dad's file and answered some of my questions," I said.

My mother did not seem thrilled. Neither did she seem entirely surprised.

"Do you like them?" she asked, as if we were discussing my new neighbors or someone at the grocery store.

"Yes, I do. I think they're good men," I said.

Mom reached over to Dad's bedside table, pulled a drawer open and removed a small box. I had no idea what was happening. She clicked open the box. And handed it to me.

There was a dental appliance inside. Dazed, I realized I was holding Dad's backup teeth.

"You might want to take this with you," she said.

I felt an instant *no* articulate itself. I wasn't ready to take responsibility for an artifact with this much weight and meaning. I'd gladly assumed ownership of Dad's Nikons and lenses, but they weren't evidence. What if I lost Dad's teeth in a move? Absolutely not. The box would be safer here. For the moment, I clasped the little package gently and examined it in wonder. His teeth had made an impression in putty, and from the subsequent mold, the prosthetic teeth in my hands had been created.

I felt something itch at my mind. "Mom, the detectives said they'd found remains somewhere in Virginia, but they wrote it off because the teeth were wrong. The body in Virginia had a full upper and a full bottom, but they said Dad had two partials on the bottom."

The denture captivated me, an intimate relic of my father that now dwelled in a bedside table. It was the same reverence that stirred me in art museums. Eddy Crane was here, in some indirect way that I could now hold.

I looked back at my mother. "This looks like a full upper and a full bottom."

Mom looked so tired, and it was my fault. "He changed dentists at some point. They must have used an old record."

My heart started to race, and I wanted to be in three places at once—in the car bound for Cold Case on Fayette Street; in the other room, calling the detectives to say I was coming; and in this room, with my mother, whom I saw so rarely. This bit of information meant that the skull in Virginia could be my father's. If they'd dismissed it based on the wrong dental records, maybe it was him after all.

Just then my sister walked in. I couldn't believe it. Some sixth sense had tipped her off to trouble. Disappointment and irritation coursed through me. I got precious little time alone with my mother. I was glad to be with her. And the window to seek her blessing for this project, in person at least, was narrow. I also knew the risk of informing my sister about my project. Ethically, as a journalist as well as her kin, I was obligated. Did I want to, though? No. I felt she was a powder keg. Today I was more than a spark—I was a whole pack of matches.

"Kate has been talking to the detectives downtown," my mother said. "They might still be able to do something for Dad."

Ignition.

She whirled to face me, color in her cheeks rising.

"You talked to the police?"

"Yes," I said, my voice hardening.

"And they're going to *do something*?"

"Possibly. It's unclear what can be done."

At this point my sister began to shout. Some of it is seared in my mind.

"You set a fire under them and now they're going to work on this!"

A wave of loathing slammed me so hard I saw spots. A garbled *ummm* choked out of me. "Time out. Let me get something straight," I said, ice cold. "You're angry that the cops might try to do something about Dad's murder?"

"You don't have to live here and be afraid!" she said in a snarl. "All you think about is yourself!"

I felt woozy with fury. I was shutting down, and my sister was still yelling.

"What good will it do? I don't care about the details! I don't care where his body is! I know what happened to him! Who cares whether or not anyone is punished!? It won't bring him back!" She launched into a brief lecture on the value of Eckhart Tolle, whom she insisted I should read.

"Well, I care where his body is," I said, flat.

I felt a blank, detached fear that my sister might lunge at me.

"His spirit is all that matters!"

My grip around Dad's teeth tightened. Straight teeth, healthy teeth, pretty teeth, were not something my mother and father took as a given like I did. Losing one's natural teeth at a fairly young age was not uncommon for my parents' generation.

Maybe if we never found his body, we could bury his backup denture. I stifled an awful, choking laugh.

"Well, in cultures the world over, when a loved one dies," I said, shaking, aware of the disdain in my tone, "there is some aspect of ceremony and ritual. Whether someone is cremated or buried, his or her loved ones take special care of their remains."

My mother had been sitting with her head in her hands listening to my sister rage. For the first time in what could have either been ten minutes or an hour, she spoke: "It's the final act of respect."

My sister ignored her. "You don't care about my safety or Mom's. You moved away! You left! You don't have to be afraid of Augie anymore!"

In that room, Dad's backup teeth in one clenched fist, I was certain my hatred for my sister could turn the Chesapeake Bay into a vat of acid.

It took me years to understand a bigger fact, the overwhelming fact in the room that day in summer 2007: We were two halves of a warped whole, two sides of a cheated coin. Two children, one twelve, the other ten, had lost a parent.

I left. She stayed. I was desperate to get to the bottom of Dad's disappearance—and maybe even find him. She was desperate to stay grounded.

Same trauma, different survival strategies. It wasn't for me to condemn hers. At the same time, I could not predict which version of my sister I might encounter on visits. I did not feel safe, and it was wearing thin.

My sister rushed out of my mother's bedroom. I braced myself. One of two things might unfold: She would shove me later in the bathroom or give me the silent treatment for the rest of my visit. I wouldn't know until it was happening. One thing was certain: She would never apologize. Should I bring it up in the future, she would likely claim it never happened and suggest I seek mental health care. Danger hung in the air. The windows of connection, with my mother over Dad's false teeth and my sister over the gift of clean sheets, had shut with a bang.

Dad's denture sat on the bed, somehow having left my fist, another mouth that couldn't talk.

# DOO-WOP

SOMETIMES I FELT like I was dog-paddling with sharks, or trying to build a skyscraper with pen and paper. This new reality was a steady short-circuiting. A voice in my head kept repeating: *There's nothing to say, there's nothing to say. There is no story here beyond my old fifty-word narrative.* What I can only describe as an abject sense of nothingness would take over. Yet as I pondered questions about the past, I also got flashes of somehow becoming more myself. Those flashes were better than the fog—there was an aliveness to them. But all in all, I felt less able to relate to other people. My world was too strange.

I was surrounded by writers, and all of them had an opinion on what I should do. One friend insisted I write a book. Another connected me to the editor of *Fortune Small Business* magazine, who assigned me a feature, saying, "Your angle for this is: What happens when a business partnership goes wrong?" This felt absurd. There was another problem. The editor wanted me to call Augie.

"I'm pretty sure that contacting my father's business partner would endanger not only my life, but also that of my uncle, mother and sister," I told him on the phone, coursing with the adrenaline that felt permanent. "I'm not saying I'm never going to do it, but I'm not there right now. Too much of the situation is unclear to me. I can't make a phone call like that until I have a lot more information."

Then I said something that surprised me. "I don't care if I find out my dad was a criminal." I meant it. Tracking down some answers mattered more than whether or not what I learned conformed with my sense of right and wrong. Much less anyone else's.

"I'm not going to stop looking into this," I told the editor. "I'm just not sure if I can give you the story you want the way you want it."

The editor didn't kill the piece on the spot. "Just keep going and be in touch as you find things out," he said.

Somehow, I doubted I would.

The kinds of jobs I had in New York were unimaginable to most of the people I'd grown up around, and often to me as well. I had neither a journalism degree nor, at first, any connections. On mostly talent, I was winging it. Now, having slammed the brakes on an assignment with a legitimate publication, I had no idea where I was headed. But for the moment, I was relieved to be back on my own again. Even if the unknown was daunting.

I needed to drop off some film at my lab, Duggal, on 23rd Street. Strolling out of the office, onto Broadway and across 57th Street, at a languid pace that any non–New Yorker would call a full-on charge, I descended the subway stairs and darted onto a downtown R train. I slid into a seat, let my eyes slip shut and breathed the familiar scent of subway air.

I barely registered the troupe of doo-wop singers who entered the car. Until they began to sing. My eyes opened back up.

When I drove around with Dad, I had two favorite songs I always pestered him to play. There was the one about the one-eyed, one-horned, flyin' purple people eater. And there was the one I was listening to now, for the first time since 1987. "The Lion Sleeps Tonight." Of all the singers and all the songs in all the cars on all the trains on all the subway lines . . . Maybe it's a subway-singer standard, but in my decade-plus riding the trains, I had never once heard it.

Dad.

The song was first recorded in 1939 under the title "Mbube," by Solomon Linda, a South African songwriter. The lion in the song is metaphorical. Legend held that a Zulu king, Shaka the Lion, didn't die after the British invasion. He was just sleeping—one day he'd wake up and return.

After running away from his absence for twenty years, I had turned to embrace my lost father. I was now with him 24/7. Where was I in time? The air around me felt unreliable and the hard plastic seat beneath me, overly malleable. I was twelve and thirty-two all at once. I had not felt Dad in Curtis Bay. But he was here with me now on the subway—I was sure of it.

The doo-wop troupe was inching toward me, locked in the impeccable New York City trick of harmonizing while shuffling past knees, backpacks, a Yorkie poking out of a Balducci's tote. Panic rose like an algae bloom from somewhere deep. My face went sheet white. I was surrounded by people in their own R-train bubbles; no one registered my reaction. I could not bear for the musicians to come any closer, could not bear it, and what could I do? The singers were singing. Oh, God, the singers were looking straight at me.

No longer sure if I was in my dad's 1975 Mercedes or on the train, I started to cry.

Tears struck my cheeks in a salty flash flood. I held my breath, I screwed my eyes shut, I bowed my head, but, having started, the tears had no intention of stopping.

And neither did those doo-wop singers.

Closer and closer they shuffled, swaying with the train as we hurtled through a tunnel, until they were standing in front of me, doo-wopping their hearts out.

The repeated keening of *wimoweh, wimoweh, wimoweh, wimoweh* . . . I couldn't bear it.

*Wimoweh* doesn't even *mean* anything. When other musicians adapted Linda's song, they misunderstood *uyimbube*—"You are a lion." And now, four or five big men, hovering in front of me and swaying with the twin motions of the train and the song in the narrow aisle of an R train, were singing *wimoweh*, some of the first sounds I'd ever sung myself.

The lion might be sleeping tonight. But what about tomorrow?

I looked around with the expression every New Yorker understands to mean, "I'm getting off at this stop, make room or get shoved." What stop? Didn't know or care. I couldn't stand that song and its bittersweetness. I had to get off the train.

Dad had sent me a singing telegram from the other side: *As you find out about me, don't forget about us.*

The doors opened. I gulped reassuring New York City air and fled.

# BRYANT PARK

READING THAT DIALOGUE from *The Wire* had changed my feelings toward David Simon in a way that was electric. His act of remembering, of memorializing my father, decades after his disappearance, had washed clean my resentment about the *Homicide* episode. I'd reached out to David's office soon after finding that script.

*Someone else remembers*, I kept thinking. *Someone else cares.* I secreted this small joy away, as if talking about it too much might cause it to vanish.

We found a time and date when David would be in New York, and I suggested meeting at Bryant Park. His team had offered up the HBO cafeteria as a quiet, private backup in case of bad weather. Now I was kicking myself. I should have jumped at the suggestion. I had enough experience to know that quiet and private are preferable for an interview.

Beyond that, I was bone weary with a sinus infection. I got them every month—to some degree I was always sick.

David and someone from HBO were waiting for me on the northeast corner of Sixth Avenue and 42nd Street. He was dressed comfortably. Social studies teacher who coaches softball vibes. By some miracle we found a free table and settled in. I turned on my audio recorder.

"The key things that I remember are the desk, the dog, the chair," he said. David meant my dad's desk with its puttied-over bullet holes; Sherlock the Rottweiler, the mute witness who was lost and then found; and Dad's desk chair, which his killers had in all likelihood used to wheel his three-hundred-pound body out of E & M.

"These were the things that convinced the detectives that the night watchman was the actual doer," David continued. "According to the file, your father made statements to your mother and uncle that he would not go anywhere with Augie—he'd told your mom he didn't trust him. He thought the guy was enough of a sociopath to try to kill him. He said, 'I'm not gonna go anywhere with him. I'm not letting him take me out of that office.' Which is one of the things that made the detectives go back and really consider the office as the crime scene. And then they found it. They turned over the desk and found the bullet holes and realized the chair was missing.

"Then there was the dog. Your dad was by all accounts extremely attached to this dog. He's not going to park at the airport and leave the dog. Just let him off the leash, let him wander around."

"No," I said, and a smile, sad and weak like the October light, filled my face. "Absolutely not. And if Dad were going to leave the state or the country, he would've left Sherlock at home. He was Dad's dog first but the family dog too . . . I don't believe he would have put his kids through losing their dad and their puppy at the same time. We all suspect Augie may have poisoned the first Rottweiler. I don't know if that's true or not. But that's the only time I ever saw my father cry. He was crushed. He loved his dogs."

I remember that day. We still lived on Silver Spring Road. Dad came into the little bedroom I shared with my sister, wearing his standard stretchy work shirt and trousers. He sat next to me on the edge of my twin bed, which made it sag precariously. "Katy, Brutus was very sick and we had to put him to sleep," he said. Then my father broke down and cried, great wrenching sobs. I heard his heart cracking in two.

"The idea of somebody stealing a chair and a mop and a pail is just ridiculous on its face," David said, bringing me back. "And then the compulsion to leave the dog alive."

"What did you make of that?" I asked. "I've never understood why."

No hesitation. "There's a lot of people who, forgive me, who'll kill a person . . ." David trailed off. Hesitation.

"But not an animal," I said.

"But not an animal," he said.

"It's like the guy couldn't bear to kill the dog. He knew leaving the dog in the car would kill the dog. So he decided to let him go at the airport."

I thought of Sherlock, Rottweiler tough, but a family dog, used to Iams kibble, the adoration of little girls and car rides with Dad. How confused and scared and lost he must have felt.

Bryant Park was loud. Conversations and car horns flowed all around us. And David was definitely getting recognized. It was fall 2007; *The Wire* was being hailed as the best TV show in history. I braced for interruption as passing faces registered interest.

"Augie was the business partner, right?" David asked. I nodded. "Well, I met him once. And I was young. It happened in late '87, am I right?"

"September 10," I said.

"I came into the Homicide Unit in January of '88," he said. "So it didn't happen the year I was there."

A longtime reporter at *The Sun*, David took a leave of absence and shadowed the Homicide Unit of the Baltimore Police Department in 1988, a year of 234 murders. His experiences are chronicled in his book *Homicide: A Year on the Killing Streets*, which was later adapted to the television series that ran for seven seasons and 122 episodes. The book is a riveting window into Baltimore that holds up decades later.

In its pages: the preposterous tale of Geraldine Parrish, a fifty-five-year-old lay preacher with almost as many husbands as life insurance policies naming her as beneficiary. It was a case of contract killing fit for a circus. Miss Geraldine got eight life sentences and died in custody of natural causes.

*Homicide* also tells the story of La-Tonya Wallace, an eleven-year-old West Baltimore honor student and book lover who vanished after leaving the Park Avenue branch of the Enoch Pratt Free Library. Instead of fulfilling her dreams of becoming a dancer, La-Tonya became known as the Angel of Reservoir Hill. Despite the diligence and determination of Detective Tom Pellegrini, Sergeant Jay Landsman and colleagues, her rape and killing remain unsolved.

Simon continued. "Ed Brown was still very involved. And Ed and Donald Kincaid were in no way fools. They put down their share of cases. There were guys in that unit that could have been mistaken for Sherlock Holmes, they were so good. There were guys in that unit that could carry a whole squad—Donald Worden or Kevin Davis. But in all the years that I knew Ed Brown, he never dogged a case. The fact that he was still dealing with your dad's case in January when I came into the unit shows a certain healthy regard for it. Because a lot of shit gets dropped after a week."

"And also at the end of the year," I said.

"That's right. The reason it came up in conversation when I was around—they had gone to Timothy Doory to urge him to charge the night watchman. There was not enough to charge Augie under any circumstances. Ed and Kincaid wanted to charge. It was Tim Doory who wouldn't.

"Augie was never going to give anything up. But they could charge the night watchman and have him convicted, and then try to roll him. The night watchman was scared of Augie. And scared of the cops too. They felt they could rattle him a little more than they had.

"I never met the night watchman," David continued. "But Augie, I met. Because I went to try and get a quote from him."

I knew this, because it's in David's 1992 *Sun* article. David is fifteen years older than me, and was twenty-eight when he shadowed the Homicide Unit. I was ravenous for his impressions of Augie.

"What did you make of him?" I asked. "I mean, this is a guy I called *uncle* when I was a kid. I had savings bonds that just matured from him, which is creepy."

David sighed. "It's very creepy. My impression of him is colored by the fact that Eddie Brown thought he was guilty. So I thought he was guilty. And I was going there ostensibly to get a comment. I never thought he'd talk about it in any detail."

"Did you go to his house?" I asked.

"No. I went to the business. There was two guys there. I don't know if the other guy was the night watchman or somebody else. But there was one other guy doing something at the end of the yard because I asked him, 'Where's Mr. So and So?' What was his last name?"

"Augustin."

"Augustin," David repeated. "'Where's Mr. Augustin?' And he said, 'Oh, I dunno.'

"Then I watched him walk over and talk to another guy who was under the hood of a truck. He stood up from under the hood and wiped the engine grime from his hands with a rag. Came over to me."

I could picture my "Uncle" Augie, a lean, imposing figure over six feet tall, olive skin reddened and tough from decades of hard work with heavy machinery out in the sun. His black pompadour was agleam with styling potion. His strong hands reached for a rag he kept near the engine he was working on. Slowly, deliberately, he removed the truck grease from his hands, the gears of his mind turning. It was spring 1992, and the sky over the E & M Machinery lot shone a piercing, icy blue over the bony white of the gravel.

A chill ran through me and I shook off the vision.

"I said, 'I'm from *The Sun*. I'm doing a story on your business partner's disappearance a couple years ago.' He sort of listened. I said, 'You know, there's a lot in the police file to suggest that you had something to do with it.'

"He said, 'You gonna print that?' I said, 'I'm gonna print that possibility. I'm not gonna say for sure you had something to do with it. But I'm definitely gonna print something about the police scenario of what they think may have happened.' The move that I was trying with him was, 'Look. All the bad shit the cops are saying, that's gonna be in the story. Now's your chance to speak for yourself.'

"He just shook his head and walked away. Then he did the most startling thing. It's the thing I remember most clearly . . . . You'll understand, as a reporter, how savvy it was. He came back as I was leaving. He said, 'Can I ask if you're a reporter?' And I said, 'Yeah.' He says, 'Well, I got something that I want to talk to you about.' And he starts talking about a zoning problem where the city councilmen were fucking him over. 'You ought to do a story on this,' he said.

"I said to him, 'But you don't want to talk about the disappearance of Eddy Crane?' He said, 'No. I really can't talk about that. I've got a lawyer who says I'm not supposed to talk about it. But this other thing. I'd be happy to talk to you about that. There's a good story in there for you.'

"Excuse me. *There's a good story in there for you.* And I was like, *You ballsy motherfucker.* There was something about that. With that black pompadour . . ."

David shook his head. "When did I write the story?"

"May 1992."

"So I was thirty-one. I'd been a police reporter for a while. I took the precaution of telling my editor where I was going. I said: 'If I'm not back here in five hours, you fucking call the police.'

"But I didn't really believe there was any problem. He had nothing to gain. Anything I knew, the police knew. He was no fool."

David shifted gears, looked me straight in the eye.

"If you try to talk to this guy, emotions will come up for you."

I held his gaze. "Yes."

"To the extent that you try to have a conversation with him, I don't think you'll succeed. But I don't think you need to fear him physically," David went on. "That moment of turning around and trying to engage me on some other bullshit is so calculated, and he'll be just as calculating with anybody who approaches him about this issue."

"Did you ever meet my uncle? Bob?" I asked. "He worked for my dad and Augie for seven years."

"I never did," he said.

"Bob scared the living hell out of me."

"Telling you not to go to see Augie?"

"He said, 'They would think nothing of picking you up, raping you, cutting your throat. If you try to talk to Augie, you're gonna get us all killed.' He said that, for years, Augie and his people harassed my uncle. Blew up his mailbox. Left sticks of dynamite on his front doorstep."

"Why would they do that after Augie had obtained the business?" David asked. "What's the gain for doing that?"

"I don't know," I said. For the millionth time since July, I wondered, could I get my family killed? If there was even a chance, what kind of monster was I?

*YOU DON'T CARE ABOUT US YOU DON'T HAVE TO LIVE HERE ALL YOU CARE ABOUT IS YOURSELF.*

My sister's voice jutted into my mind, coalescing with the hammering of the sinus infection and the din of Bryant Park. It was then that I received one of the most peculiar mentoring sessions of my life.

"If you decide to do this," David said, "you could begin by being blunt. First you say, 'Everybody told me not to come out here. I talked to my mom and my uncle. The Baltimore City Homicide Unit knows I'm here right now. And Sergeant Nolan said for me to call when I got back.' You make it very clear that Roger Nolan knows where you are. And do it. I would call Roger Nolan."

I nodded.

"You say Sergeant Nolan was concerned. 'But I just can't see me not having a conversation with you.' You put it all in the preamble."

I said: "I thought about the approach of 'You were my uncle. Why would they say all this about you? You were family to me. I grew up playing in your garage.'"

"Right," he said. "And you might end up getting more out of him with that. You won't get anything incriminating. But you may get some exculpatory bullshit. You may get more of an interaction with him than anybody could.

"If this guy did it, he is the most calculating motherfucker you'll ever encounter. All you have to do is put the integers into his calculation. He may not talk to you. And he may say, 'Get off my property.' But I don't think a visit by you, after all these years, is going to result in physical harm."

I was listening so hard my ears hurt. This counsel was invaluable. For this dot in time, it was just me and someone with singular insight into the quest I'd undertaken. I listened. And I begged my foggy mind to record it.

"There's all different ways to try to get the reluctant to say the first word," he continued. "But you can rely on the historical semifamilial ties that you do not feel but that you might be able to guilt him with.

"This is so personal to you that I can't give you advice," said David. "I can only tell you how to be tactical if you choose to do it."

"I appreciate that," I said.

"I'd be curious to know where the night watchman is. 'Cause that is the only link in the case that you could still turn proactive. Augie's never talking. I don't believe in deathbed guilt."

I agreed. At no point was I expecting Augie to express remorse. David suggested a call to the Office of the Chief Medical Examiner to see if I could track down a death record for Roscoe Woolard.

"It's my sense that there was an element of organized crime involved in this," I said. "Whether it was formal or informal. With that sort of business, and from what I've found out, E & M was not on the up-and-up. Theft, creepy characters. But I don't know if it was large scale or hyperlocal."

David shrugged. "I just don't know. I learned very little about that aspect of the business. And I don't think the detectives spent a lot of time on that. They knew about the financial interests that Augie had in the business as a result of your father's death. That was sufficient motive for them.

"There's a saying in homicide. *Motive is not important*. What it means is: You show me opportunity. You show me lies. You show me witness statements. You show me physical evidence. Detectives don't care why. *We know he shot him. That's all we care about.* Those detectives felt as if your father's body were disposed of at a chemical plant in Curtis Bay," David said.

"That's one theory, yes," I said. "There was an acid vat on the premises. A ready-made body disposal. That came up in *The Wire* last season. Do you remember that?"

"What?" David looked surprised.

"My father was mentioned by name in a fourth-season episode of *The Wire*." I wasn't trying to sandbag him. Both times he'd used Dad in his TV shows had had a significant impact on me in polar-opposite ways. I was curious what he'd been thinking when he made the decisions to include Dad in his own creative work about Baltimore.

"Oh, when they had a case where they weren't going to charge because there was no body." It came back to him. "It would've been in my head when I was writing dialogue because I actually heard your father's name invoked, years later, by detectives who had not worked your dad's case. *We've gotta find a body. 'Cause otherwise we got Eddy Crane.*

"Your dad became a paradigm for taking a murder case into court without a body. Tim Doory's logic was, *I can only do this once. I think this guy's guilty. If I do it now, I don't think I'll win without the body.*

"The good part about that is that he was trying to give the case the best possible chance in the future. The bad part of it is, the future is always cluttered with other cases and other ambitions. You get taken off the front burner. But for years afterward, the Eddy Crane parable was one that said: *We don't trust Baltimore City juries enough. If we don't have a body, we ain't going. We didn't go on Eddy Crane. We're not going on this one.*"

"Did you agree with that?" I asked.

"Well, I'm not sure Doory is wrong. Baltimore City juries are the most incredulous juries in the state of Maryland, certainly. If E & M were located in Baltimore County, Sandra O'Connor would have charged that case, and there's a 70 or 80 percent chance she'd have gotten a conviction. Even without a body. But that's a Baltimore County jury, and it's very different. I had a conversation with Doory about it once, and he was very persuasive in his way. He's a good guy. But he was also a political animal . . ."

"He's a judge now," I said.

"Yeah. And he's related to Ann Marie Doory."

From January 1987 to July 2010, I later learned, Ann Marie Doory was a member of the Maryland House of Delegates. A public servant with a résumé a mile long . . . I got David's point. Timothy Doory, an assistant state's attorney at the time of my father's murder, who'd gone on to become an associate judge in the Baltimore City Circuit Court, was part of a prominent Maryland family. A family of politicians. It wasn't a positive or a negative, just a fact: Politicians think and act like politicians. I suspected the decision not to charge anyone in my father's case was calculated in part according to Doory's career. He would have charged if he was sure of a win.

"He was not a guy who took a lot of chances. Those guys don't like to lose in public."

I wanted to look into this skull story with David. "Do you remember going down to Virginia? Sergeant Nolan said you went with them. Does this ring any bells? They found remains in Virginia in March '88."

"He's absolutely right. I would have forgotten about that had he not told you about it. We drove out to Frederick and then went south on 15. They found the remains of a white male. I seem to recall we went to your dad's dentist. Got the dental records for comparison. There was that brief spasm of hoping, because it was the right age. Right demographic. Right approximate bone structure. But it wasn't him. They had full teeth, and it came back negative. I don't know if they ever identified those remains."

*YOU DON'T CARE ABOUT US YOU DON'T HAVE TO LIVE HERE ALL YOU CARE ABOUT IS YOURSELF.*

My sister's rage felt stiflingly close. And I felt guilty—I was supposed to figure out the teeth.

"But I do remember the trip now. God, Roger's got a better memory than me."

"He's a sharp guy," I said. I had many thoughts and emotions around Roger Nolan. Those were the only words I could find.

David agreed. "He is. He's a very sharp guy. The only Black Republican in Baltimore, as Rich Garvey used to call him. He's an ex-Marine. He was one of the better squad supervisors out there. He doesn't drink. He doesn't socialize with the men. He's the boss."

"He doesn't even drink coffee," I said.

"I respect Roger a lot. Although I'll never admit it to him because he'd run a mile with that," he said. "Because he was the supervisor, your dad definitely got a better shake than most.

"Given the murder scene they uncovered in that office, I'd have loved to have seen a jury deal with that. To me it defies anything but one explanation. I'd love to hear what a defense attorney could've done to put smoke in front of that."

"Well, the evidence room destroyed all the evidence in the nineties. So it's gone." I tried to state this fact as if it were not still messing with my sleep months later.

"You're kidding? I'm not surprised," although I saw it flash across his face, just a second, aghast. "Fucked-up police department. So the desktop is gone? And—"

"It's all gone," I said. "And no one asked Homicide."

"Roger told you that?" David asked. I nodded. "At least he's being honest with you. There's no reason not to show you the file now. For purposes of your journalism. Because they can never make a case. Absent a confession."

"What if they actually found a body after all this time?" I asked. I didn't think it was possible, but I couldn't help hoping.

David said: "They'd have to find something with the body that is as evidentiary as what was destroyed. They'd identify the body. They say he died of gunshot wounds. I guess they still have the photographs, right? They still have a file?" Again, I nodded.

"So they can show the stuff in the file . . ." He trailed off. "Listen, it makes the case harder. I'm overstating it. They would have to go in and say, 'We don't have the desktop for your examination, but we have the officer's reports and we have these photographs showing you the bullet holes. And we have the results of the blood test in the office showing the same blood type.'

"Then they have the absence of the chair and what happened with the dog. And where the car was stolen. Then they would have whatever statements put them over the top. No. They should've kept the desktop. They could still have a case. But again, it's more smoke for a defense attorney to say, *Oh, you destroyed the evidence. How convenient*," David said. "You can just hear a defense attorney running a million miles."

"Do you regularly use real cases in your work, just because of the time you spent in Baltimore Homicide and because of your years as a police reporter?" I asked.

"Real cases probably come up in my head because I'm a little bit frustrated as a storyteller . . . Frustrated at not knowing the end of a story," he said. "I covered other cases where they never came up with a body. A couple of drug murders where people were dismembered, and they invoked your dad. The psychological precedent in Baltimore of, 'Well, we didn't charge Eddy Crane. We're definitely not charging this.' And so it became a standard. When I have fictional detectives and they're discussing whether they can charge something when they're missing the body . . ." He trailed off. "I didn't think it would offend you or your mom if you heard it," he said.

"My mother is sensitive," I said. "But it doesn't offend me." And immediately couldn't believe myself. Both of us, not just my mother, had been leveled.

"I remember she called me after the *Homicide* thing and I

said, 'Was that OK?' Actually, I called her before then. I said, 'Is it OK if I reference . . . I won't say Eddy Crane, but I'm just going to use the pieces of it.'"

"You talked to her after," I said.

"Oh, I did."

"It was a total surprise," I said.

"I'm sorry," said David. "Then I did it—"

"It was a total surprise," I said, not meaning to cut him off. But now the words were tumbling out, with some of the old shock.

"That's right. She called me after," David agreed. "I didn't think it would be recognizable without the name."

I just looked at him, said something about how I watched it religiously, and trailed off.

"So it just blew your mind," he said.

"Oh, I immediately knew what it was. As soon as the scene started, I said, 'I'm watching my father's murder.'"

"I apologize."

"It's OK."

That night in 1998 when I'd watched Dad's last night play out on prime-time television, I felt betrayed, caught off guard. Now I was on the same side of the table as David: a writer. Mining the same story that he had, arguably with murkier ethical implications. And with my family distressed and afraid at what I could set into motion, I was no longer the betrayed. I was the betrayer.

"It's a comfort that someone else remembers us," I said.

Conscious of the time, I pressed on with a final few questions.

"My uncle says my dad would leave his gun lying around the office. Bob has said to me on numerous occasions, 'It's the element of surprise that counts. And it's the element of surprise that got your father killed.'"

"Just because you're paranoid doesn't mean you don't have enemies," said David. "But I don't think your family has anything to fear anymore."

"Augie is about to turn eighty," I said, agreeing with him. "I try to keep in mind that it's not my world—criminals. I grew up in the Baltimore suburbs. And I left when I was twenty-two and moved to New York. I mean, I *did* grow up with gangsters. I just didn't know it at the time."

"Nobody's really scary when you grow up with them," said David. "Nobody seems to be a sociopath. That's part of what being a sociopath is.

"A lot of people got away with murder over the years. Most of it in the drug game. There was also something different about your dad's case in this way. Most of the guys I knew that got killed in drug murders, they fucked up the money. They stole something. They threatened another guy and the guy came back on them. They fought for territory.

"But your father's case, there was an act of betrayal. It was getting away with murder with a capital *M*. It made me angry. I feel like they caught this guy and they weren't allowed to catch him. Does that make sense?"

Yes, it made all the sense in the world.

In the watery light of a Midtown afternoon in October, I shared space with one of the only people who cared about the injustice of Dad's fate. David Simon was a singular figure in the life of my family, who, twenty years after the fact, still thought about Dad now and then, found the situation unfair and used his vast platform to say so publicly.

Daylight was fading and I wasn't sure if we'd been talking for one hour or three. We said our goodbyes, and then David stopped me as I was walking away.

"I'm not telling you to pursue this. I can imagine how fraught it is. Only you know whether there's anything to be gained by pursuing this. And who knows what emotions might come up for you. You probably don't know that yet."

I didn't.

# CHRISTMAS

POP WAS IN the rust-colored recliner, newly eighty-two years old, slim and dignified in a flannel shirt and heather-gray trousers, what little hair he had in gleaming white tufts. The sight of him melted away the five hours of driving. Looking at him, I saw everything good about my childhood: the books he bought for me at the Enoch Pratt Free Library sales, our walks to Burdick Park, the stops we made at the corner store for Nutty Buddy ice-cream cones, the afternoons I spent with him just, as he would say, "foolin' around down the basement." He used to go crabbing, that most Baltimore of pastimes. When you go crabbing, if you're lucky, you come home with live crabs. One time he brought back a massive, teeming bushel—and they got loose. I often picture a younger Pop, this trumpet-playing World War II veteran, artist and flaneur, dancing an improv Lindy Hop around the basement with its red and black tiles as he tried to recapture dozens of Maryland blue crabs and their wrathful pincers.

I leaned in and hugged him. He wasn't fragile, but he was old. My joy at our reunion was riddled with dread at the inevitable: One day he's going to die.

Pop looked debonair and radiant. I could still see the teenager who'd been a member of the American Sokol Gymnastic Union for Czechs, the twentysomething who'd mastered newspaper Linotype technology and gone to work for *The Sun*. I could also see the gravitas of a widower.

"Katy!" He roared with a gentle joy. Every time I saw him, I relived the same dazzling memory: Pop and Mee-Mom on the stoop of their little house in Hamilton, in northern Baltimore City near the county line. When Mom would drive away from their house, the two of them would stand on their stoop and wave and wave and wave. They waved at us until we got to the top of the hill on their street, and they kept waving until we made the turn and all of us were gone from each other's sight.

"Hi, Pop!" I said, almost shyly. I felt his arms around me, the embrace of a proud granddad. He had always given me boisterous, sloppy cheek kisses. If I squirmed, it was the galactic hugeness of the love. I never quite knew how to hold it along with the sadness and the anger that took up so much space in me.

Mee-Mom was gone and so were Pop's brother and sister, and many of his friends. After his life as a gymnast—he pronounced it gym-NAST—he'd become a fan of fitness expert Jack LaLanne, pursuing calisthenics, yoga and walking, and studying nutrition. "Ugh, Pop, what's that?" I once asked, staring at a glistening jar full of rank-smelling amber.

"Fish oool!" he enthused. Something I now sometimes take. Everyone teased him. He was right. Cold comfort: Pop had outlived most everyone he had loved.

"Dad, do you want a coffee?" Mom asked him. I was not a Folgers fan, but Pop partook.

"Joey, this is good coffee," he told her a few minutes later, content.

I went to the bathroom and when I came out, my sister was blocking the doorway.

"Could I please get past?" I asked. Her lip curled and her eyes, all black somehow, fixed on me. She said nothing. "Move!" I said, indignant, and tried to push past her. Taller than me by a few inches and broader, she shoulder-checked me. I fell backward and bumped my head. "What the hell!" I gasped. "What is your problem?"

She snickered and got in my face. "What's *your* problem?" she whispered. I tried to move but she was matching my stumbles, looming over me and silently laughing, all the time those black pupils boring.

I started gasping, attempts at hollers that came out in rasps, like the dogs next door who had no vocal cords. I broke away and stumbled back into the kitchen. Tears flooded my cheeks. I was stretched paper thin with this new reality—months of nightmares, the guilt at putting everyone in danger, the drive to push ahead and uncover what I could. I had come here for family, and it was just more danger. Nowhere felt safe.

"What's wrong with Kate?" Mom asked my sister.

"I didn't do anything," she said, a bland grunt. My mother and grandfather turned to me in shared disapproval.

"I don't know why you have to act like this, Kate," said my mother, disgusted.

My grandfather eyed me with disappointment. And then he looked away.

"How about I take you home, Pop?" my sister said, all compassion and concern.

"I think that's a good idea," he said stiffly.

My sister swept back into the kitchen with my grandfather's baseball jacket. "You ready, Pop?" she cooed. I saw her smirk just for me—neither my grandfather nor my mother was able or willing to read it. "Let's get you home."

## ED BROWN

Sometime that fall I received a voicemail. "Hi, Kate, this is Ed Brown. I received your message in reference to a book you're writing about your father's—" and here the voice paused "—death. It has to be Eddy Crane. You have to be his daughter."

I heard the wonder and disbelief in his voice. It was electrifying. Yet again, here was someone who remembered, and it was one of the actual lead detectives, one of the men who had visited us back in 1987. I believed everyone had forgotten. But here was Ed Brown's voice, astonished. A child from his past had grown up. Before even speaking to each other, there was a shared recognition. Both of us had been in the same place in 1987. It felt unreal to be reconnecting twenty years later.

So we made a plan for me to come and see him in Baltimore while I was "home for Christmas," a phrase that now tasted sour. I ached with longing for my grandfather. The last time I'd called him, he was cold to me on the phone. No one believed how my sister treated me when they weren't looking. Why was it easier to accuse me of lying or bad behavior than to believe me when I said she mistreated me? I knew the answer: She stayed, and I left. I had violated fundamental family doctrine. And now I was violating more.

Rage and sadness and exhaustion pressed down on me like a lead blanket as I drove across the Baltimore Beltway, 695, west toward Reisterstown.

Soon I was knee to knee with a tall Black man who looked about fifty, in a dim, cramped room that flickered—the nerve center of the Baltimore Ravens security operations, where the retired homicide detective now worked. I had not seen this man since I was twelve.

The dashboard in front of us flashed and made hypnotic robot chirps, indicating calls coming in, calls in progress. As I had no idea if or how often we would be interrupted, I got the recorder going and we settled in.

At first, our conversation largely repeated the ones I'd so far had with my uncle and David Simon. The night watchman, the desk, the chair, the dog—like a C. S. Lewis novel from hell.

But then Ed Brown remembered something that surprised me.

"Augie was real tight with a politician," Ed said. "I think he's dead now, but he used to be on the City Council and he was very popular in Southeast Baltimore."

"Willie Myers?" I thought of Uncle Bob's insistence that this longtime Curtis Bay member of the City Council had been involved in covering up Dad's disappearance.

"He was an older guy. And Augie had all types of ties with this guy. As a matter of fact, I went there to serve a search and seizure warrant. Augie made some calls, and while I'm at the scene, it came down from a higher-up. 'You can't do anything,' they told me. I said, 'What do you mean, I can't do anything?

I have a search and seizure warrant signed by a judge. I have to execute it.'"

I realized I wasn't breathing.

"I had to hold off serving the warrant until a supervisor or someone from the commissioner's office arrived at the scene—"

"That's incredible!" I blurted. You're not supposed to interrupt your interview subject when they're talking. The idea is to let people talk. For a second there, Dad's daughter had shoved the journalist out of her chair.

"Yeah, this politician called City Hall and then he called the police department," said Ed. "I ran into quite a few roadblocks in my days. But not from City Hall."

It had to be Myers. My uncle had brought him up on the phone over the summer, saying he was in Augie's pocket. I'd thought it sounded like something out of *Serpico* or a paperback spy thriller. I just couldn't tell if it was real or paranoia. Part of my strategy to find out was to see if the detail ever came up in another conversation. Here, again, was William J. Myers. The involvement of a local politician in the cover-up of Dad's murder was beginning to sound credible. *Cover-up* . . . That term was hitting me for the first time.

"It should've been classified as a homicide, right from the very beginning: Homicide/Shooting. Not Missing Person/Homicide," Ed said.

Misclassified as a missing person, with the number one suspect putting pressure on a politician to prevent the detectives from executing a search warrant. *Cover-up*, I thought again, like I was trying on a new sweater. I had always vaguely assumed that a combination of people refusing to talk, Dad's missing body, a Homicide Unit swamped with cases in a city known for killing, and maybe some police incompetence were the dominant factors in the languishing of my father's case. It was dawning on me that there could be more to it.

"Augie came up with a story that your father went to Mexico, he had a woman there, he started a new life, and all this money's missing. But we knew better—that the whole thing was a cover to make it look like your dad had left town or taken his own life," Ed said.

"We didn't buy it. And it had to be more than one person involved," he continued. "Someone disposed of the body, someone drove the car, dropped the dog off. They had to know where they were going to do that. And they dropped the dog off right in front of a kennel."

I hadn't considered that the Doberman breeder finding Sherlock was anything but pure coincidence—that someone may have left Sherlock where a Rottweiler-savvy person was likely to find him and take care of him. The humanity of the gesture rang in my head like breaking glass.

"Whoever did this, they came up with some things pretty fast. I don't think it was premeditated. Why would you want to kill a person right there in the office? It's going to bring all types of attention to you."

I had run through most of my questions. I was tired and hungry, and I didn't want to keep Ed Brown from his job for too long. It was such a charged action just to talk to him. I was thirty-three years old and terrified to defy my mother. And yet here I was doing it anyway. It awed and unnerved me that something so innocuous—a conversation in a room, however dim and chirping—could feel so traitorous.

As I was leaving, I said, "Sergeant Nolan said, 'Ed Brown won't want to talk to you.'"

He laughed, and I saw something pass across his face that I

didn't understand. "I've always wanted to solve the case," said Ed, whose voice was warm and radio-smooth. "I put a lot of time, a lot of work into it, and it's been a mystery.

"When I got that message you called, I knew right away," he said. "That has to be Eddy Crane's daughter."

# THE WALL

BALTIMORE IS A city of trees, almost three million of them. That's neck and neck with Philadelphia and about half a million more than Denver.

Some parts of the city are so green and dense with tree canopy that you feel like you're in a fairy tale. And Baltimore is nothing if not a fairy tale—the kind you keep away from your kids. I love, love beyond all reason, driving up and down the Jones Falls Expressway at night with the windows down in summer. The on-ramp from Northern Parkway onto the southbound JFX is choked with leaves and branches. It's claustrophobic. The foliage insists its way into your windows. It might take you, and you just might go willingly.

In December 2007, my former roommate Harold still lived in the same fantastical house on a one-block lane, with trees looming over and lunging down. Just as I did back in 1995, I eased over the curb, handing my car to the trunks and the branches as if they were a valet service. I crawled into the passenger seat to climb out the other side of the car.

It was late afternoon, and the sky was brimming with the wintry light, river-water gray, that bathes Baltimore from December to March. But it turned out my day had barely started. The next half hour would determine the coming year of my life.

Picking my way up the overgrown path to the front door, I once again felt like Gretel.

I thought I was alone. And then: "Oh, hey."

Harold! It had been two or three years since my last visit, but he acted like it was nothing. He opened the door and I followed him inside.

I longed for some tea and a good talk. Conversations with Harold could go on for hours and sprawl over continents and centuries. *A little decompression after a day of interviewing cops and private investigators.* The decompression involved pressure cookers: We both used them for beans.

"What are you doing down here? Visiting your mom?" Harold asked at some point, as if it took him a while to remember I no longer lived upstairs.

"I decided to work on a book about my dad," I said. "Do you remember the story?" He nodded.

I had started down this road intending to write a magazine article, maybe a story for an online publication like *Salon*. But as the months progressed, and information hit me, wave after bracing wave, as my notebooks filled with to-do lists and ideas of who to talk to, I came to understand that I was not preparing to write a couple thousand words. I faltered at times. That voice could be relentless: *There's nothing to say, there's nothing to say.* That numbing, all-erasing sense of nothingness would fog me over. And still, I could not deny the certainty rising up in my gut: I was preparing to write a book.

It was a relief to see Harold, with whom I always felt at home, where everything always made sense.

"This year is twenty years since he vanished. It was just eating me up . . . I don't really know what I'm doing, but I'm doing my best to do something. It's more than anyone else is doing, I'm realizing."

"He was down in Curtis Bay, right?" Harold asked. I nodded. "I used to have a place down there where I kept cars and parts." He pulled a map off the shelf and we looked. The spot nearly abutted E & M Machinery.

I reeled at the small-worldness of it. All that time I'd shared a house with Harold and I'd had no idea he had a Curtis Bay connection.

He started telling me about his friend Earl Crum, who worked in Curtis Bay. "I wonder if Earl knows anything about your dad's business," Harold said. He told me he'd bring it up next time they talked. We meandered back to refried beans.

In the dining room where I'd once phoned Jan Wilkotz for permission to take her Virginia Woolf class, the phone rang.

Harold got up and went to answer it.

"No way—I was just talking about you to my friend Kate!"

Feeling the *Twilight Zone* sifting in yet again, I realized the caller must be Earl.

Harold got what sounded like bad news ("Awww, that's terrible, I haven't talked to him in a year!") and then he hollered at me: "Hey, Kate! What was the name of your dad's business?"

"E & M Machinery," I said. "Like Eve and Mary."

"E & M," Harold said into the phone. And then he jumped, as if he'd backed into a hot stove. I startled too at his face, which bore an "oh hell no" expression. What had Earl told him? Harold waved the handset at me.

"You talk to him!" He set down the receiver and stormed to the refrigerator, where he retrieved a beer.

"Hello?" I said. "This is Kate Crane. Harold said we should talk?"

"Yeah, I know that business," said the voice. "Those guys put your father in a wall." What? Five minutes ago, Harold and I had been chatting about refried beans. And now some guy named Earl was telling me my dad was in a wall? This could not be real, and should not be real, and yet!

Clutching the phone, I dived for my bag, which held the notebook I'd used a couple hours ago when I met with Ed Brown. I began to scrawl, upside down, in frenetic shorthand. Earl talked fast.

"What wall?" I said, the only two words I could come up with.

"Along the side of E & M," he said, "there's a retaining wall. Along Birch Street. Your dad's business is on a hill. That wall keeps the hill from collapsing."

Yes, I could picture the wall he was talking about. Gordon and I had seen it on that five-minute visit.

I was flustered and off-balance, and my hand wasn't cooperating—some of my notes from that call are little more than slashes of fright. I was unprepared physically, mentally and emotionally for this interview.

Earl breezed on into a twenty-minute primer on the breadth and depth of Curtis Bay's lowlife culture. He'd been in Curtis Bay during the 1990s. Meth and bikers and industrial waste. Earl tipped me off to one person in particular: Petty Naff. "He was a typical biker. Did heroin and crack, was drinking all the time." He said Naff rode with Fates Assembly Motorcycle Club, which was founded in Brooklyn Park, where Augie lived, in 1974. Fates

Assembly was an offshoot of the Hells Angels Motorcycle Club with, according to *The Washington Post*, an extensive criminal history in Northern Virginia. It had had few run-ins with the law in the 1990s but was hitting law-enforcement radar screens again in the mid-2000s.

Naff wasn't just any hard-living biker. This one was tight with my dad's business partner. "He was like a son to Augie, and he looked up to that guy like a father," said Earl. "He did anything Augie told him to. And one of Naff's favorite stories when he was out drinking was to tell anyone who'd listen that when your father got killed, he helped remove a piece of that retaining wall and stashed his body in there."

"Was Augie a gangster?" I asked.

"I don't know about Augie," he said, "but my father was a gangster. He was a big-time numbers runner. He took bets from Al Capone."

Earl said that when people did murders in Curtis Bay, they'd put the victim's feet into buckets of wet concrete, slice the bodies up the middle so they wouldn't float, and dump them in the water: harbor markers.

He described Curtis Bay in Wild West terms: "People would fire machine guns down there for fun. Bullets flying everywhere." Illegal dumping, according to him, was rampant. "Once the circus came through town and an elephant died. One of the waste plants took the elephant. No one asked questions about how they disposed of it.

"You can't build on the land down there," he said. "It's so toxic. If you walked around in tennis shoes, within a couple months the soles would get eaten away. I really hope I don't get cancer."

Earl came back to Naff. "He couldn't get a driver's license out of a Cracker Jack box." According to Earl, he once killed two people while driving drunk, which I later confirmed. On another occasion, he got arrested for dragging his girlfriend alongside his car on a highway on-ramp.

"Oh my God," I murmured.

Harold shouted from the next room: "That guy is the worst person ever on the planet!"

What on earth were the chances of Earl calling while I was in Harold's kitchen? If I wrote this as fiction, everyone would call bullshit.

"All right, hon. Hope it helps. Leave my name out of it, 'kay?"

I hung up the phone.

"What the hell," I said to Harold, sitting back down, stunned.

"Yeah, that was weird, huh?"

Harold leaned back in his chair and studied the ceiling. He looked at me and said, "So, anyhow—turmeric is the first thing, then cumin—I grind my own seeds in that grinder right there, but you can use powder—then coriander, then as much cayenne as you want to make it spicy."

Back to refried beans? Right. I guess it was just another night in Baltimore.

WHEN I LEFT HAROLD'S, I dialed Cold Case from my flip phone the second I was back in the car.

"Sergeant Nolan, you will never believe what just happened," I said, buzzing to tell him the unbelievable story and pass along a genuine lead. "Petty Naff," I said, spelling out the name. "OK, I'll see you tomorrow." The next day, I drove back to 601 East Fayette.

Sergeant Nolan and Donald Worden were ready when I got there. Worden opened a slim manila folder; inside was a sheaf of computer printouts. They had looked into Petty Naff, all right. "Three dates of birth, thirteen Social Security numbers."

I looked at him, eyebrows raised, and waited. "The biker I told you about?"

"Franklin H. 'Petty' Naff. The guy has three DOBs and thirteen SSNs." Naff's court cases in the Maryland Judiciary database went back to 1982. There were 176 of them. His infractions included speeding, driving under the influence, driving with a suspended license, first- and second-degree assault, battery, bankruptcy, resisting arrest, unlawful possession, paraphernalia possession, nonpayment of child support and intention to harm with a deadly weapon.

Of note was a case for manslaughter and vehicular homicide while intoxicated. As Earl had said, Naff killed a woman and her child while driving drunk. He was found guilty on the manslaughter charge and did time.

In 2003, Naff was sentenced to ten years in prison, with all but three years of the sentence suspended, for conspiracy to commit kidnapping. There was a perjury charge in there somewhere too. Naff told police he was a bondsman and had deputized others as bounty hunters. When it looked like someone he'd posted bail for was going to skip, Naff plotted to abduct them. Baltimore is desensitized to the absurd, but a note of incredulity is detectable in the media reports.

In a 2009 video about "eyesore" front lawns, Naff wore a blue ball cap and work jacket; he had bushy sideburns, and his dark brown hair was pulled back in a ponytail. After numerous code violation warnings, he was fined eighty-nine days of jail time. He got out after eleven days, once his family had cleared the property of trucks, a porta potty and a boat that had seen better days.

"Stay away from that guy," Nolan and Worden told me. "We'll look into him. This is a good lead."

I readily agreed.

I wanted to hug them both. I had become fond of them. These older gentlemen who exuded integrity were making time for me. They took me seriously.

# BOB CRANE

I STAYED IN TOUCH with my Uncle Bob over the latter half of 2007. He remained torn over how much he could help me. "I can't talk about it, baby. I just got over it. I just stopped taking a gun with me to church last year," he would say.

*I understand*, I would say, *maybe another time*. Then, without skipping a beat, Bob would launch straight into his account of his brother's disappearance. I could practically hear the cassette deck in his mind clicking play. I listened hard for divergences, conflicts, discrepancies in my uncle's soliloquy. Every detail was consistent.

That Christmas, I'd seen my mother, Gordon and Marie. I'd interviewed Ed Brown, visited Harold, had the strangest phone call of my life with Earl and visited Donald Worden and Roger Nolan at Cold Case. My last planned visit: Uncle Bob. I met him and one of his daughters at an eatery in a labyrinthine shopping center near White Marsh Mall.

I shuffled in through the glass doors. It was cold but not miserably so. Uncle Bob and my cousin were wearing light jackets, while I, always freezing, wore a trusty shapeless black puffy coat that doubled as a security blanket.

We settled into a booth. Across the tabletop, my uncle and my cousin could have been twins.

"Honey, do you want breadsticks?" Oh no.

"I'm, uhhh, allergic to bread," I said, fearing the word *gluten* would make me sound like a snoot.

Once we ordered, traditional pasta dishes for them and a Chevy Tahoe–size chicken salad for me, my uncle began to speak. He didn't stop until the check came.

What follows is Bob Crane's story, in his own words, edited for clarity. He begins in the summer of 1987.

SATURDAY MORNING, EDDY called me, and he said, "You know, I thought about what we talked about last night. I want you to go down the office with me. Bring one of your guns along. Go down the office with me." I said OK.

Well, I go down the office with him. And he realizes that Augie was the one doing all the stealing. All this stuff we dug up and went over. And he realizes. He even accused Augie's daughter, without proof, of doing the stealing, which she denied. She worked there for a while. And Augie had to fire his own daughter because your father thought it was her doing the stealing.

So. When he realizes what an asshole Augie's been making out of him, *he . . . was . . . unbearable.*

He got into a big screaming match with Augie out on the parking lot in front of the whole god-durned place. From that day forth, it was like your father had a mad dog in the corner and he was poking him with a stick. He couldn't get enough of aggravating Augie, of pissing him off.

That brand-new Mercedes that was in your mother's garage . . . [pauses to flirt with the waitress] He bought that Mercedes just to piss him off. He didn't need it. He didn't really have the money to buy that car.

He started coming in to work later and later and later. Augie would come in early, and as soon as your father would come in, Augie would leave. They couldn't stand the sight of each other anymore.

Well, a couple weeks before your father disappeared, the guy that I know was the shooter came into the office and he tried to pick a fight with your father. When he realized your father had a gun, he backed down and left. That's Archie McAleese. I know he shot your father as if I saw it with my own eyes.

Anyway.

[Gets quiet for a few moments.]

Your father was hit at head height with a .44 Magnum, right in that add-on brick office. The slug hit the brick wall and ricocheted up into the ceiling. The police recovered that slug with your father's blood type.

Roscoe Woolard, as if I were there and saw it with my own eyes, was the one that got the drop on him and shot him in the knee, the bullet holes the cops found in the desk. Roscoe had a .38 pistol, which was missing. The holster was there, there was an empty box of shells, but the pistol was missing. These thieves, they favor certain handguns. McAleese was a .44 Magnum guy; Roscoe was a .38 guy.

Well, there were three .38 bullets fired. Two of them in the front of the desk where your father sat at night. It was the secretary and bookkeeper's desk.

Roscoe disabled him and then McAleese killed him.

Those bullet holes were filled that night, and the furniture was restained. Well, when your mother called me, I canceled my reservations in Ocean City and I ran down there and I called 911.

An officer came in, and I said, "My brother was murdered here last night."

He said, “You’ll have to fill out a missing persons report. We can’t do anything for at least thirty days.”

I said, “No. You get your sergeant.” The sergeant came in. I said, “My brother was murdered here last night.”

“Why do you say that?”

“He called home at nine o’clock, said he was on his way. He never made it. No one’s ever kicked my brother’s ass. My brother was murdered here.”

“Well, we have to fill out a missing persons form.”

I said, “No. Get your lieutenant.”

And that’s when Lieutenant Green came on. I tell Lieutenant Green the story. Lieutenant Green was in a little disbelief . . . Your father was in touch with an FBI agent and had given him some kind of a heads-up about what was going on. So Lieutenant Green called him.

Lieutenant Green said, “Come on down to the station with me.”

So I jump into a police car with Lieutenant Green. He calls in Detective Ed Brown. I was probably there for four hours. And I’m telling them this story.

They look at each other, and Ed Brown says, “Mr. Crane, your brother probably ran off with some young girl.”

I slammed my fist down on that desk. I said, “I’m telling you, my brother was murdered there last night!”

I said, “Five minutes. Can’t you just give me five minutes? Can’t you come down there and look around? Can’t you spare five minutes? Just give me five minutes!”

They looked at each other, and it was a big joke at that point. That’s when they both asked me, “Could his wife have been involved in this?” No, no, no . . . Well, after they heard the whole story—I mean, they interrogated me for hours and hours. I didn't work for two weeks. I was down at that station on Fayette every day for two weeks.

Ed Brown says, "OK. We'll give you five minutes. Fiiiiiiiiiiiiiiiiiiiive minutes." It was a big joke.

So I got in Ed Brown's car and we go down there. And Ed Brown walks into the office. Brown isn't in there five minutes when he runs out and says, "My God, there wasn't a little foul play in there last night. There was a lot!" He had already found blood spattered on the TV in the office. Within minutes, cops and lab guys were crawling all over the office. I was there for 100 percent of that lab investigation.

Right below the two bullet holes that were in the front of that desk . . . You know they sprinkle this powder down and it turns colors, and I'm color-blind . . . And there was a puddle of blood there, and then there were droplets of blood across the carpet leading out to that room where he was actually killed.

I knew Roscoe Woolard, the night watchman, got the drop on him. Roscoe Woolard was a hillbilly, a North Carolina white-trash hillbilly. And apparently, your father didn't take Roscoe seriously, tried to get his gun away from him or whatever, and Roscoe fired three bullets. Your father was hit in at least one leg below the knee, from the height of the holes that were in the desk. Then they were trying to get him out of the office. Archie McAleese had to be standing outside that office door. Apparently your father was getting the best of them, because he could kick ass.

McAleese blew him away—he didn't have any choice.

They didn't intend to kill him there; they didn't want to kill him there; they wanted to take him somewhere else and get rid of him.

Maryland State Police gave me a permit to carry a handgun, while I waited, with no restrictions, when Brown and Green realized I knew what the hell I was talking about. Ed Brown personally drove me over to the State Police in Pikesville. I didn't renew it anymore after we moved away.

Augie's people came after me several times. Ed Brown told me to divorce myself of all the people, of everything that had anything to do with E & M Machinery.

Roscoe called me at some point when I'd gotten another job. Augie had fired him, and he wanted to get together with me, and this and that. I wanted the BCPD to wire me up, and the state's attorney said no, he can't do that. They wouldn't let me do that.

They said I wasn't a police officer . . . It would be life-threatening to me, and they weren't allowed to do that.

Ed Brown said, "Bob, please. Don't go meet him. Don't try to be Superman."

I said, "Ed, I have no intention of meeting him unless you can wire me up and back me up!"

What Augie wanted to do was kill Roscoe and me. Roscoe, when the very first police officer came up and questioned him, admitted being there all night. He admitted calling Augie around midnight because a car drove on the lot, and he thought maybe they were trying to steal something. Augie admitted to being there. Roscoe admitted being there. I think Homicide drew up indictment papers twice. But Augie had political ties all the way up to William Donald Schaefer. And there was some city councilman, Willie Myers. He's since died. There's a lot of dirt that you have to take as hearsay. There was a dump across the street from E & M. Willie Myers was getting big money to keep quiet about them illegally disposing of toxic waste. The watchman at the dump was getting paid off, Willie Myers was getting paid off, and I, personally, with my own ears, heard Augie talking to Willie Myers on the telephone, screaming at him: "Take care of this!"

Buzz Berg, the wrecker, was involved in it. Buzz Berg went to jail. Buzz Berg kept his mouth shut. The night watchman was going to run his mouth. He opened his door one night, got a 12-gauge shotgun in the chest. Augie murdered him for Willie Myers. There ain't any doubt in my mind he did that. Because I heard Mr. Augustin talk about it over and over and over and over. But it's hearsay. It's strictly hearsay.

All I know as fact is that Augie had political ties all the way up to Governor William Donald Schaefer. And that's why nothing's ever been done. No question in my mind.

There are so many possibilities on how they could have disposed of your father's body. McAleese at the time was driving a reefer for Montford Packing. He could have put Eddy's body in a reefer. That's the kind of crap they'd do and get away with it. There was a rendering plant across the street, and Augie was buddy-buddy with a guy. They disposed of biomedical waste and contaminated body parts. There's also that landfill a couple miles away. They could have rolled him up in a carpet. The chair that was damaged by gunfire, because of your father's weight, it was easier to handle him, they sat him in this chair that was missing. You could see the scrape marks across the tile, and across the concrete for just a short distance. They put his body in the back of the pickup truck. Police sprayed the back of the pickup truck that Roscoe used most of the time and it turned that color.

So, you know, where did the chair go, where did the body go . . . The possibilities were so . . . mind-boggling. THE WATER! I mean, there's water all over the place. There's woods all over the place. I mean, my God, you could dig a hole, bury him and plant a tree on top of it for God's sakes.

Between the water, the woods, the rendering plant, the waste plant and the landfill, I drove myself crazy. For years. I mean, for at least two years, I had nightmares every night. I wanted to get even with that bastard so bad. I thought of every way in the world of killing that SOB and getting away with it. The police even gave me tips on how to do it. [laughs] Honest to God! My best one was Halloween. Augie loved to give out candy to the kids. And give him a .44 Magnum right in the face . . .

For the first year, my mother begged me, begged me not to get even. "Please, please . . . Your brother never treated you right anyway. Leave that man alone. Please, please. I need you. Your daughters need you."

I said, "Mom, I know. I'm not gonna." But you couldn't help but want to get even.

Shortly after your father disappeared, we were living in the Ridge Gardens apartments. They put a stick of dynamite in a newspaper box near us. It blew up and landed way down the street. The next morning, we had *The Sun* paper on our doormat. We weren't subscribers. One of the detectives said, "That's a message for you to stop spreading the news."

I didn't go anywhere without a handgun on my person for years. It's a hell of a way to live. And every time you come home and you see a strange car or a strange truck . . . You are forever looking over your shoulder.

As long as Augie is still alive, you are a threat to his family. That man is just as dangerous at eighty as he was at fifty-nine. He doesn't want anybody stirring up anything from the past, or in any way becoming a threat to his family. Just suppose they recovered your father's body right now, and they did indict him on first-degree murder. And he knows his life is almost over, but he has his daughter, his son, his grandchildren . . .

I'm concerned about YOU. You go poking your nose around too much and he gets wind of it . . . It could be life-threatening. There's no question. I'm serious. No ifs, ands, buts. He is a cold-hearted, ruthless man.

SLICES OF COCONUT cake fluttered to the table, and I drank coffee while my two relatives ate. Bob's chilling warning gave way to lighter conversation. My cousin smiled at me and said: "I just think what you do and where you live . . . your lifestyle is so intriguing."

My life as it was flashed before my eyes: Working at a magazine until one thirty in the morning three weeks a month. Trudging through rain or sleet to get to and from the PATH train. Bad relationships, bad dates, friends that moved away. Loud neighbors, expensive apartments.

"Thank you," I said. "But to me it just seems like a grind."

"You're independent," said Uncle Bob, "and you're standing on your own two feet."

The check came. My uncle refused to let me pay. He flirted again with the waitress—one more innuendo for the road.

*They would think nothing of picking you up, raping you, cutting your throat.* The words rang in my ears as we exited into a wintry parking lot. Yes, I was afraid, and what he was saying made me more afraid. For now, I had one last request of my uncle. I held up one of his brother's Nikons and gave it a festive shake. "I need a photo of you two!" I grinned.

Later, when I got my negatives back, I found I had captured

two smiling full-color Cranes, beak noses carved from the same sculptor's clay.

What was I doing? What was the point? With no evidence, the chances that Cold Case could make any noteworthy progress now were negligible. That said, my primary goal was information. I sure got it in this statement from my uncle. What did it mean? What could I do with it? What came next?

Long-distance driving in torrential rain or dense fog is stressful but possible: You focus on what's immediately ahead. The same maxim applied here. I had a list: Try to talk to a handful of other detectives. See if anything came of this skull in Virginia. Uncle Bob had mentioned Dad contacting the FBI. Maybe there was information beyond that out-of-reach Homicide folder. To my list I added: Consider filing a Freedom of Information Act, or FOIA, request.

Even with clear bullet points contained safely in a notebook, the prospect of it all made me want to go to sleep for a hundred years. I'd been in Baltimore barely a week and it felt like a month. My head was pounding from overwhelm and cat allergies. As I left the Beltway and merged onto 95 North, the impulse to forget everything I'd done for the past few days bore down like an 18-wheeler filling the rearview.

"Do I still love this man?" I spoke my racing mind into a recorder I used for notes and interviews. "My mother is the one that raised me. But it's my dad, the one that's gone, that I can't let go of. I'm doing this for him. I buy what my uncle says, that to a degree my dad brought this on himself. And that hatred he describes . . . never forgive, never forget, got to get even. Uncle Bob said Grandmom Hilda raised them with a philosophy: 'You've got to let them run with the wolves.' My mom's philosophy was more like: 'That's not a good idea.'"

The worst of Uncle Bob's warnings hit me again as I tried to sleep that night: These people would rape me and slit my throat without hesitation. There was no way to fully weed out the myth from reality, to distinguish the man from the bogeyman. My heart cracked open, thinking of my uncle's desperation—first to get Baltimore police to take him seriously as they laughed him off, then for revenge. Dad's little brother had waged a one-man campaign for justice. Then, finally, he'd put down his handgun and searched for peace. Until I came along with my own desperation, an echo of his own, decades out.

# DREAM

I DREAMED I VISITED AUGIE. I was armed. I encountered a group of women who knew him and took me to his house. He was shrunken and infirm. It felt so real. I didn't want to breathe. He was lying down on the couch, and I was frightened but didn't think he was dangerous. He drew me to him, but I didn't want to touch him—his face seemed on the verge of rotting. I forgot my recorder, but he admitted everything.

I woke up. I had to speak with him.

# SERGEANT NOLAN

I CALLED SERGEANT NOLAN early in January 2008 from my desk at *SmartMoney.*

"Hi, Sergeant Nolan, happy new year," I said. "I'm following up about that guy we discussed over Christmas. You said you were going to look into it?"

"Unfortunately, Ms. Crane, we're not able to do anything here," he said.

I was taken aback. "What do you mean?"

"The state's attorney won't permit us to talk to Petty Naff," he replied. "He says we're treating a missing persons case like a murder." I was dumbfounded, and angry. This sounded like bullshit. Since when did detectives need a permission slip from the state's attorney to have a conversation with someone? I thought Cold Case would jump at new information, the chance, however slight, of a break in a twenty-year-old case.

I bit my tongue. I feared losing access to Cold Case if I was demanding. And as frustrated as I was, I was sure Nolan cared. "Hang in there," he said, and we agreed to talk again soon. I turned my focus on the wall that Earl had mentioned. It was, in fact, all I could think about.

I knew where the wall was located in part because I'd spent so much time at E & M in my childhood. Besides which, it could be in only one place—on the side of the hill it was meant to hold up. Gordon and I had glimpsed it during that brief visit. I understood that Naff's boast could be a tall tale, that this wall was only one of many places where my father's remains could be hidden.

But why would this Naff guy brag about putting my father in this wall if he had not, in fact, put my father in this wall?

On the other hand, attempting to ascribe rational behavior to bona fide criminals was a waste of brain cells. Dangerous too. I didn't want to think too hard about how criminals thought. It made me anxious and afraid. Above all, Petty Naff's posturing reminded me that I needed to be careful. Naff's voluminous criminal record made me edgy.

The week I'd seen Uncle Bob, Harold and Ed Brown, I'd also visited a private investigation firm recommended by a retired detective. I posed the question: "Are these people actively dangerous or just historically dangerous?"

I wrote them a check for the amount of the savings bonds from Augie.

Their report had just come back. It was unclear, they said, if anyone presented an active threat. The investigators had confirmed the death of the E & M night watchman Roscoe Woolard in 1997, at age 61, in North Carolina, which was new information. Archie McAleese appeared to be alive, though the investigators could not pin down a current address. I shared these findings with Sergeant Nolan.

I was glad that Augie's money no longer burned a hole in my pocket. I had not, however, purchased reassurance.

The wall continued to grow in my mind. I pictured it as tall and made of concrete. By now it would be worn, cloaked in coarse shrubbery and ground cover. But through the overgrowth, maybe I'd spot a section not quite like the rest. An indication that the biker's tall tale might hold a truth.

A few weeks later, I ran into a former colleague on the PATH train. We'd first met at *New York Press*, and still crossed paths now and again. As we hurtled through the tunnel beneath the Hudson River, I filled him in on what I'd been up to. I got to the detail about the wall as our train pulled in to Christopher Street.

"You know you've got to knock that wall down, right?" he said.

It was such a Hunter S. Thompson thing to say. *Knock it down . . .* I bristled. Only I could figure out what I *had* to do.

The only thing I knew for sure: I had to get a good look at that wall.

# SKULL

SERGEANT ROGER NOLAN was dogged in his attempts to track down the skull.

My letter had upset the medical examiner's office in Virginia, he said. Although someone later claimed the letter had never arrived. Multiple Virginia towns pointed the finger at each other. One person insisted the sergeant needed to talk to someone else, who then put it off on a third person. They complained about the denture, presumably because I'd implied an error. "I told them to forget about the denture," Nolan said. "All we need is a chip of bone. We're after DNA." Exhumation might be necessary, Nolan said, but he doubted it was possible to track down the body. "That skull had to go somewhere," he said, exasperated.

I was living in a state of adrenaline. The specter of the lost evidence sickened me. I felt as if Baltimore itself had risen up, a sea monster, to steal from me. The sadness felt as old and as cold as the Chesapeake. At the same time, I was no longer entirely alone. Cold Case was not, in fact, there to clear cases, Sergeant Nolan had once clarified. They were there to answer phones—to talk to families. Yet Nolan was working hard—doing tedious, time-consuming work.

He was frank about how politics interfered with his role.

"Baltimore's always been very corrupt," he said. Of the people overseeing the Homicide unit, he said not one had ever cleared a homicide. He lamented the lack of a system of apprenticeship, and the inability of newer officers to document a crime scene: "Some reports aren't even remedial writing."

Some days Sergeant Nolan called me twice. His frustration with the runaround was palpable. "I spent twenty minutes explaining something to someone, and they can't or won't help," he said. "If they don't have records, say so. But someone should know what the process was."

One set of conversations with the ME's office, said Nolan, did not go well. "He's spouting off about bone weight," said Nolan, "that the bones were not the weight of a man your father's size. He still hasn't answered the twenty-four-thousand-dollar question: Where's the darn skull?"

Winter turned to spring. I could have helped Sergeant Nolan more. And the missing skull distressed me. I didn't know how to handle that on top of job pressures. Nolan was getting nowhere with the ME's office. At some point, we let it go.

In the absence of evidence, I still had a to-do list of interviews. That list was a lifeboat. It gave me a sense of purpose. I was ticking the items off slowly. Cold Case, Ed Brown, David Simon, Uncle Bob. One call petrified me more than all those conversations put together. More than anything I had ever done. But I'd worked up my courage. I was going to call Augie, my childhood uncle, Dad's business partner.

When that magazine editor had asked me to do it, the answer was no. I can't map the chain of events that got me ready. Every external action I was taking in these months had internal, often inscrutable counterparts. One day I could not make that call. Another day, about ten months into my project, I woke up and I could.

It was May 13, 2008.

I left the apartment in Jersey City for *SmartMoney* that morning, thrumming with a sense of purpose, and as corny as it might sound, also of fate. I knew I had not been in my right mind since the previous July. I also knew that my efforts were momentous in my life. I turned the dead bolt knowing that when I came back that night, I would in some way be a different person. I would make the call from my office phone.

All day I fidgeted, trying to get my work done. I'd gotten another promotion, to deputy managing editor, and I had to forsake my cave at the far end of the hall for an office with windows closer to the rest of the staff. I was awed and grateful to have views of New York City—my office even had a mini couch—and I dearly missed my shadowy lair. The increase in noise and interruptions made my workload feel insurmountable. Today I was at a loss to edit what seemed like forty-two fact-check changes into a 140-word product review. As quitting time approached, though, the staff was scattering.

Except, that is, for my manager. A mercurial newspaper veteran, this editor thought that mentoring required scorching castigations, at least it seemed to me. There was no telling when my phone might bleat with the dreaded:

"Got a minute?"

It was never a minute.

With everyone leaving, I would soon have privacy. But I was also more of a target if my boss felt like chatting.

I shuddered. What was worse—trying to call the man who'd had my father killed or getting hauled into that editor's office for the third time in one day? I took a deep, resigned breath.

The phone call I was about to make would shatter the ultimate family taboo. I could never have asked my mother what she thought about me trying to interview Augie. The voice of my sister shrieked on permaloop in my mind: *You don't have to live here! You don't have to live here and be afraid! You left! You don't care about us! You left!* Her accusations weighed on me constantly. So did the guilt that I was proceeding anyhow.

I gave the recording device in my hand a skeptical once-over. It was just some funky little cord with a switch. Who was I kidding—I was no journalist.

I tried to figure out how the device worked. OK, the cork-screw cord end clicked into the handset, and the other end connected to my cassette recorder. Genius.

Then, as I was taking a breath to pick up the phone . . .

*BLEEEEEEP BLEEEEEEEEEEP*

*BLEEEEEEP BLEEEEEEEEEEP*

My boss. The recording device clattered from my trembling hands. I could ignore him, but he would either keep calling or come bouldering down the hallway. In which case, I would also have to explain why I hadn't picked up.

I picked up the phone, defeated.

"Got a minute?"

I looked at the clock. It was about five fifteen. What time did suspected murderers eat dinner in Baltimore? I was guessing no later than six. If my boss took me to task for longer than average, I would have to gear up for this all over again some other day.

Twenty minutes later I collapsed back into my ergonomic chair. Do it? Bail? To hell with it—I was already eggshells. I was going for it.

Besides which, I figured Augie was expecting my call.

Ever since I had started this quest, I felt a bone-deep conviction that I had flipped an invisible breaker. We've all had that experience where we think of someone and then they call five minutes later. I felt that Augie, in whatever role he'd played in my father's murder, had created a cord between us, one that had lain dormant for decades. I was certain my inquiries had reactivated it.

I looked at my notebook. This was one of several in a group of notebooks that would multiply over the coming years. I carried one everywhere I went, but I could never fully capture the contours of the cyclone. The more overwhelmed I got, the less I wrote or dictated. Survive now, take notes later.

My notebook was open to the page with the phone number I'd taken down in my favorite Pilot P-700 pen. Once again, I fastened the recording device. Then I picked up that handset, tentative, as if it might shock me, and dialed.

The phone rang and rang. I almost gave up.

And then a man said hello. I did and didn't recognize his voice. There's a boom, a musical resonance, to the voices of older Baltimore men. Part cigarettes, part suspicion.

"Hi, may I speak to Mr. Augie?"

"He's not—he doesn't live—at this number."

"Oohhkay . . ." I said, cautiously, my voice shaking. "No Augustin at this number?"

"Who?"

"Augustin?"

He was hostile now. "Which one?"

"Um . . . Augie?"

Now he was shouting.

"No! He doesn't live at this number!"

"OK!" I flinched out the syllables, my shoulders tensing and my eyes squeezing shut.

"What's this in reference to?"

I thought about the conversation I'd had last October with David Simon. The guileless route. I'm daddy's little girl.

"I . . . just wanted to ask him a question. I apologize for bothering you. Do you know where I could reach him?"

"That depends on what it's in reference to." The storm had subsided, but this man was on edge.

"He worked with my dad, and—"

With that, I was certain this man knew who I was. I didn't get the rest of my sentence out.

"He worked with your dad?"

"He worked with my dad, yeah." I could hardly breathe now. I didn't know how I was speaking when my chest had frozen.

"And who's that?"

"Eddy Crane." My voice was so, so small.

The man on the other line snarled. "Yeah, what about him?" He might have been defensive or just suspicious or angry. But he knew who I was.

"He's the one person who knew my dad, and I'm just wondering if he would tell me what kind of person he was."

Before I could take my daddy's girl spiel any further, the man stopped me. "If you want to give me a number, I'll give it to him, but I don't give his home number out."

"OK, that's wonderful," I chirped. "I appreciate it." Like I was talking to the dry cleaner.

"Let me get a piece of paper."

He was gone for about half a minute. Who was this guy? It definitely wasn't Augie. Despite the decades, I would have known his voice anywhere. And this man was too young, maybe fifty. If they lived in the same house but had different numbers, it must be Augie's son-in-law, I thought. There was a dull pounding in my ears, and I kept gulping for air, like I'd been under water. I wanted to steady my breath and my voice before he got back.

When he did, I recited my phone number.

"And could I leave a message? Could you just tell him that—" I faltered "—I don't want to ask any upsetting or difficult questions? I honestly just want to know what he remembers about my dad. Because no one will talk to me. My mom won't, my uncle won't."

I was racing to get the words out, knowing this phone call would soon end.

"He's the one person who remembers my father. He died before I really got to know him. It probably seems extremely odd after all these years. I'm an adult now and no one will talk to me, and I remember Augie fondly from when I was a child."

"Right." I detected a note of sympathy.

"So," I felt myself spinning out, "I don't need to know about September '87."

He cut me off. "You don't want to know about '87. Because what you would hear and what we have found out . . . You wouldn't like."

I suddenly couldn't see. There was brown static where my notebook had been. If I had stood up, I could not have made it to the door of my office. My chair shifted and I felt myself lurching. I dug my heels into the comforting ordinary of office carpet and tried to find words.

"Well, that's the other thing—I don't need pleasantries."

"Right."

"Whatever he wants to tell me, I'm open to it."

"I'll give him the message when I see him."

And that was it.

When I hung up the phone, I sat in silence. I watched through my glass walls as straggler colleagues filed past, en route to the elevators.

I didn't know what to do. Something big had happened.

Or was it little? Had I done a big thing or had I done nothing? I had no clue.

I adamantly could not call my mother. I tried to call Gordon, but he didn't pick up. There wasn't really anyone else to call.

Why did I feel so . . . cold?

I packed up my things for the night, making sure I left no trace of what I had just done.

Half an hour later, I was perched on a stool on Prince and Lafayette streets, an Anne Carson paperback balanced in my lap as I breathed in the perfect medicine.

Dosa. Eighteen inches of it, stretched sumptuously across a green plastic lunchroom tray.

The ends were a light and crisp filigree. I always cut a piece off the end and ate that first. Crunch: flawless. Inside was chicken, arugula and tomatoes. I had pumpkin chutney and this moment also called for coconut chutney: I paid extra.

I was leading a double life. Magazine editor by day. Reluctant cold case investigator by night. In taking on the work around my dad, I was trying to build a bridge between my past and present. This phone call shot me out of both lives and into a borderless unknown.

So in that familiar nook a block away from McNally Jackson, my favorite bookstore, I regained my grounding. With each steaming bite, I put more distance between myself and Baltimore, more distance between myself and 1987, more distance between me and this wrenching, nameless terror. The dosa was so delicious, it brought tears to my eyes. It wasn't enough, but it was something.

# DREAM

I DREAMED ABOUT MY DAD. We were driving through a tunnel, beneath its chrome and deco elements, on the way to work. We stopped at the Inner Harbor and he used his tickets, pink and orange, to pay the toll. The city of Baltimore sparkled out before us, and I marveled at its beauty.

Long ago it dawned on me that whenever I drove around Baltimore, I was probably within a dozen miles of his bones. This knowledge became so fundamental that it no longer took me off guard. But on waking from this dream, the thought resurfaced like a bell. All of Baltimore is Dad's grave.

# CHRISTMAS

THE EAST COAST can dish out holiday blizzards. But a Baltimore Christmas is just as likely to be bone-dry cold or sleeting. That year, 2008, brought rain. Sheets and sheets and sheets of it. The drive down the turnpike from Jersey City had taken over five hours, the rain often blinding. All the way down, I could barely see two car lengths in front of me. I clicked into a deep, sweaty hyperfocus, listening with my body as much as my ears to how the tires were relating to the slick roadway, watching for signs of reckless motorists in the rearview, scanning the murk ahead for the worst-case scenarios: stopped vehicles or a wrong-way driver.

As my silver hatchback crept through the stormy peril, I thought about what was waiting for me at my mother's house.

I was constantly trying to calibrate how much to tell Mom. She had discouraged any discussion of my father for so long that my pursuit of his disappearance felt like a betrayal. I felt many internal shifts—the sense of betrayal did not budge. My mother never asked about it, yet when discoveries, however minor, piled up, I felt like a liar in witholding them. It was a hellish merry-go-round. I settled on occasionally telling her very little and gauging her reaction as a compass to help me assess how much more to tell her.

"You're here! You're here!" she called. Now in her late sixties, she jangled out of the garage with a sturdy black umbrella extended.

I was hopeful for a happy Christmas. Gifts exchanged, a simple dinner, conking out in front of the TV next to my mom on the couch. The Christmases before my dad disappeared were idyllic. We would leave a snack out for Santa—a couple Chips Ahoy cookies, some milk in a blue glass tumbler. We'd get a real tree, and my sister and I hung our handmade stockings from the fireplace. One year at the old house, Mom and Dad had surprised us with two Strawberry Shortcake dollhouses. The best presents ever. Dollhouses are spaces for growing brains to experiment with character and narrative. I loved creating adventure stories, and those houses had so many rooms.

After Dad disappeared, Christmas became unbearable for me. Black leaden depressions every time. My mother tried to make things normal. Tree, thoughtfully wrapped presents. I wanted to participate, told myself it was just a fabricated calendar event with no more meaning than I lent it. Still, I got depressed.

I was cautiously optimistic this might be a good one. As I settled in, I discovered that my sister had once again washed the sheets for me and made up my bed. The laundry gesture felt so welcoming. I seized on her courtesy as a good omen.

My godmother and her partner arrived for a visit soon after I did. Yvonne had been the administrative assistant for Roland Park Country School since 1984 and was nearing retirement. She and Martin were living in Pennsylvania, where Martin had built a lovely house for Yvonne and her cats. Auntie called me hon and sent me a card and a check for twenty dollars every birthday and Christmas. Her artful cursive with its strong slanting lines made me feel safe. Auntie remembered every holiday and always, always sent me mail. Martin didn't always come along on visits. I was glad to see him.

Glad, then surprised. Out of his pocket, Martin pulled a rolled-up copy of *SmartMoney* and pointed at the masthead.

**DEPUTY MANAGING EDITOR: KATE CRANE**

"How did you do this?" he asked.

I understood exactly what Martin was asking. People like us didn't get our names in national magazines, much less ones with *The Wall Street Journal* on the cover. I might as well have built a kayak to the moon.

I was taking in more than just his question. Without turning my head, I felt my sister stiffen on the couch a couple feet away. I sensed the air around her change, grow cold.

I told Martin how when I first got to New York, my friend John showed me the ropes about temping, which led to the full-time researcher job at Burson-Marsteller. I'd worked up a sloping corridor from the old office of Thomas Mosser. Ted Kaczynski, the Unabomber, killed him with a mail bomb in 1994. My boss had a friend at *The Wall Street Journal*, and they needed a proofreader. That's where I was working the day the planes struck the World Trade Center. Under a year later, my entire department was eliminated. My first layoff. I went by my full name then. Next came *New York Press* and a couple more proofreader gigs. Finally, I took a full-time job at *SmartMoney* after freelancing there for a while.

I stopped to take a breath. It all sounded unreal when I spoke it out loud. I really was not supposed to have done any of that. And now my name was in a glossy *Wall Street Journal* publication.

"It was just this weird combination of luck and being good at things and one person referring me to the next person," I said.

I glanced over at my sister and started. Her face was a mask of cold fury.

The visit with Martin and Auntie Yvonne brought me gladness. I wished with all my heart that I saw them more. After they left, my mother and I settled down on the floor in front of the Christmas tree to exchange gifts. We invited my sister. She ignored us.

"Hey," I said to her. "Could you turn off the television?" It was a big TV and it was right behind my head.

She ignored me. My mother asked next. She ignored my mother too.

I went over to where she was sitting, tried a second and third time. "Could we please just have the TV off for ten minutes?" I asked.

And then she was on her feet, and then she was in my face.

"You're sick, you know that?"

"Not that I know of," I replied. "I need you to get out of my face and back up, though."

But she didn't back up. She got closer. And I got scared. I started retreating, trying not to fall. She moved in lockstep with me, forcing me into the kitchen. This room had more space—and a path to escape. I broke into a run across the kitchen, a short distance into the laundry room, and banged the door shut behind me. It had no lock. I grasped the doorknob and held tight.

Then I felt like my body was taking speed bumps too fast, my arms and neck and shoulders bearing the brunt like unwilling pistons. The door, which I was trying to hold shut, was alive—and angry with invisible hornets. The tugging and rattling reverberated through my muscles and bones.

"Mom! Help me!" I gasped. I saw her on the other side of the door through the flash of space when my sister yanked the door in her direction. "You're standing right there! Stop her!"

The violent shaking halted. I heard a soft, animal huff of derision, inches from my face.

"*Shiidntgunna help you*," my sister whispered through the crack in the door, quiet so that only I could hear. A shiv.

Translation: *She isn't going to help you.* I tightened my grip on the doorknob and tried to ignore the rivulets of snot that were making my face itch. No matter what: I could not let go.

Through the door I heard a sniff of delight, a sound that seemed to me like that of hunter closing in on prey, lapping up my fear like a cat tonguing milk. I caught a momentary glimpse of her dirty blond hair.

I held tight to that doorknob and started gasping for breath. Where was the air? Panic.

The door kept rocking.

*You're sick*

*You need help*

*You're sick*

*You need help*

she chanted through the crack.

"Open the door and I'll help you, SISTER!" she jeered.

This was the same person who had washed my sheets so I wouldn't have an allergy attack. Now I feared she was trying to do me real harm. Was it just the adrenaline, or was I about to be choked out on the laundry room floor? That question—is it just fear, or is the danger real?—had marked all of us for two decades.

I believed this was about the copy of *SmartMoney* magazine and what it symbolized. I'd gone out into the world and done something that made Yvonne and Martin proud. My sister had the house and my mother. I had this other thing—concrete proof that my talents were valuable outside that house, beyond the borders of Baltimore. Both of us paid a price for the ongoing absence of our father.

*Thump thump*

*Rattle rattle*

went the door.

I shifted my grip and nearly lost a fingertip as the door slipped open and slammed back shut from the tugging.

My sister cackled. "Whoops! Watch your fingers, *Kate*!"

This was what Jane Eyre heard coming from that attic, I thought. My head was a helium balloon, bobbing with the door. I was feeling lighter and lighter. Like I would drift away.

"MOM!" I cried. "DO SOMETHING!"

*Thump thump*

*Rattle rattle*

went the door.

*You're sick you need help you're sick you need help*

Finally, I heard my mother say, "Stop it." She repeated my sister's name a few times. I was crying and holding on too. But . . . no relief. My mother's voice was a cup of cold Lipton tea. And my sister would not stop until she'd had enough.

# THE WALL

TIME WAS PASSING.

I'd made changes to my life. In the previous year, I'd left *SmartMoney*, broken up with the boyfriend and moved three times.

I now lived in a bright, spacious apartment a block from the Holland Tunnel approach in Jersey City. Late-afternoon sun drenched the living room in a rippling liquid gold. In the distance, the gas stations and motels leading up to the Holland looked gilded.

At the same time, Pop moved from his house in Hamilton to a retirement community called Oak Crest. It was emotional. He and my grandmother had moved from the city into their house when it was built in 1955. Mom was around twelve, the same age I was when we moved into our new house. But Mee-Mom was gone, and Pop was more than ninety years old, spry but slowing. We worried about him falling on the front steps or getting mugged. Oak Crest was safer.

Still—letting go of that sweet little house broke our hearts.

Some of it was with me now: an armoire and a white Hoosier, a freestanding kitchen cabinet popular from the late 1800s to the 1940s. Mee-Mom had always said, mournful and theatric: "When I die, they're yours." Earlier in the day I'd made her apple cake, a low bronze confection strewn with cubes of white apple, like bits of exposed bone. The scents of cinnamon and apples rupturing from raw to boiling suffused the space. I cut a textbook-size slab and sat down to phone Pop.

I longed for my grandfather. To claw my way back to the postage stamp living room of their house in Hamilton, where he and my grandmother enthroned me in a recliner with a puffy Sears comforter and christened me Queen for a Day.

"How's Oak Crest, Pop?" I asked.

"I call it the stalag," he said, using a German term for POW camps. "But they were going to sue me, so now I just call it the barracks." I roared. He was handling the transition better than I think I would.

I told him about the new place, and where I put his furniture, and that, yes, I had enough to eat (true) and enough money coming in (less true).

"On a clear day, Katy, when I look out my window, I can see the creek . . . It's a band o' gold, a band o' gold, glimmering and shimmering."

Pop could see the Susquehanna River from the windows in his new apartment, and I could see the New Jersey Turnpike from the windows in mine. Sunbeams connected us. Comforted by the belly full of warm apple cake and the sound of Pop's voice, I told him I loved him and hung up.

Living alone again, as I'd done on Metropolitan Avenue in Brooklyn, I was a fish back in water. I did freelance copyediting and tried to figure out what I was doing with my Dad project. I couldn't get a handle on it.

At my feet was the big blue notebook, journals and pages of notes. My discussions with Worden and Nolan surrounded me. In my hand was a transcript of my conversation with Detective

Ed Brown. I couldn't tell if all of it added up to something or nothing, and I didn't know where to go next.

*Take small actions that feel doable*, I told myself. Forward motion, even just an inch, often illuminated the next step. I had a note to go back to Curtis Bay. Gazing out at the sun setting over the turnpike, I felt ready.

So in fall 2010, I went back to Baltimore, where Gordon and I set off again in my five-speed hatchback. On this second and final drive, I was less afraid.

"How you feeling?" Gordon asked. It had been another quiet ride. I was centered and even-keeled, but pointing the car in this direction was still heavy.

I took in the sky, gray on gray. "I'm pretty OK," I said. My eyes skimmed over the blur of worn storefronts on Pennington Avenue. Had any of them been a lunch spot for Dad? I couldn't remember visiting any Curtis Bay businesses as a child. It was home to E & M and back, occasionally an afternoon playing video games in Uncle Augie's garage. My only tie to this neighborhood was waiting for us around the next turn.

As we approached Birch Street, I got ready.

Sometime before he moved, Pop had offered me a VHS tape while I was visiting him at his house. The masking tape on the side said: *April 16, 1988, Eddy Crane.* A segment of *Crime Stoppers.* Standing right here under the E & M sign, where Gordon and I now idled in my car, Uncle Bob, dressed in a good suit I'd never seen, pleaded with the camera. He was earnest, desperate. On that day in spring of 1988, the street was lonesome and dreary just like today, a junkyard on the moon, colors bleached out by time. Bob's pain, raw and jagged, scorched through the decades: "If anybody knows what happened to my brother, please call."

"What do you think, little girl?" Gordon asked. "Do you want to stop?"

The image of my uncle, stricken and alone, flickered away. "Yeah," I said. "I'm good."

Up on the lot, a man balanced atop a dry-docked boat, fiddling with something in his hands. I tensed, but he either didn't notice that we were there or didn't care.

At the base of the property was a gate blocking a paved road. I saw a rail-trestle bridge about fifty feet off the ground, level with where E & M sat. The whole property was bounded by a high, weeded hill. Peering back a ways, I got a better look at what I'd rushed away from three years ago.

Gordon was leaning against the car, lighting a Carlton. The silence down there was eerie. Nothingness cut by the occasional engine, tires skimming pavement.

"Gor, take a look. You see that?" Exhaling smoke, he squinted to where I was pointing.

The thing that held up E & M, that kept the property from a catastrophic slide, was a large, long wall. *The* wall. This was the thing I'd been wondering about and worrying over ever since that electrifying call with Earl Crum in Harold's dining room. I had to get a closer look. And this time, the desire to satisfy my curiosity outweighed any urge to get back in the car and flee.

"Would you look at that," said Gordon. "I never would have noticed it." Time had weathered it into a facet of the natural landscape. Wall and hill were one, and set off from the main road, which was itself no kind of major throughway.

The only way forward was by car. Gordon and I got back in and proceeded slowly up Curtis Avenue, almost on the shoulder, hazard lights flashing. Cars passed us. I prayed for a cloak of invisibility.

"Hey, turn there," Gordon said. The hint of an entrance beckoned. It was paved but barely wide enough for two cars. A hot-purple truck cab, sans trailer, nearly clipped us as it passed. I flinched. The driver, up high and partially obscured behind tinted glass, was the only person we'd seen other than the guy astride the boat.

The path we chose led us to a desolate branch of this desolate place that led us almost to the bay. On the other side: W. R. Grace, the chemicals company. That day at Harold's house, Earl had told me: "Down in there at night, I'd put on my floodlights. One night it would be a green haze." This, he said, was manageable. "Other nights it would be a purple haze. And I'd get out of there, because when that stuff blew over you, you'd be itching and crawling."

Gordon and I drove by warehouses, abandoned cars and lots of nothing. No street signs. We kept seeing a water tower and a silo, and began to map this place according to those landmarks. There had to be a back way, an alternate route into the rear of E & M, to that area beyond the gate. We reversed course, this time with purpose.

Ahead of us were railroad tracks. "Let's leave the car and walk," said Gordon. "If we head down those tracks, we'll eventually reach your dad's company." I agreed, reluctantly. Those tracks screamed tetanus. Maybe I should have asked his daughter, also named Kate, for permission to drag her seventy-three-year-old father on this expedition. But Gor was adamant that we keep going.

We started walking. It was slow going . . . weeds, busted track, garbage. Here, an abandoned mattress. There, a lone Chuck Taylor, disintegrating. All along the way I shot color film photos with one of Dad's cameras.

"You could hide a body anywhere," I said. "There could be bodies all around us." I felt an unexpected rush of relief. For so much of my life, I'd wondered, *Where is he?* It was a revelation to be in a place where I could reasonably say, *He might be here.*

Gor marveled at the plants, whose existence in this soil was an act of resistance. He leaned down to one hardy shrub, cigarette in hand. I thought of the riotous Victorian garden that he and Marie grew back in Hamilton, a world away. Their annual act of late-life creation birthed a rumpus of vines, textures and hues, its rainbow of blooms hosting a botanical Mardi Gras for birds, bees, snakes and Jake the remarkably large cat. Each spring, the alchemists putted around in Gordon's own Honda Civic to garden centers, collecting plants, seeds and other supplies, and then spent days plunging their arms into fragrant sacks of fresh soil. "Keep it up!" Gordon roared in admiration to the defiant sprig of life.

Then we saw that metal bridge. Rail trestle and iron mesh, inert and forbidding. We assessed the position of our north star, the water tower: E & M was nearly in view.

The bridge didn't look flimsy, but I was no civil engineer. Was it fifty years old or a hundred? Was it designed to hold pedestrians? The ground was visible through the rusted mesh; the whole thing was about half a city block long over a twenty-foot drop. I couldn't decide if this moment in my quest was anticlimactic or potentially fatal.

I turned to Gordon. "I've got to cross that thing, but you don't have to," I said.

"I'm coming with you," he replied. "It'll be fine. Let's just take it slow." And so, one father in my head and the other picking his way carefully along next to me, we set out.

The going was troubling. Gor and I both kept getting caught up in the fact that we could see the ground. It was a disorienting crawl, in a place that felt both alien and ours alone. *Gordon gets it now, what he's doing for me*, I thought. We were suspended in midair, on dubious footing, on a ghost hunt. I banished thoughts of bridge failure and men with guns.

I felt something shift. It might have been five minutes or twenty. Looking down, what had been a blur of concrete through the mesh was now weeds and meager shrubbery, tall grass that could double as makeshift knives. I took my eyes off the blessing of solid ground and looked up.

"We're almost there, Gor," I whispered. I had no idea if anyone could hear us. I didn't have much to say, anyway. For the first time in twenty-three years, I had a workable view of E & M Machinery. I stared into that near-empty parking lot where I used to play, where Dad had most likely died after his associates shot him. That wall bordered the rear of it.

I thought back to what Earl had said: *"One of Naff's favorite stories when he was out drinking was to tell anyone who'd listen that when your father got killed, he helped remove a piece of that retaining wall and stashed his body in there."*

When I hear *wall*, I think bricks, or at least a whole comprising smaller parts. This one was built of architectural sheet metal set into a long, solid concrete slab, parts of which bowed outward like a beer gut. The metal panels could maybe be manipulated, but you couldn't remove a piece of the concrete component without a serious tool. And even if the sheet metal budged, it didn't look to me like there was sufficient space to conceal a three-hundred-pound man. The E & M property ended abruptly in this metal-and-concrete structure. Maybe someone could have hidden a body back there as the wall was being built, but after? I had a hard time picturing it.

After all this time, it was a relief to be there and assess it for myself in person: to weigh the boasts of a criminal against a three-dimensional expanse of concrete and rust. The wall I'd built up in my mind talked but never had anything helpful to say: "You're not doing enough. You failed your dad. You're too chickenshit to knock that wall down. Hunter S. Thompson would be down there with a sledgehammer."

We hadn't heard a car in ages. The silence was suffocating.

"What do you think, Katy?" Gor was holding on to my arm. He had not enjoyed that bridge any more than I had, and I said a prayer that my car was still waiting for us.

"I'm glad to get a look," I said, "but I don't know what to think. Look at all that concrete! How would anyone open that thing up? And those guys would have been in a hurry. Those sections of metal look heavy."

That rickety iron bridge was a time machine, ferrying me as close as I would ever get to the moment when Dad had vanished. For the past few years, I'd been approaching the things that scared me most with questions, with my big blue notebook, with phone calls and nightmares and rides down I-95 in a stick-shift Civic. Now I was approaching it on foot. I had eyes on a vault of answers I could never unlock. It meant something to share space with that for a minute. And I felt the pull of a hot meal and a scalding shower. I was standing in the past and I couldn't think of a good reason to stay any longer. I doubted this was any grave site. Just another dead end.

Slowly and carefully, Gordon and I made our way back across the bridge, back to the silver hatchback, out of Curtis Bay and to the Chameleon for dinner. Out of 1987 and into the present.

# SSN

ONE DAY I was standing next to my mother, next to our cars, in the Oak Crest parking lot. Pop stood at a distance, waving, then left to slowly walk back to his apartment.

My mother turned to me and said, "What's this about wanting Dad's Social Security number?"

This caught me off guard. I had been putting off the FOIA request for four years, and I'd been putting off asking Mom for Dad's SSN for just as long. A few months previous, I had finally asked her for it over email. She hadn't responded. I let it go.

"I want to do a Freedom of Information Act request," I said. "If the government has any information about Dad, I'm more likely to get it if I include his Social Security number."

The back-and-forth was tense and brief. Expecting a no, I turned to get in the car.

"Well, I'm not going to email it to you," my mother said. I stopped, turned back around and stared at her. She shot me an impatient look. "Don't you have a notebook?"

I kept staring. Yes, at all times, I had a notebook. I got it out of the front seat. My mother rattled off my father's Social Security number. Twenty-plus years later, she still knew it by heart.

# KINCAIDS

THE WORD *INVESTIGATION* still felt phony. I had never wanted to play girl detective, and, if anything, I felt more strongly about it now, almost four years since I'd started.

I had a psychological block the size of Mount Everest around the FOIA. It wasn't the how of it: I'd taken a workshop on FOIAs from *Wall Street Journal* lawyers, and plenty of other journalists would have gladly walked me through it. But again and again, I balked. And I had to work. Copy chief hours were brutal. I spent two weeks a month or more hunched over page proofs near cold pizza and bleary-eyed, stubble-cheeked colleagues until two in the morning. Then I'd hand a stranger a voucher and huddle in the back of a town car, dozing to Kavinsky, Zoo Kid and Booker T. Jones on a playlist from my friend Dacus. In the climate-controlled hush of the roll down Varick Street and through the Holland Tunnel, I clung to silence.

I would make a little money and then a bill would come and the money would be gone. Again I would say, "Next week I'll focus on Dad. I just have to make a little more money."

I had a second mystery on my hands: the case of the cataclysmic pain collapses. In the past eighteen months, I'd been struck to the ground three times by a thunderclap of abdominal pain. Annihilating, all-consuming pain. Each time, I was certain I'd die. I was on 8th and Broadway when it first happened. I dragged myself into an ATM vestibule and sheltered until I could walk. The second time was on the PATH after the twenty-fifth anniversary concert of my beloved and renowned cousin, pianist Sara Davis Buechner, at Merkin Hall. Most recently, I was having lunch with my friend Martin's dad, Patrick, at the de Young Museum in San Francisco. I sensed an episode coming and knew I had about ten minutes to get flat and brace for impact. I stood up and heard the voice of a ghost say, "I have to go right now." I collapsed in the parking garage next to the rental Ford Focus and struggled into the back seat.

Somehow I got my gynecologist on the phone. She asked me a few questions. Then she started yelling in the dialect I call New York Mother. The gist: I need you in my office now.

A couple days later, Dr. Dena Harris hugged me tight and said, "You're very sick, but I'm not going to let you die."

Uh . . . die?

I wasn't afraid until that moment. Through years of illness and a kaleidoscope of infections, MDs had insisted it was all in my head. When they couldn't figure out what was wrong with me, they advised: Talk to a psychiatrist. Medical gaslighting defined my sense of self as much as losing Dad. So, naturally, I had assumed these episodes, which lasted for hours and left me haggard for days, were stress. All in my head! Except this time, an ultrasound revealed the culprit. Dr. Harris would operate on me at NYU to remove an ovarian cyst.

The night before the surgery in January of 2011, I opened a closet I seldom used. I wanted to get out some blankets and set up a cozy nest in the living room, where I planned to recover on my sofa. I squinted and blinked, thinking I'd gotten something in my eye. What were all those little black dots? Oh, God, no. Mouse droppings. Hundreds and hundreds of mouse droppings. The ramifications of a mouse infestation hit me. I was having abdominal surgery in twelve hours. I couldn't fix this. How had I not realized? I went into the kitchen and began moving small appliances and inspecting classic hiding spots. Mouse droppings were everywhere. I'd been working seven days a week for so long, I hadn't discovered the problem until the worst possible moment.

There was a minor complication during the surgery, and I couldn't walk at all for weeks. The pain was ghastly. I struggled to make it between my bed, bathroom and couch, while the mice grew in number and boldness. When I went back to work, the copy chief role at *Men's Journal*, near Rockefeller Center, I had to inch across a sheet of ice roughly ten blocks long on my mile walk to the PATH train.

That winter unfurled into a dark night of the soul. A sense of failure blanketed me, like that daunting sheet of sidewalk ice. My ovaries had tried to kill me and rodents had overtaken my home. The endometrioma and the infestation felt like outward manifestations of my worthlessness. I wasn't suicidal, but I felt that coming. All that time and energy, and for what? I was tired to the marrow, and I couldn't see a story in any of it. The days were heavy with futility.

I began my search in July 2007, and here it was, March 2011. My adrenaline-drenched plans of asking some questions about Dad and writing about it were steamrollered—by life. Digging into Dad's death could be its own full-time job, while I also needed to work full-time to stay afloat. Then there were apartment moves and breakups and health crises. And every single fact I gleaned about Dad required time to reflect. Lost and unsure what was next, I couldn't tell if I had done, was doing, anything meaningful. My project rolled at a snail's pace. Years were passing.

I had taken it slow until Dr. Harris said my stitches were healing and I could handle a mile of walking and short days at work with the subway and PATH commute. I was still scared of getting stranded in the city. Eight weeks after the surgery, I was not walking normally or remotely free of pain. I shuffled around, stiff and aching. But I could move. I made plans to go see Donald Kincaid, who had worked with Ed Brown as the lead detectives on Dad's case.

I pulled into a driveway on a quiet country road. This former Baltimore City homicide detective had retired to fresh air, expansive skies and beagles.

Donald and his wife, Diane, were a trim, attractive couple. They bred those beagles. One slept at our feet the whole afternoon, as the others barked outside.

Diane set a glass of water in front of me.

"What have you heard from Cold Case?" Donald asked me, as we all settled into our kitchen chairs.

I sighed.

"Well . . . They told me it's the only missing persons file in the Homicide Unit," I said, reaching for the first fact that came to mind.

"That's saying something," said Donald.

"It's saying something," I agreed, "but . . . what does it say? I mean, they're still holding on to the file twenty-three years later. I haven't met with them in probably two and a half years. The last time I was down there, Roger Nolan was still sergeant, still head of Cold Case, but he's now retired.

"I called them around the same time I called you, in December, and left a message, and they didn't call me back."

It stung. Sergeant Nolan was gone now. I hadn't said goodbye before he retired, which hurt somehow. He had exhausted all avenues of inquiry on the skull. Without the evidence or new developments, I didn't expect that Cold Case could do much. And I'd still hoped they would be there if I needed them.

"Did you get a chance to see the folder?" Donald asked. I let out another deep sigh. Yes and no. I shook my head and told him what happened on my visits with Sergeant Nolan and the other Donald. His eyebrows went up and Diane winced.

"They wouldn't let you look at it." Donald sounded floored. "Was he holding you up from looking at it?"

"Yes. He said, 'It's still an active case.' Which in a way—OK, that's nice to hear, but it's been twenty-three years."

Donald said, "It's still an active case because it's open but nobody's actively working on it."

"That's right," I said.

"That's just a phrase he's using. That's a word game. That's not an active case."

"I know," I said, and then, my voice going up slightly: "I know." This was central to why I'd come here: to see how my own impressions of what I had heard and experienced would line up with those of another insider. It was both a relief and salt in the wound that he agreed with me. Why had Nolan prevented me from reviewing that folder?

"Let's lay out the basics of this case," said Donald. "Here's a man, calls his wife and says, 'I'm on my way home.'"

"Which he did every night," I said.

"Exactly. He works in an enclosed area, with a ten- or twelve-foot chain-link fence around the whole property. There's a security guard on the premises. And there's a cover-up. It's very evident that a shoot-out took place in the office. His chair's missing. He's missing, his dog's missing, his car's missing. They even took the time to cover up the bullet holes in the wood by puttying over everything.

"They cleaned up the bloody floor. This was not a missing persons case. But Timothy Doory said there was not enough probable cause for a warrant."

The point of conversations like this wasn't just to learn something new—it was also to consider what I already knew from a different vantage point. At the Kincaids' kitchen table, surrounded by beagles, that happened again and again.

"Do you think Doory was prioritizing his career?" I asked.

"I dealt with Doory a lot. He'd seen my investigation, and when I presented him with someone to indict, I was really shocked that he turned me down."

"You mean, you were shocked because you thought you and Ed Brown had enough of the right evidence to implicate Augie?" I asked.

He nodded emphatically. "It was all there. At least he could have given us a search and seizure warrant. I had enough probable cause based on the office and the truck."

"Wait," I interrupted, confused. "But there was a search of the premises."

"Oh yeah, I *did* get it, but not from him," said Donald. "I got it from the judge. We showed all the probable cause and the judge signed off on the search."

If that's how it went down, and I had no reason to believe it wasn't, then what David Simon had told me was true: Dad had gotten a decent shake. When Donald Kincaid heard no from Timothy Doory on the search warrant, he sidestepped the obstacle and got what he needed from someone else. I recognized this: persistence.

"You told me on the phone that this was the strangest case, or one of the strangest cases, you worked in your career. Why was that?" I asked.

Donald didn't hesitate. "Because of all the evidence . . . I've never had any missing persons report that's handled by Homicide. And when we initially went down there, we got resistance at the gate. The security guard didn't want to let us in."

I nodded. "That's what Ed Brown said."

Donald went on. "We threatened him with the search and seizure warrant. He called Augie, and Augie came down, and we were still outside the gate. We got in through him and started looking around. That's when I did go get that warrant.

"Ed Brown and I did a real thorough job. We took it as far as we could. The puzzle pieces were there. I just couldn't get the state's attorney's office to see it."

*We did a real thorough job. We took it as far as we could.* I believed Donald Kincaid. It also seemed like the kind of thing a retired detective would say to the daughter of a murdered man who had gotten crumbs from the justice system. I suspected everyone I spoke to told me what they wanted me to hear. The degree to which that aligned with the truth would always nag at me. *Am I naive or not paranoid enough?* It was a constant calibration. By all accounts, Doory was the roadblock. I'd left a few messages at his office and gotten no reply.

"One of the workers made a statement off the record, which might not be in the folder. Down the street, I never knew about it, was a company that made dog food. He said, 'If I bet my money, that's where he went.'"

Valley Proteins. It was the region's only rendering plant. In 1995, longtime *City Paper* reporter Van Smith wrote a stomach-churning deep dive into "a phenomenon that many have heard of but few are tempted to ponder" that "answers a vital societal question: What to do with the prodigious amounts of carrion, offal, and fat that our society leaves in its dietary wake?"

*Consider these items: Bozman, the Baltimore City Police Department quarter horse who died last summer in the line of duty. The grill grease and used frying oil from Camden Yards, the city's summer ethnic festivals, and nearly all Baltimore-area and Ocean City restaurants and hotels. A baby circus elephant who died while in Baltimore this summer. Millions of tons of waste meat and inedible animal parts from the region's supermarkets and slaughterhouses. Carcasses from the Baltimore Zoo. The thousands of dead dogs, cats, raccoons, possums, deer, foxes, snakes, and the rest that local animal shelters and road-kill patrols must dispose of each month.*

Valley Proteins processed all this and more into profitable products—including, in what Smith called a "gruesomely ironic twist," food for pets. Cooker operator Bud Kellner told Smith: "If it don't go here, it'd be laying on the side of the street somewhere."

A vital service to society and a potential boon for a local murderer in a hurry. No one's ever going to find a body that doesn't exist. Again, this subject sparked an anguish beyond words. If I touched it too long, I would break from reality or cease to survive. Knowing these details fed legions of "murder fans" made me seethe. I had a reason to wade into this hole of damnation: to emerge from it more whole.

Donald had a determined expression, and I saw the gears working in his mind.

"It's a shame you didn't get a chance to see the folder, because what I wrote up and presented to the state's attorney's office," he said, "I thought it was pretty decent."

I could see him weighing something, trying to make a decision.

"I'm going to try again to obtain the folder."

There it was: a kernel of hope. Maybe Donald Kincaid would actually gain access to Dad's file. I also knew in this moment that it was highly unlikely. Not because the retired detective didn't mean it. I believed he was entirely sincere. But people are busy. People have their own lives. People are disinclined to get involved. I already knew that Donald, content to spend his retirement days in this peaceful, rural place, didn't enjoy driving back to Baltimore.

"If you were me, what would you do?"

Donald thought for a minute.

"Me, I think right now, I would pursue this guy who says the body's in the retaining wall. And see how far you want to pursue the fact as to why the Cold Case squad didn't pursue your lead."

His face changed. "You know what? Make a stink. You're a journalist. Call *The Sun* paper. Pull some strings—"

(as if I were a puller of strings)

"—and get with one of these reporters, because every now and then, they'll have an article in the paper about a missing person. And just see if they'll print an article. And put in there about going to the Baltimore City Police Cold Case squad with information that you were able to develop, that your father could possibly be buried in a retaining wall on the property where he worked."

Donald looked at me expectantly. "What do you got to lose?"

"No, nothing," I conceded.

"Let somebody down there in the police department read that. Let the commissioner read that. Let them sweat over it. Worst thing police hate is publicity. Especially publicity like that. They don't like that. They get all shook up."

As much as I wanted to, I didn't fully buy it. But I didn't say that.

"I want to make sure that I don't lose access," I said. "I don't want to become persona non grata down there. So I want to try to get a look at that folder before I go pissing them off."

"No, it would be the opposite. You'd have them all scared to death."

This seemed dubious. Why would the Baltimore Police care if I ran my mouth to *The Baltimore Sun*? Why would *The Baltimore Sun* care about a decades-old case and the claim that BPD was not devoting resources to it? Baltimore had bigger problems. But I told Donald I'd think about it.

Diane called me brave, and Donald said he respected what I was doing. I hadn't known how starved I was to hear this.

As we were saying goodbye, I told the two how vehemently my sister opposed my project.

"You tell her," Diane said, hugging me hard, "'Then don't ever read my book.'"

The rural love nest of a retired homicide detective and his wife and beagles had charm. This was a normal life. I had been so laser focused on Dad that I didn't or couldn't always acknowledge that I might want a life like this. For a second I felt lonely and needy.

Gordon, the punk scene, Harold, a bunch of homicide detectives . . . I'd sought family generally and fathers specifically in ways both subtle and overt. Across the board, I was looking for dads I was never going to find. Taking on this quest was a remedy. I'd traded heartache and paralysis for a sense of agency—along with considerable guilt and anxiety. But as hard as I tried to find family, nothing ever quite stuck.

# GASLIGHT

TWO MONTHS HAD passed since I'd met with the Kincaids. The debilitating post-surgery fatigue felt endless. I wondered if my energy was gone for good. I'd always been unwell, and to cope I had developed an array of strategies—from acupuncture to strong-tasting Chinese herbs. Somehow I had always found a way to power through, give or take a week in bed. Now I was a dead battery.

As I reckoned with physical limitation, I began to question how much more of this project around Dad I could take. I'd been at my meandering, part-time, amorphous quest for nearly four years. I was not James Ellroy. I was just some woman. I was thirty-six and I got lonely sometimes. If I wanted children, the window was fast closing. But working on this project made it hard to date.

A year or so previous, I'd had lunch with my old mentor, Maer Roshan, the gay Iranian media icon who founded *Radar* magazine, at Cafe Orlin in the East Village. Maer encouraged me to get out more. I improvised the conversations I had with new people:

DATE: *Oh, you're writing a book, how exciting! What's it about?*

ME: *You don't want to know. It's kind of a downer.*

DATE: *Oh, now I have to know!*

ME: *My dad was murdered by his business partner when I was twelve. There came a point when I realized my survival hinged on seeking out the truth. So I'm digging up everything I can, in the hopes of finding some answers and maybe some peace.*

DATE: *[shocked silence] Damn. That's . . . awful. Waiter, check!*

Maer looked at me with a mixture of affection and humor and sadness and "I give up."

I still tried. Today, in fact, I'd gotten the afternoon off to see someone I'd been casually dating. But instead of inviting me back to his apartment after lunch, he'd performed a flowery lamentation about leaving to work in Europe for the summer and feeling honor bound to protect my feelings. I was up to my eyeballs in a morass around my dad's murder. The idea that I'd be decimated by the loss of some guy I'd hung out with maybe four times? I was incensed. I couldn't tell if it was more about a fun afternoon spoiled or the fact that this person understood so little about me.

It was a beautiful day, technically still spring, but the heat was suffocating. Disappointed and sweating bullets, I began making my way across 9th Street toward the PATH. It was June 1, 2011, the fourteenth anniversary of my move from Baltimore to New York City. That morning I'd met survival expert Bear Grylls, who was being photographed for a *Men's Journal* cover story. I was such a fan. I opened my flip phone to text a friend about it. At which point I saw missed calls—three of them. All from my mother.

Someone was dead.

My grandfather was hale. He was also ninety-four.

"Call me back, Mom," I said to her answering machine. I made no attempt to hide my alarm. "Call me back and tell me what's wrong."

I felt myself bracing for impact, desperate to know and desperate to flee. Three missed Mom calls—someone was 1000 percent dead. Now I was charging across 9th, my tall black biker boots a blur of brisk steps. I knocked elbows with someone going eastbound and the jostle ignited a current of hatred. The seconds ticked by like hours, and my mother did not call back. I was not ready to lose Pop. I could not imagine descending the steps at 9th and 6th and holding a dead phone for twenty or thirty minutes while I got a train back to Jersey City. And all around me, Manhattan was acting like everything was fine.

At 9th Street and 3rd Avenue, across from St. Mark's Bookshop, the phone buzzed in my damp palm.

"Mom, what's wrong?"

Silence.

"Mom! What's wrong? Who's dead? Where's Pop?"

More silence. I opened my mouth again, but she spoke.

"Augie hung himself."

*Hanged. Augie hanged himself.* The copy chief of *Men's Journal* corrected her mother's grammar, a cuckoo clock, and sank to the sidewalk.

It hadn't taken long for the news to reach us. Someone knew someone who knew someone who'd handled the 911 call. One of those someones called my uncle; my uncle called my mother. A grapevine of fate. Now here I was, crouched in a ball on the concrete outside of St. Mark's Bookshop in the East Village of New York City.

Sometime the day before, on May 31, 2011, William Walter Augustin Jr., eighty-three, my father's business partner, my de facto godfather and the man whom detectives suspected had my father killed, hanged himself in the garage of his home near E & M. A family member found him and made the call to 911. It was nineteen years to the day since David Simon's feature article on Dad had run in *The Sun*.

And just like that, the bogeyman was gone. Twenty-three years, all of us believing we were next. One day, when our guard was down, Augie would get rid of us too.

East Villagers stepped carefully past me on the sidewalk where I had planted myself next to a pole. A minute before, I had been frustrated with some meaningless guy. I was trying to reel in my brain. Haze, pounding chest. Could I just go to sleep right here? The few blocks to the PATH train felt too far to manage.

Only a few seconds had passed since my mother spoke those three words.

Everything was different. Everything was the same.

"I wanted to interview him!" I sputtered.

Then I whispered: "I don't have to be afraid of him anymore." I said "holy shit" repeatedly, the apparent sum total of my vocabulary from my pavement crouch. My mother was silent. Which is not to say that my mother had nothing to say. But to confide in me her thoughts and feelings would be to violate her own infinitely private code.

We shared space on the phone, nothing more. As always, a wall separated us. On the occasion of a world-rocking event, there was no rush of words, no cascade of confidences, no exchange of feelings. My feeble interjections were a placeholder for thoughts that would take years to fully form.

I rose up in a woozy spiral from my sidewalk crouch.

"I'm going to that funeral!" I chattered, alive again, pacing and pressing my bag to my torso for balance, emotional and physical.

"Oh, no you're not!" my mother gasped. Here was an authentic declaration of emotion. She spoke in an over-my-dead-body tone. That gasp was sheer horror.

Standing outside St. Mark's Bookshop, I gave the East Village a performance fit for any hole-in-the-wall theater. "That man killed my father!" I bellowed, not at the top of my lungs but close. "And I'm going to his funeral! *That is my prerogative as a thirty-six-year-old woman!*"

Time froze. My patch of the city, my speck of time-space, halted. Faces flickered. I registered no judgment. If anything, I perceived a ripple of respect. My fellow New Yorkers, in telepathic unison: *Do what you got to do. I'd go too.*

It took me almost an hour to complete what is typically a ten-minute walk. I made a few phone calls and sent a handful of regrettable text messages: "Augie hanged himself."

Texting was still pretty new to me. In those days, you could text your tweets to 40404 and, marvelously, they posted on twitter.com. I'd been meaning to hang out with my neighbor Finn. I took the flip phone back out and sent a text: **Hey, are you around tonight? I need a drink.** He confirmed.

When we met at our elevator, Finn raised his eyebrows. I was still in my work clothes. I looked bedraggled and I smelled.

"Rough day at the office?"

"No. The guy who killed my dad just hanged himself."

Finn nodded neutrally, as if I'd said I needed blue corn chips from the bodega. After a year of saying hello in the hallway, and bonding over the mouse invasion, this was our first official hangout. He was probably regretting it, but I didn't have it in me to feel guilty. Tonight, my aversion to discussing Dad was out the window. I needed company. Few of my friends lived in Jersey City—I always took the train to meet up with them in Brooklyn or Manhattan. I thought I could trust Finn and had to try. We walked to the Hamilton Inn, a nearby spot with a solid menu.

I rarely drank to excess. On Friday nights I went to the Ten Bells. I'd drink a glass or two of biodynamic red over a French novel I could chat with my bartenders about. "You speak French like my grandmother," one of them told me one night. Not knowing or caring if it was flirtation or insult, I beamed with pride. I'd come home again with a sack of gluten-free treats from BabyCakes, the bakery next door. That was a wonderful routine. My empty attempts at marking the anniversary of Dad's death with alcohol were in the distant past, and I drank the offbeat French wines at Ten Bells in moderation. Tonight I intended on oblivion, and I had no doubt it was the right call.

Two Jamesons on an empty stomach in a state of shock, and I got there quickly.

Finn, an engineer a couple years older than me, was excellent company and one hell of a good sport. I told him everything. And I drank that amber Irish forgetting serum.

A couple hours in, when I stumbled into the ladies' room, the adrenaline and sweat were still pulsing off me. But the sheet-white figure swaying slightly in the mirror looked considerably less like a deer caught in headlights. No longer feral, just drunk. Finn got me home.

I sprawled, fully clothed, across my mattress, silent and frozen, for the duration of the night.

Augie never called me back after I tried his house that day in May 2008. I guess I didn't really expect him to. All the same, I had eyed my cell phone warily for months after making that call. I watched my back, and I waited for something bad to happen. By my mother's and uncle's telling, the mere act of making that phone call sealed a bloody fate for us all. They'd told me over and over that any attempt at contacting Augie would result in all of our deaths. I thought that was unlikely, but I still didn't tell either one of them what I'd done.

We didn't die.

What now? I still longed to talk to him. He may have engineered the event that destroyed my childhood and shaped my life path. Augie had answers, and now I could never again try, however futilely, to get them.

I knew he was dead, and I wanted to see him.

I was determined to track down that funeral. I told my boss I'd need to take a personal day on Friday or Monday, and the morning of Thursday, June 2, I started casting a net for the obituary. A colleague checked LexisNexis, and I asked Gordon in Baltimore to check *The Sun* paper. After my performance outside St. Mark's Bookshop, I doubted my mother would call to volunteer the contents of that obit.

It didn't strike me or anyone else as odd that there was no obituary on Thursday. There may not have been time for his family to place a death notice. All the same, what if there wasn't going to be one? I decided to see if my contacts in Cold Case would help me. First, I left a message at home for Donald Kincaid. Then I called Cold Case.

By then, Sergeant Roger Nolan and Donald Worden were both retired, but there was a chance that Worden still freelanced for the unit.

"Cold Case."

"Hi there . . . Is Donald Worden still with the unit?"

"Who wants to know?"

I told the man, a detective who said his name was Todd Corriveau, that Worden had worked on my father's case and I had a question for him. I didn't want to tell a stranger that I was looking for help finding the funeral of the man who'd killed my father. I realized I'd sound like a crackpot. But I had to do just that—the man refused to tell me anything until I disclosed who I was and what I wanted.

"Who?" he asked.

"Eddy Crane. He's the only missing persons case in Homicide. It's a famous case."

"Never heard of it."

That stung. But whatever. I suggested he call Sergeant Nolan or Donald Worden, as either of them could clear this up.

"No," he said. I started to get the feeling he was enjoying himself. "I'm going to do an internet search on you and your father to check out your story."

I shook my head at the phone. "That's not going to help you. There's nothing about it on the internet, and all you're going to find about me is that I'm a journalist writing about my father's murder." I told him David Simon had written a feature in 1992, and if he'd give me an email address, I'd send it to him.

"I'm not giving you any email address."

My chest clenched. What? Why wouldn't a detective at Cold Case give me an email address? Wasn't there one for the whole department if he didn't want to share his own? But why would that be a problem? This detective was a public servant and I was the daughter of a murder victim. I backed off and said, fine, check me out however you want. I gave him my office number and my cell number. I wasn't making anything up, and it would be easy for him to confirm my identity. Certainly he'd be friendlier when he called back.

The phone rang about fifteen minutes later.

"Hi, Ms. Crane, I'm just calling as a courtesy to let you know that I'm not helping you with anything."

I felt kicked in the teeth. It defied comprehension. How, why, would any detective speak to the family member of a victim with what felt to me like unbridled malice?

"I don't understand. Why won't you tell Donald Worden that I called?"

He said, "I have no reason to believe you're not making this whole thing up."

It was one of the more difficult days of my life. I was experiencing a crippling episode of post-traumatic stress disorder. This exchange broke me.

"You claim you know David Simon?" he asked, in a mocking tone. "Well, why don't you call him, then?"

"OK," I stammered. "That's fine."

Detective Corriveau hung up on me. (In a phone conversation years later, Corriveau denied ever having spoken to me.)

Year after year, the silence and the inaction of the Baltimore Police Department telegraphed to me and my mother and sister: What happened to Eddy Crane doesn't matter. Now there was a postscript: "And by the way? Fuck you."

I thought of something Sergeant Nolan had said: "You lost

your father and not much was done about it." I'd been trying to figure out how to carry the weight of that for two-thirds of my life. I already knew my father was gone forever. But now the people who were supposed to help were displaying what I perceived as cruelty.

I hung up the phone I was still holding, dial tone buzzing in my ear, and calmly went to the women's room. There, on a busted leather couch, I lost it. The sorrow, usually secured on my highest emotional shelves, poured out of me in uncontrollable sobs. I wished my cries could break my bones . . . That kind of pain made sense; that kind of pain would heal.

Later on, after I got home, I hit up my friend Dacus, who also worked at *Men's Journal*, on gchat and explained my predicament. I hadn't found an obituary. I had called twenty funeral homes looking for the service and come up empty-handed. Either there was none, or the information was under wraps. I was strongly considering throwing a bag in the car and hitting the New Jersey Turnpike. Dacus suggested I call Augie's family to be polite and give them a heads-up that I wished to attend the funeral. I suggested this might not be wise. Dacus pressed me on my motivations for going to Baltimore.

DACUS: what would you see?
ME: the six-foot-five body of the person who stole my childhood
DACUS: I don't think you should get in the car
DACUS: and there's about a 1 percent chance of you finding the funeral
DACUS: by the time you get to Baltimore it'll be late afternoon

DACUS: by the time you find the place, if you find the place, there's a huge chance that the service and everything will be over

Then he added:

DACUS: that man is probably in the ground
DACUS: the thing you want, Kate, probably doesn't exist anymore
DACUS: I think you need to let this one go

I thanked Dacus for his friendship, and I went back to bed and cried for a while. In the end I did not drive to Baltimore. But I did, in fact, reach out to David Simon. His reply:

*I spoke with a Det. Alston at Cold Case and strongly criticized the way in which you were treated. He said you should call him and he'll do what he can. Cold Case should be interested in the suicide; Augie may have left stuff around that is relevant to the crime that might now be recovered and other associates might now speak openly about what they know. And it is possible that other confederates to the murder are still alive to be charged, if so.*

*But the truth is that because the case was never officially ruled a murder, they're under no pressure to clear the case.*

*Indeed by clearing the case, they add to the murder rate for that year, which, while not a big deal, certainly doesn't help them with the current workload. Do not look for impassioned police work.*

*See if you can make a friend of Det. Alston.*

I made that call a month or two later. I got a wall of ice. Detective Alston told me: "Go through official channels if you have questions for us."

I never called Cold Case again. The exchange with Todd

Corriveau had infected me with shame. A couple friends said, "Why not just call back and talk to someone else? You're likely to get what you need from the official channels, right?"

If I had been working on anything other than this, that's exactly what I would have done. When I advise younger reporters, I tell them that if they need one source, reach out to ten or fifteen people and prepare to do a second round if no one replies.

This was different. I hadn't wanted to face facts. The brief window of hope I knew with Sergeant Nolan and Detective Worden no longer existed.

# MEMORIAL

Once or twice, when I was a teenager, Mom asked me if I wanted a memorial service for Dad. I said no. I knew he wasn't coming back, and I still wanted to wait for him. A service would confirm he was gone forever. I couldn't face it back then. Now it was past time.

I called my mother. "What would you think about doing a service for Dad?" I asked.

Silence on the line. Then: "A memorial?"

"I think I'd like to call it a funeral, for myself, but yes, a memorial."

I handed the reins to my mother and sister. I would be an attendee, not an organizer. They made arrangements for a service to take place in November of 2011, in the chapel at St. Joseph, the same place where I attended pre-K.

I cried a lot in the days leading up, mind fuzzy, joints stiff. I'd gotten sick in September, and one night at work around midnight, I started itching. When I pulled up my shirt in the women's room, I couldn't believe my eyes. Hives. Over my entire body, the size of saucers and dinner plates. Since then, the hives had flared and receded, like jellyfish in the tides. Washed-out and weak, I made my way down the turnpike the night before the service and checked in to a Fells Point hotel. I lay awake the entire night.

I forgot the camera, I texted Alex, my old *New York Press* partner, when I parked at St. Joe's in the morning.

Forget the camera, he said. Use your notebook! I'd left the big blue notebook in Jersey City. For running around, I mostly used palm-size reporter's notebooks with hard black covers. I gripped mine like a security blanket and headed for the chapel.

I've never smelled anything else like the St. Joe's chapel—clean with notes of incense. It had not changed a bit. The second I was inside, I felt safer.

I watched in awe as people began to stream in. Gordon and Marie, who needed help walking but was in good spirits. Uncle Bob and his wife, who traveled from another state. Bob's twin daughters. Yvonne and Martin, in from Pennsylvania. Mom's childhood friend Nancy. Ken Glenn and Walt Bain, who'd worked at E & M. All these people who had not been in the same room together for decades, some of them ever, were congregating to honor Dad.

"It's the final act of respect," Mom had said the day she placed Dad's denture into my hands, about my hopes for finding his body. We could not bury him, but with this gathering, we could say goodbye on consecrated ground.

An elegant flower arrangement adorned the altar. Deacon Charlie Baynes, whom I'd known my entire life, conducted the service. I held my grandfather's hand.

My mother, grandfather, uncle and sister spoke. From the lectern, Pop said, "We are here to honor Eddy Crane." He spoke of Dad as a good father, loving husband, wonderful son-in-law. When it was my sister's turn, she was initially too emotional to speak. She read from passages she'd carefully selected: Lao Tzu, *The Tao of Pooh.* When she finished speaking, she hugged our uncle.

I declined to go up and speak. I felt peaceful. There was nothing I wanted to say. At last, Dad had a proper and official ritual to mark his passing, twenty-four years after that horrible night in 1987. If nothing else, I had done this. Something valuable, something good.

Most everyone went back to my mother's house. It was the biggest crowd since Dad had died. As conversation buzzed and people filled their plates with deli meats and cheese, Ken Glenn and I made our way down the hallway back to my little yellow room. I lugged a kitchen chair for him. It was odd to have anyone else in that room. But there we were, me and this clean-cut white man in his fifties, dressed in a nice sport coat for his friend's decades-late quasi-funeral.

Ken began to fill in some of the blanks I had about E & M. He'd met Dad when he was working on trucks at a Ford dealership. Dad gave him a salesman job, similar to my uncle, in August 1981. E & M had no more than twenty employees at the time, he said.

I asked about his impression of Dad and Augie's relationship. He said it was good at first. "Then things over time deteriorated. Augie really became a nuisance to the business."

He brought up the time after the fight. "Sometimes your father would just not come in. It actually got to be quite funny. Because he would call in the morning and say, 'Everything OK?' I'd say, 'Yeah, everything's fine.' We'd talk for a few minutes on the phone. He'd say, 'I'll be there in a while.' Then he would call maybe somewhere around eleven, eleven thirty. 'I'll be there in a little while.' All right. About three o'clock he'd call. 'Yeah, I don't think I'm going to make it in.'

"Yeah, no shit, bro."

My face twisted into a grin. This reminded me so much of myself, it was uncanny. No one would have used the word *neurodivergent* back then, but that's how I read this. No, Dad did not want to see his estranged business partner. And I also perceived flickers of someone who was attached to the private rhythms of his day, and with less of a reason to align to a nine-to-five reality, increasingly declined it.

"Did Augie know he was a nuisance?" I asked.

"No. He thought he was the greatest thing since sliced bread. He would try to be overbearing. He would try to impress people with knowledge that he really didn't have," Ken said. "He seemed to surround himself with ex-cons and people of limited abilities. Like he wanted to be the Pied Piper with all his minions. He was a decent mechanic. He just . . . I don't know if it was delusions of grandeur, or what."

How had it not occurred to me to have this conversation first, not tenth? I always thought of Dad as having few friends. In reality, his close friends were the people he worked with. In this way too, we were alike.

Ken went on to say that at some point, Dad decided he'd leave and start another business on his own. The problem for Augie was that Dad brought in the cash, and Augie would not be able to keep the business going without Eddy running it.

"I think that's when push came to shove. He wasn't going to allow Eddy to basically take it away from him. If Eddy went and opened up this new company, he would take 80 percent of the business, at least, there with it. That's where the customers would go.

"The good customers of E & M Machinery dealt with Eddy and me and Bob and Walt, not Augie. The lowlife scumbag customers would deal with Augie. But they were 10 percent of the customers."

I thought about the story of the fight on the front lot, which I always pictured as taking place under hot sun, the white gravel glinting. With Ken, a single snapshot was transforming into a photo album.

"One of the cutest little things that always sticks in my mind . . . A lowlife buddy of Augie's owed the company money. He sent a Christmas card one time. Your dad took the card and wrote on it, on the card itself, 'Thanks for the card, but a check would have been nicer.' And put it in an envelope and mailed it back to him.

"Your uncle says, 'You can't do that, you can't do that!' and your dad says, 'Watch me.'"

A jolt of electricity coursed through me. Ken was describing me. *Watch me.* This was how I reacted when people told me what I could and could not do. To the letter. The defiance, the directness, the swagger. *I really am my father's daughter,* I thought, there in my little bedroom.

My mother had never told me these kinds of stories about Dad—or that he and I so resembled each other in character and will and demeanor. She had witheld more than information about Dad's disappearance. It was also our alikeness. I was the black sheep in the absence of Dad. If he'd lived, I might have had a twin.

"Your dad was a good guy, and I loved your dad, but there's

sides of him that you don't know, and there's maybe sides of him you don't want to know."

"Oh no, I want to know," I insisted, trying to keep the alarm out of my voice. This was the pot of gold at the end of the rainbow. I did not want Ken to stop talking.

"He could be a very coarse individual," said Ken. "If you were close to him, he was one of the greatest people you'd ever known. OK?" I nodded in a way that felt solemn. "But if you were on the wrong side, watch out. Here's a perfect instance." And Ken launched into another story.

*They had put an engine in a customer's truck. And the guy hadn't paid for it. Well, now it's getting like 60 days, and the guy still hasn't paid for it. OK?*

*Calling, calling, calling. "Yeah, yeah, yeah." Fortunately, when the truck was there getting the engine, your dad had a spare key made to the truck.*

*So one night, he went out. Found the truck, got it and was driving it back to the shop. He stopped at a pay phone, 'cause this was well before cell phones. Called this guy up at home. Said, "Here it is." And he held the phone outside the phone booth at the truck stop: "That's my engine running in your truck. Be down here tomorrow morning with the cash, or it's coming out."*

*The guy says, "You can't do that." And he said, "Watch me." The guy was there the next day to pay for it. OK?*

It felt so real, like I was watching from the truck Dad had temporarily repo'd as he called the delinquent customer on a pay phone. I could picture it in Technicolor, smell the Chloraseptic lozenges that Dad often sucked on, smell the Viceroy cigarette cupped in the palm of his hand. I could picture myself in one of my Holly Hobbie nightgowns in the truck's front seat. It was impossible. Dad never once brought me along on this kind of outing. I would have been asleep in bed, probably in the house on Silver Spring Road. And yet the scene spooled across my mind like a home movie as Ken spoke.

As much as I was searching for clues about my Dad's disappearance, I was also searching for this. Ken had gifted me memories. I absorbed them hungrily.

"One more thing," I said. "We were all terrified of Augie until he died. Do you think there was a legitimate reason to be afraid?"

Ken thought for a moment. "Concerned, watchful. Scared might be pushing it. Maybe at first. Because your mom was pushing the issue—"

I stopped him. "What do you mean?"

"Well, she pushed the issue that your dad was really killed there, and pushed the police to do as much as they did." Then, he said, the danger to the rest of us might have been quite real.

"But at that point, you gotta look at it the other way," Ken continued. "Augie wasn't an overly intellectual person, but he was smart enough to know that it'd be pretty obvious if then something were to happen to your mother and Bob . . ." Our eyes met. Yes, and to two little girls.

"That would have brought all the rain down on him."

I had not always thought of my mother as someone who pushed. In my mind, Bob more frequently played this role. Now I could see it differently. I knew she pushed when she sought for Dad to be legally declared dead—the waiting period was seven years. I was beginning to grasp an active quality to her silence and her withdrawal. Push, then retreat. With Ken's telling, I could credit my mom with more agency.

"It would have been more scary if they'd charged him with

the crime," Ken added. "Because at that point, he really wouldn't have anything to lose."

*YOU LIT A FIRE UNDER THEM AND NOW THEY'RE GOING TO DO SOMETHING. YOU DON'T LIVE HERE YOU DON'T HAVE TO BE AFRAID YOU LEFT.*

My sister's accusation jangled in my head. Ken was articulating my central concern, and hearing it spoken aloud . . . I shivered. Through the windows, daylight was waning. Dark fell fast in November.

I thanked Ken, and we got up to join the others in the kitchen. "My peace is that the one person whose head I'd like to put a bullet in is no longer alive," he said.

# GREEN LIGHT

I WAS STILL COPY CHIEFING, now at *WSJ Magazine*. On a slow week, I summoned the courage to call Donald Worden again. He was no longer freelancing for Cold Case, and I had an instinct that he might speak more frankly to me.

"Well, hello, Miss Kate," he said, sunshine and roses. I smiled. He always sounded glad to hear from me, even when I knew full well he was going to put me off. I launched in.

"I'd like to come down and see you," I said. "You've known Dad's case for years. You may not be able to tell me anything new, but I respect your thoughts. I'd bet anything you have strong opinions."

Quiet on the line.

"Maybe, maybe," he said.

And then the old dance. Donald Worden reiterated that he didn't want to waste my time. "You might be making a drive all the way down here for nothing," he said.

"I love to drive. You know this about me! I'm looking at the New Jersey Turnpike from my kitchen window right now. It's an easy trip," I assured him.

Miraculously: Donald Worden agreed to meet with me. I

did a little dance and started to toss notebooks and pens in a bag while we hashed out details.

Just as we were about to hang up, Donald Worden dropped some parting words:

"You know your father led a double life, right?"

# WORDEN

I MET THE BIG MAN at Spoons, a diner in Federal Hill.

"Hi, Detective Worden," I said, giving him a hug. "Great to see you."

"Hello, Miss Kate."

Donald Worden never called me Kate, even after four-plus years. It was usually Miss Crane. Once in a while, I got Miss Kate. And I always called him Detective Worden.

Spoons was cheerful, with brick accent walls and two-tops in glowing cherry. Worden and I chose a table. "Test, test, test," I said, paranoid that my recorder would glitch. I showed him the device. "If you want to stop it, you just press that."

He nodded almost imperceptibly and began to speak.

"The initial investigation, in my opinion, was to avoid getting what they call a number, a statistic. And it was unnecessary. I mean, he *is* missing, but he didn't just disappear. Your mother finally succeeded in having him declared dead.

"Unfortunately, your father didn't lead the best lifestyle. As far as his partner in business goes, his reputation wasn't that great. He had a convicted murderer working for him," Worden said. I'd heard rumors of this—I was pretty sure this was Archie McAleese—and here was the confirmation.

I had tracked down some information on the night watchman. My memories of the man I'd called Mr. Roscoe were few and vague. He visited the house on Silver Spring Road once and brought me a brown paper bag. Inside: a box of Crayolas. By the age of sixteen, Roscoe Woolard had been arrested ten times in his native North Carolina. Soon after, a judge saw fit to lock him up for ten years, for larceny and breaking and entering. During that time, Woolard received another sentence, to be served upon completion of the first. In September 1969, *The Sanford Herald* declared: "Two inmates are missing from Advancement Center." He'd spent roughly as many years incarcerated as free. Six years later, and eight months after I was born, a docket list in the same newspaper said of Roscoe Woolard, escapee: nol pros. Case abandoned.

Woolard, according to the newspaper, was not considered dangerous.

"Augie had control of everybody. There was nobody talking," said Worden. "But here's what you don't know. Here's what I meant when I said your father was living a double life: Your father was an informant for the FBI."

I took this in. Everything made more sense. Here was a missing piece that helped organize a twenty-five-year puzzle. I didn't gasp, or drop my fork, or telegraph any alarm. I accepted this information that I'd fought so hard for.

"We think his partner found that out. But it couldn't be proven. All the circumstances do point back to it being a murder, and his partner was more than likely involved."

Dad was an FBI informant. I had no doubt Augie would have killed him over trying to start a new business—that alone was enough. Informing on him to the feds? The ramifications flooded my mind. FBI would mean crimes across state lines.

I thought back to that 1970 notice in *The Evening Sun*. Stolen truck: New Jersey. Attempt to get a new title: Pennsylvania.

The FBI had likely given him a choice: Inform for us or go to prison. Dad had been stuck.

Then, so was the Homicide unit. Because, Worden told me, the FBI waited ten years to tell Homicide that Dad worked for them. Ten years. As if anything at that point could be done.

I felt small and old and tired. Outside Spoons, I snapped a picture of the white-haired Hampden native.

"What's the photo for?" he grumbled.

"Because we'll blink and it'll be ten years and I don't have any pictures of you," I said. That explanation apparently sufficed, because Donald Worden smiled for my phone camera. It's a beautiful black-and-white snapshot.

I went back to my rental in Mount Vernon and climbed into my bed. I felt like a lake of static—no feelings, no thoughts, just nothingness.

No more of this. I was done.

# MOTHER

I WALKED IN AND saw my mother waiting in a booth, looking a little older and also entirely the same as she always had. Thin, watchful, erect, as if someone might be scrutinizing her posture. She lit up when she saw me approach. "Kate, Kate!" We hugged, me stiffly. My mother was always happy to see me. Shouldn't that be enough? I felt a stab of agony. It should be enough, but I could never quite melt into those moments of greeting.

We were having lunch at The Bowman, a bar-and-grill with great crab cakes. As soon as I sat down, I knew.

"No!" I said, eyeing the exit, turning to go, calculating if I could get up and bolt.

She began to chortle softly.

"I told you I *wouldn't*!" I said, raising my voice. "I told you I would not see you unless you promised. You PROMISED!" I felt desperate tears flooding my eyes. Heat rising, voice rising. And hatred.

My mother and I had an ongoing battle over "going through boxes." Every time I saw her, she wanted me to go through childhood things on visits. I found this distressing. My mother would not take no for an answer.

My mother produced a series of bags and boxes. The scent of cellar wafted up. "It's just a few things, Kate. You won't mind. It'll just take a minute."

I had come there to tell her what I found out about Dad, and she wanted me to sort through items from the basement. I did not want to look at and smell and touch the artifacts of a childhood with my dad or the suicidal teenage years when he was newly gone. The only way to elude the boxes was to refuse to visit her house, which is why I had suggested lunch at the Bowman.

I had set up this meeting to say: "Look, here's what I uncovered about my childhood." And my mother showed up with her carefully packaged memorabilia to say: "Look. Here is your orange comb from fourth grade. Here are the stories you wrote for Mrs. Jedlicka. Here is a rosary from Uncle John in Hawaii. This is your childhood."

I felt anxious, exhausted, ashamed. I'd retraumatized my seventy-year-old mother, fully against her will, for the past five years. This was the woman who kept me clothed and fed, and got me to and from school every day after the unthinkable happened. The daredevil who'd turned my Tercel into a rocket ship on an icy driveway when I loved her against my will.

It felt a little absurd. All my questions, all my questing, the terror diarrhea and insomnia and long drives and derailed career and botched relationships. My investigation was concluding over crab cakes and coleslaw on Harford Road.

My mother said, in a guarded, fake-upbeat voice: "So, what did you want to tell me?"

Haltingly, feeling like a bad child, I laid out my process and the simple facts of what I had found. I went over everything—

Augie's connection on the City Council, the medical examiner in Virginia, the lowlife who bragged about putting Dad's body in a wall. Then I shared the key revelation.

"I found out that Dad was an informant for the FBI," I said. "So, if Augie found out, that would be the reason Dad got killed."

She eyed me warily, saying nothing for some time. Everything I had done again seemed small. Why had I ever even considered this project, when it would only upset my mother? I couldn't think of a single good reason. It's not like I found Dad. It's not like I brought anyone to justice.

"Dad. An FBI informant," I repeated.

"I could have told you all that," she said, and looked at me, wholly unimpressed.

I sat back in disbelief.

What if my mother had been straight with me from day one? What if she had shared what she knew . . . shared her fears . . . looped me in? I can't say who I would have become, but I have some guesses. Maybe a chasm of question marks would not have dominated my life. Maybe the silence would not have stifled me. And maybe, maybe, I would not have dedicated my thirties to seeking answers, and, instead, sought out a partner and had kids.

My mother was not unlike me. I was nearing the age she was when Dad first disappeared. How would I have handled it? My mother was dealt a ghastly hand. She played her cards as she saw fit.

"I could have told you all that," she said again.

"But you didn't," I said, and ate my crab cake.

# EPILOGUE

One Sunday afternoon before the new house was done, Dad and I took a drive to see the four horses who lived in an adjacent field. When we parked the tan Mercedes, he casually unhooked the barbed-wire fence and helped me under. We were surely trespassing. And we strode the field together companionably, a businessman in his forties with his ten-year-old firstborn daughter, our future house visible through the trees and dense brush beyond the stream. I felt content and proud to be with my father. I was not afraid of the horses, who approached us slowly as we approached them.

A soft, silver-brown horse with a white lightning bolt on her face was stepping lightly to us, all grace for a creature who loomed over me so large. "Daddy, can I pet her?"

"Go 'head, Katy," he said. He was relaxed, wearing the same outfit as always: the stretchy black pants and short-sleeved Oxford. "She likes you."

The horse's face was a study in velvet. Her nostrils puffed warm psalms into my small hands. I thought, *This place will be my secret.* Together with Dad, I had entered a fairy tale where the horses had been waiting for their girl. I was enchanted.

Not long after, the spell broke, and instead of *Anne of Green*

*Gables* or *Misty of Chincoteague*, I found myself living out an echo of a Tana French or Donna Tartt novel. Or one of my beloved Nero Wolfe books. I was blessed with the ornery genius of Roger Nolan and Donald Worden. And there was no tidy pulp-fiction ending. Just a handful of men who'd done what they could and wished they could somehow have done more.

"WHY DIDN'T YOU charge anyone in Dad's case?"

I could guess the answer, having heard it already from Ed Brown, Donald Kincaid, Roger Nolan, Donald Worden, David Simon and, most recently, Lieutenant Terry McLarney, the current head of the Cold Case Unit. Now, in April 2025, I finally posed the question directly to Timothy Doory.

"We did not have enough evidence to expect a conviction," Timothy told me by phone. After his time as assistant state's attorney, a role he held from 1974 to 1996, he'd become an associate judge, also in Baltimore City, retiring in 2019. "In the world of murder, there's always the possibility that something will develop over time. You have to make a decision based on the evidence you have. If you can't win, you're not doing anyone any favors to go ahead and charge.

"We had the best evidence against Roscoe. Brown and Kincaid leaned on him hard. He was a drunk, and we didn't think the jury would buy that he killed your father and also disposed of the body," he said. Dad was six feet tall and three hundred pounds, in contrast to Roscoe Woolard's five foot ten and one hundred sixty-five pounds. String beans don't move mountains.

"We had a confrontational meeting with Augie and got nothing out of him," said Timothy. "From there we hoped someone would rat him out.

"When we made an arrest and went for prosecution, we were playing to win. We didn't have enough."

"I ALWAYS FELT we had enough," Ed Brown told me recently by phone. "They tied my hands. People just don't disappear." He said the fingerprints they lifted matched only people with access to the premises. "It was clearly an inside job. This was not a complicated case. I wanted to at least charge them with conspiracy to commit murder. Let a jury decide.

"It's always haunted me."

Ed had misgivings about the FBI angle. "I would've found out if your dad was an informant. I don't see why the FBI would hide it for ten years."

It made more sense to Timothy Doory, who said: "Baltimore does not have organized crime; it has so much disorganized crime. In the world of trucking in which your father and Augie moved, it's not a stretch that they could have had information about a lot of people."

DAVID SIMON AND Ed Brown diverge on the subject of Curtis Bay politician Willie Myers.

In early September 1987, days before Dad disappeared, David took a ride in Willie Myers's Chrysler New Yorker with him, Joe DiBlasi and Timothy Murphy as they campaigned for reelection to City Council in South Baltimore's 6th District. Myers, the driver, was "using two lanes at once as only an eighty-three-year-old City Councilman can." The soundtrack: *Don Ho's Greatest Hits.*

"By that time, Myers was a mentally inert submenial hack who could barely negotiate a council meeting. He voted only how Schaefer, his mayor, told him to vote, and he was carried to that last election victory by Murphy, who was the only smart and functional guy in the 6th," said David by email. "Myers only said one thing in all the council meetings I ever attended: 'I am behind Mayor Schaefer 1000 percent.' That was his only quote. He was never an intellect on the council, and by 1987, he was on his last legs mentally and physically. Even if Augie had a friend in Willie Myers, he had a friend in the most do-nothing inconsequential councilmember—with absolutely no pull inside a police department that was by then largely indifferent to pressure from back-bench councilmen."

I shared this with Ed Brown, who remains adamant that Myers interfered with his investigation. "I wanted to charge Myers too," said Ed. "Charge them all and let them get lawyers."

Augie is quoted in a January 11, 1990, *Sun* paper obituary of Willie Myers: "If everyone he helped showed up for the funeral, you wouldn't be able to get them in the church." The obit said Augie visited Myers every day in the weeks leading up to his death.

ANY CHANCE OF arrest and prosecution is dead and buried. I never tracked down my father's body, and I do not expect to.

Van Smith, the journalist, weighed in recently by text on the Valley Proteins theory. "The route truck is the way into the production line. Be hard to get a body into the line without it being brought into the yard in a route truck. So the driver'd be key," he told me. "Once it's in the back of the truck, mixed in with the rest of what's in there, even the video that monitors what's going out of those trucks into the cooker would be hard-pressed to show a human body distinct from what-all else."

Of all the potential answers to the question of what happened to Dad, Valley Proteins makes the most sense to me.

A FRIEND ONCE QUIPPED: "You know the abyss. You're from Baltimore." A part of me has perched for all these years at the edge of the abyss, swinging my ankles and wondering how to escape—or if I should jump.

I used to resent Baltimore for wronging me. I pictured the city as a sea monster and accused: *You stole my childhood, you took my father, and you hid him where I can't find him.* I stand by Baltimore as a sea monster, but she's not to blame for my father's death or the lurch my young life took in 1987. Terrible things happen. If it exists at all, justice is rare.

I could not handle filing the FOIA request. The emotional prospect of the task paralyzed me. It was too much weight on top of all the other weight.

I spoke to Augie's daughter by phone in 2015. When I identified myself, she shouted, and told me that Dad had been the one who embezzled from E & M. The business still operates, under different ownership, who were not involved with the potentially unlawful activities I described.

Robert Rodriguez, the landlord of Camden Sylvia and Michael Sullivan, went to prison for several years for identity theft and tax fraud but was never charged in the disappearance of his tenants. Camden's mother, Laurie Sylvia, who spoke out about her missing daughter for twenty-five years, died in 2023.

I've laid to rest the hope that anyone will face justice as defined by the American court system over the disappearance and likely murder of Eddy Robert Crane.

After the 2019 exoneration of three Black men who'd served a total of 108 years for a 1983 murder they did not commit, two retired Baltimore detectives were named in a federal lawsuit alleging constitutional violations, which led to the largest settlement in Maryland history in 2023. In the reinvestigation of the case, the state's attorney found that a detective and the prosecutor coached witness testimony that was later recanted.

Roger Nolan died in 2023. Donald Worden is fully retired and doing his best to keep on moving. Dad's brother, Bob, is retired and lives a quiet life. David Simon continues to make television shows. I still haven't seen *The Wire*.

For close to twenty years, I plodded away at a quest that my remaining family perceived as betrayal. I am certain I would have eventually killed myself if I had not embarked on this project in 2007. So I succeeded in saving my own life. To do so, I dragged myself through hell. I did it while working full-time jobs and moving apartments repeatedly, navigating health issues and relationships—propelled by the forward motion of time while also ensnared in the past. Along the way, I lost the ability to have children. Following the path outlined in these pages meant declining other paths.

All that weight is enough. I would not learn anything from the FOIA that would make a tremendous difference to me at this point. I did, however, get an unexpected gift in 2016. After reading a story I'd written about Dad in a now-defunct digital publication, Nick Feugy tracked me down on Facebook, saying he'd worked for my father when he was twenty-one. When we got on the phone on a warm spring day, I was in the front seat of the same stick-shift Honda Civic I'd driven so many times up and down the New Jersey Turnpike, to Curtis Bay with Gordon Porterfield and to police headquarters on Fayette, but now parked on a side street in Mountain View, California.

Nick was concerned I had the wrong impression of my dad, that I judged him in too harsh a light. "Your dad was a good guy. Smart guy. Of him and Augie, your dad was the sanity. I think the only place your father failed was underestimating Augie—I saw him as the crime boss of Curtis Bay."

When Nick had been at E & M for a year or two, he wanted to move out of his parents' home but didn't have enough for first month's rent plus security. He went to my dad to ask for an advance on his paycheck. "Eddy opened his wallet and gave it to me," Nick recalled. At Christmas, Dad gave him a bonus. "I signed the check over to him and paid him back.

"He was a decent guy," said Nick. "I'd see him in his Mercedes, sitting in front of E & M Machinery cranking up classical music, or laying across the hood of the car, shooting rats with his handgun."

Decades and thousands of miles away, I could see it like I was there. Nick was right. I'd come down hard on Dad in my mind, and closed off my heart to him. I didn't judge him for the seemingly illegal activity of E & M; rather, for miscalculating the risk Augie posed, and leaving us. It's hard to get the balance of anger and compassion right. It's hard to get the emphasis on decent-guy Dad versus angry-bull Dad right. I've tried to replace a lifetime of relationship with a limited number of interviews. It neither brings back my father nor accurately renders him.

I could have pursued somehow demolishing the retaining wall at E & M, but why? The idea that Dad might be in there was the boast of a criminal, who, as of 2021, is also dead. That wall was on private property—E & M Machinery changed ownership after Dad disappeared. Even if I could have somehow gotten permission to interfere with it, the money, time and stress would have been extraordinary. Petty Naff was dangerous. And that task would have eaten up even more years of my life.

In the years of my searching, I got more information than I ever thought possible, and less than I'd hoped. After I spoke to Donald Worden that day at Spoons, it was time to stop.

On September 10, 1987, we were late to school, and I didn't run in and kiss Dad goodbye. For years, this failure haunted me. I saw myself in my plaid school uniform, backpack overflowing with textbooks, standing in the open door, facing Dad's blue velvet armchair. I'd see him after school, I told myself. I went out to Mom's car.

I realized at some point that this memory was faulty. On the day he disappeared, we'd already been living in the new house for close to a year. The doorway there didn't face his chair. My decision to run out to the car instead of saying goodbye took place in a different house, in a different doorway.

Losing a parent at a young age is foundational. I have no video or audio of my father, but I remember his voice. In our kitchen, cigarette burning in the ashtray, making work calls. Or in the armchair, calling people who were selling cars through the classifieds. Walking with me at E & M to hunt for tadpoles. Standing next to me in that field petting horses. One day when I was around kindergarten age, I was sitting in his lap and he told me: "When you grow up, you'll be able to count your true friends on one hand." He was right.

Those memories run through my mind like old movies, flickers from my first twelve years in a life that has now spanned more than fifty. Since that call with Nick Feugy, I see Dad leaning across the hood of the 1975 Mercedes, shooting rats, or sitting in the front seat, car vibrating from the music he loved. Those images are so electric it's as if the memories are mine.

All is not lost, but something irreplaceable was obliterated. I missed my dad in 1987 and I miss my dad today. *What are you going to do about it?* I have had to ask myself over and over and over again. This is the devastating question facing every child who has lost a parent. Millions of people before me and after me and alongside me carry this grief and face a similar quandary: Figure out a way to keep going, or not. Reach for the sweetness in life when the world is full of bitter blows . . . or not.

Live or die, but don't poison everything.

Dad was stuck. He was stuck because of the FBI and also because of money. He couldn't walk away. Instead, he died.

The hardest things I've learned: How great he was. How alike we are. My sister got to keep her likeness. Mine is lost, except in the life I've built and the person I've tried to become. No one would talk to me about Dad, and that dearth of stories about him compounded the loss.

If I made any mistakes, it was to focus on his death, and the people who knew him only in death. The detectives knew crime; Dad's friends knew him. Eddy came back to life in my conversations with Ken Glenn and Nick Feugy, both fellow storytellers.

What would Dad have been like as he aged? What would our relationship have been like? I have a hard time picturing my father in a context other than Baltimore. I can imagine Dad barking a jovial order for bratwurst and bear claws over the counter at Mueller's Delicatessen on Harford Road. But I cannot see my father hiking with me in a redwood forest, or standing in line at a taqueria in the Mission District of San Francisco. In these landscapes my father looks out of place, baffled, lost.

Would he have left his comfort zone to cheer me on in New York City and Silicon Valley, where I moved in 2015? Or would he have treated my career with disdain and suspicion? Would I have even left Baltimore if he had lived?

These questions have no answers. I'll never know.

I have a good life and good friends, and I'm fairly solitary. Many of the people who loved me the most are gone. Pop, my grandfather, died in 2014. Gordon Porterfield died in 2019. The morning that Marie Collins died in 2021, an owl came to my windowsill and called in to me. My godmother, Yvonne Hughes, died in December 2023, almost two years to the day after her soulmate, Martin Poska. Deacon Charlie Baynes, who held the service for Dad, died three years after the memorial, abruptly, at a young sixty-five. The obituary by the archdiocese called him a down-to-earth churchman.

If I'd written this book as fiction, it might go like this: Kate solves the mystery of her father's disappearance and lives happily ever after.

The reality is messier and more authentic: Kate does not solve the mystery of her father's disappearance and, quite possibly, lives happily ever after. The questions are less poisonous after the years I devoted to exploring them. "Investigation is nothing but the truth and being able to prove it," Ed Brown said to me recently. The real wall in this story was silence. I knocked that down. In doing so, I bettered my chances of surviving.

The clock is ticking. I won't forgive and I won't forget. And I want to write other books, tend a garden, care for some cats and dogs, and be of service to young people. Maybe I didn't kiss my father goodbye on September 10, 1987, but for more than eighteen years I have done what I could for him. This book is the goodbye kiss and the forever I love you.

My job now is to keep living.

Watch me.

★ ★ ★ ★ ★

# AUTHOR'S NOTE

THIS BOOK IS a work of journalism, and this book is a memoir. I say journalism first because of my training and experience, which stretch back to the early 2000s. I taught myself memoir writing over the past seven years by studying books about the form, taking workshops, reading dozens of autobiographies and writing, at minimum, hundreds of birdcage-worthy pages. The two forms have separate standards and conventions that intertwine in this book, with the dominance of memoir versus journalism shifting throughout.

Part one is predominantly memoir, which relies on remembering. I meditated at times for months on some of the scenes in part one. Memory is a trickster. Since Hermann Ebbinghaus in the late nineteenth century, many have studied memory and concluded: It's weird. An event takes place and the brain quickly casts off swaths of information.

When I spoke to Harold recently to tell him the book was nearly finished, I mentioned the call I did with Earl Crum (not his real name) in his dining room. Harold said, "Wait a minute." He swears that Earl, not me, was in his kitchen when I, not Earl, called on the phone. I have my upside-down pages of notes and the transcription I did of that frenzied scrawl when

I got back to Gordon's—neatly labeled as the call I did from Harold's dining room with Earl. I have my schedule from that week. I was in Baltimore. I was with Ed Brown before going to Harold's, and I drove to Cold Case the next day. I know I'm right. Harold knows he's right. Memory is weird.

Some memoirists discuss their recollections in depth with family members. They compare notes. Mostly, I could not. My mother wanted nothing to do with this project. I could not omit her from a story to which she is integral, but I did my best to limit my questions. That said, she claims no recollection of some of my most foundational memories. She says some things did not happen, and remembers others quite differently from me.

There is a power imbalance in being the one to tell a story that involves family members who did not control or actively inform the narrative. I did my best to frame these other family members with compassion and as complex human beings who struggled with the same trauma as me.

Much of this book is also journalism. I conducted interviews, in person and by phone, and did extensive research. I have kept a journal for forty-plus years, and I have filled many notebooks over the course of this project, including the big blue one I referenced throughout the book.

I first found that incredible headline about flowers wilting and nylons running in a file about Curtis Bay at the central branch of the Enoch Pratt Free Library on Cathedral Street. I combed newspaper archives and court records, and hired an investigator at the outset for information not publicly available. Wherever possible, I cited the source of a stated fact.

Not all dialogue in this book came about in the same way. In part one, I largely constructed dialogue from memory, building it out from the bits of speech I remembered and my best recollection of how an event unfolded. That dialogue is no kind of transcription—it's crafted to represent my best recollection.

In dialogue-heavy scenes later in the book, such as those with Donald Kincaid, Ed Brown and David Simon, I recorded an interview and then built a scene from the transcript. I deleted immense amounts of material to avoid repetition, as well as to distill those conversations down to the most meaningful and impactful words. I then tried to craft the edited conversations into worthwhile reading that contributed to the greater narrative.

In some cases, I took notes during conversations, such as phone calls with my Uncle Bob, and upon hanging up, I typed the notes into a legible document.

I wrote about finding the Mercedes on the street in Williamsburg when it happened—that scene is based not only on a memory but also on a journal entry. The two dreams are edited from journal entries.

I often indicated if a memory was clear, or vague, or if I could not recall certain elements. Where my memory drives the text, I did my best to be truthful and accurate.

# ACKNOWLEDGMENTS

IN LATE 2015, I was beyond drained, working punishing hours at a start-up. I all but decided to abandon this project. I told myself I would continue toward a book only if I met a literary agent who made me feel excited to forge ahead. Excited? Preposterous. Surely, I was off the hook. Then William LoTurco approached me. Halfway into our first phone call, I knew. He shared my vision for what this book could be. In the decade since, William has been a stalwart partner, sage in his guidance, generous in his time, unwavering in his support. This book is for William as much as it is for the loved ones named in the dedication. Words cannot express my gratitude—the existence of this book is the expression of gratitude.

William and I faced a particular challenge: selling a book without a splashy finish. John Glynn shared our vision. I had no idea how to write memoir; John became my mentor as well as my editor. His skill and wisdom illuminated every facet of this book as it came—slowly—to life. John trusted my instincts and my process. In turn, I trusted his guidance. Our work has been a rewarding collaboration. I thank John with all my heart for his immense patience and for believing in me. I am lucky as hell.

By the time David Simon showed up in our living room in

1992, I knew I wanted to be a writer. With his *Sun* story, I began to better understand why. Words on a page not only transported me to other worlds, but they could also help me make sense of mine. David has played a singular recurring role in my life. That someone else remembers has been invaluable. I am grateful for his generosity and encouragement.

The detectives I worked with at the Cold Case Unit were thoughtful and empathetic. Thank you to Donald Worden and Roger Nolan. Thank you to Ed Brown and Donald Kincaid, who had both retired from the Baltimore Police Department by the time I reached out. They could have turned me away and instead were so kind. Thank you to Diane Worden and Diane Kincaid. The gift of their time and care put tools in my hands that I needed to make the loss of my father survivable.

Thank you also to Lieutenant Terrence McLarney.

I could promise Andrew Gillings only an initial schedule for fact-checking. He rolled with the uncertainty and took meticulous care of my book. My cries of "Great catch!" will echo into eternity.

For years, I worked at magazines alongside top-tier copy editors Stephanie Makrias, Laura Siciliano-Rosen and Amelia Weiss. Each of them contributed to the book. I treasure our long friendships and their inimitable skills.

I've had a wonderful experience with Hanover Square Press. Thank you to the art team, including Quinn Banting, and the production teams, including Victoria Hulzinga and Kristen Salciccia, for their excellence, to Eden Railsback for her kindness and professionalism, and to Ronnie Kutys for her enthusiasm.

One door down from the *New York Press* bullpen was the lair of our staff columnist, a reclusive smoker in a fedora who was mostly blind. "Jim got a box of *Slackjaw* in German," Alex Zaitchik said one day, referring to the mystery man's memoir of retinitis pigmentosa. "Ask him to autograph one for you." More than twenty years later, Jim Knipfel is one of the people my father meant when he told me I'd count my true friends on one hand. In a field full of posturing and gatekeeping, Jim has always welcomed me. He made the journey of this book far less lonely.

In 2007, Joe Queenan was adamant that I write a book and helped me set off in the right direction. A few years later, when doors were closing left and right, Celia Johnson shared meaningful feedback and encouragement that kept my hope alive. Jess Row read an early draft and gave me outstanding edits. When I was petrified over a critical deadline in fall 2024, Cristin Stickles delivered a rousing pep talk that unearthed in me a baffling twenty-eight-day gust of stamina.

Thank you to Paul Barker, Steph Becker, Roxanna Bikadoroff, Thomas Bloink, Dennis, Maryellen, and Michael Brady, Tonja Brown, Sara Davis Buechner, Andre Clarke, Diane Cluck, Nelson Cooney, Earl Crum, Mary V. Dearborn, Kate and Zoë Deshmukh, Kevin and Timothy Doory, Mary Feaster, Nick Feugy, Beth Forgosh, Andrew Gilroy, Ken Glenn, Harold Goldman, J. P. Gownder, Matthew Heimer, Denice Hilty, the Hiltz family, Ellie Jones, Lonnie Jordan, Leah Kidd, Charles King, Rene Kock, Eric Laursen, Nori Li, James Lochart, Adeline, Tess, Julia Lovell, Liam Madden, William Mellott, Ben Meyers, Monica Norton, Faith O'Neal, Rebecca Parker, Larry Peterson, Kate Porterfield, Victoria Porterfield, James Power, Raisa Punkki, Adams Puryear, Rhonda Rafuse, Dana Rashidi, Reena Rexrode, Richard Robertshaw, Kora Chacha Robinson, Stephen Rodriguez,

Lucia Roncalli, Thomas Sabia, Paul Scanlon, Blake Schwarzenbach, Jamie Scotto, Judy Segal, Autumn Seguin, Corey Seymour, Benjamin Heim Shepard, Tony Smith, Van Smith, Nadia Soraya, Russell Steinert, James B. Stewart, Cristin Stickles, Blue Telusma, Dr. Shanéa Thomas, Zeyah Thomas, Dacus Thompson, Sara Valentine, Joan Wasser, Viola Wengrofsky, Jacqueline Wilkotz, Alsvid Wotansdottir, Alexander Zaitchik.